Reshaping Social W

Series Editors: **Robert Adams, L**   **ne**

The **Reshaping Social Work** serie
base for critical, reflective practiti   book is designed to
support students on qualifying social work programmes and update
practitioners on crucial issues in today's social work, strengthening
research knowledge, critical analysis and skilled practice to shape
social   to meet future challenges.

Published   es

Anti-Racist P ice in Social Work Kish Bhatti-Sinclair
Social Work Spirituality Margaret Holloway and Bernard Moss
Social Work R arch for Social Justice Beth Humphries
Social Work an Social Policy under Austerity Bill Jordan and Mark Drakeford
Social Care Pr ice in Context Malcolm Payne
Critical Issues Social Work with Older People Mo Ray, Judith Phillips and
    Miriam Ber rd
Social Work ar ower Roger Smith

Invitation to authors

The Serie itors welcome proposals for new books within the *Reshaping
Social Wc ries*. Please contact one of the series editors for an initial
discussion:

- Robert Adams at rvadams@rvadams.karoo.co.uk
- Lena Dominelli at lena.dominelli@durham.ac.uk
- Malcolm Payne at M.Payne@stchristophers.org.uk

Reshaping Social Work
Series Editors: **Robert Adams, Lena Dominelli and Malcolm Payne**
Series Standing Order ISBN 1–4039–4878–X
(outside North America only)

You can receive future titles in this series as they are published by placing a standing order. Please contact your bookseller or, in the case of difficulty, write to us at the address below with your name and address, the title of the series and the ISBN quoted above.

Customer Services Department
Macmillan Distribution Ltd
Houndmills
Basingstoke
Hampshire
RG21 6XS
England

Social Work and Social Policy under Austerity

Bill Jordan

and

Mark Drakeford

First published 2012 by
PALGRAVE MACMILLAN

Palgrave Macmillan in the UK is an imprint of Macmillan Publishers Limited, registered in England, company number 785998, of Houndmills, Basingstoke, Hampshire RG21 6XS.

Palgrave Macmillan in the US is a division of St Martin's Press LLC, 175 Fifth Avenue, New York, NY 10010.

Palgrave Macmillan is the global academic imprint of the above companies and has companies and representatives throughout the world.

Palgrave® and Macmillan® are registered trademarks in the United States, the United Kingdom, Europe and other countries

ISBN: 9781137020635

This book is printed on paper suitable for recycling and made from fully managed and sustained forest sources. Logging, pulping and manufacturing processes are expected to conform to the environmental regulations of the country of origin.

A catalogue record for this book is available from the British Library.

A catalog record for this book is available from the Library of Congress.

10 9 8 7 6 5 4 3 2 1
21 20 19 18 17 16 15 14 13 12

Printed in China

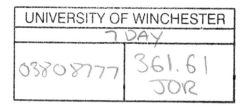

Contents

Preface

Devolution: Policy Variations and Common Themes

Devolution in the United Kingdom is more than a decade old, and with it comes a fresh set of challenges for the analysis of both social work and social policy. In many ways, the present text is a book about England, especially in the particularities of policy it discusses and the practice examples it provides. Fee regimes in Higher Education, for example, vary between each of the four nations. There is no longer a 'National' Health Service (NHS), as patterns of administration in health and social services are different in place. But devolution means more than variation in organisation. The policy purpose behind fee regimes is different in Scotland, Wales and England. The ending of the NHS is much more than the difference between Foundation Trusts in England, integrated Local Health Boards in Wales and Scotland, and single bodies covering both health and social services in Northern Ireland. It is rooted in the retention of a recognisably publicly funded, publicly provided, publicly planned Health Service in the devolved administrations and the wholesale marketisation of health services in England. Where we draw on evidence from outside England, we say so. Otherwise the specifics of policy and practice elsewhere in the United Kingdom are best pursued through reference to texts which specialise in different localities, including those noted at the end of this preface.

Yet, it is just as important to be clear that the key linking themes which form the core of our discussion apply across the whole of the United Kingdom and, often, beyond. Our main concern is to interrogate the causes of the global economic crisis of the post-2008 period, and to suggest a future in which the relationship between work, income and citizenship are radically reformed and realigned, in order to create a more equal, sustainable and successful society. In doing so, we map out a contribution which revitalised social work might make to help resolve the dilemmas of an economically bankrupt, socially divided and environmentally compromised present day, and then to model and reshape the relationships which would characterise a different sort of future. Of course, different parts of the United Kingdom would have further to travel in responding to the fundamental changes we outline – but the challenge is common to us all.

Mark Drakeford

Suggested Reading

- Heenan, D. and Birrell, D. (2011) *Social Work in Northern Ireland: Conflict and Change*, Bristol, Policy Press.
- Mooney, G. and Scott, G. (eds) (2012) *Social Justice and Social Policy in Scotland*, Bristol, Policy Press.
- Williams, C.F. (ed) (2011) *Social Policy for Social Welfare Practice in a Devolved Wales*, Birmingham, Venture Press.
- Readers might also consult the August 2012 issue of Critical Social Policy, 32:3, which carries a series of papers on devolution and social policy in the United Kingdom.

Introduction

Only 20 years after the 'victory' of capitalism over state socialism, marked by the collapse of the Soviet Bloc in 1989–91, an even bigger convulsion shook the affluent states of Europe, North America and Australasia. The twin crises of banking and government threatened the prosperity and stability which seemed to have settled on these societies, some of them were faced with upheavals that paralleled events in the USSR and its satellites in the early 1990s. Above all, the complacent view of the institutions of liberal democratic welfare states (suitably 'modernised' in recent decades) as the blueprint for future global development was dealt a mortal blow.

This book starts from the idea that the crisis which began in 2008 represented an entirely new challenge to social policy, social work and the relationship between them. Whereas the market-minded political orthodoxies of the previous 30 years had forced significant scaling back of the ambitious goals of redistribution, inclusion and social justice which prevailed in the 1960s (Judt, 2010, chapter 17), it was possible to see all this as much in terms of continuity as change (Pierson, 1994). The new situation demanded something more radical, in the form either of retrenchment or of transformation.

The dominant media metaphor for that protracted drama was the household living beyond its means, with the public services represented as a troop of idle skivvies and flunkeys, draining the resources accumulated by the hard-working members of the family (the private sector). Austerity implied sacking some of these and cutting the wages and salaries of the rest, along with the pensions paid to superannuated retainers. In order to be more competitive with each other and with the rising industrial powers of the east and south, these economies had to be 'rebalanced' towards production and export of goods (preferably high-value, high-tech ones) and away from self-indulgent services – to be more like Germany in Europe, or China in the wider world.

But this metaphor disguised what was really at stake in the crisis. This book will argue that global capitalist development had finally confronted affluent societies with the contradiction between their lofty ethical goals – equal citizenship, fairness for all, the common good – and the realities of their economic dynamic. As demonstrators occupying squares in the financial capitals of these countries proclaimed, their elites had run out of ideas about how to save the system from itself, and lost the will to protect the vast majority of their populations from unemployment and declining living standards

Worse than this, we shall argue, there was a real threat that the very instruments of income redistribution and social care were being redeployed to enforce a new regime of intensified exploitation at work and welfare discipline in society. In this, the role of social work – brought back into the front line of social policy from its more modest position in postwar welfare states, and refurbished by the incorporation of new resources from the commercial and charitable sectors – was emerging as a prominent feature of a new authoritarianism in public life.

Indeed, a more apt version of the metaphoric narrative of the crisis (think Jane Austen) would have the father of a prosperous family (the government) going abroad, leaving his dissolute eldest son (the financial sector) to run up huge gambling debts, and also make loans he could not afford to relatives who could not afford to repay them. On his return, the father pays off his debts, while making the thriftless relatives work to repay their loans with interest, under the authority of his bailiffs.

The disciplinary and punitive vein running through all the measures taken in response to the crisis in the eurozone – the most dramatic of these chaotic events – extended from the very top of the European political order to the local regimes facing benefits claimants and public service users. Democratic processes were set aside and established social rights ignored as a financial elite took control of decisions, insisting that treasuries must take action to shore up the currency. As *The Guardian* (9 November 2011, p.34) put it in a leader entitled 'Punishment Europe':

> The realisation is dawning that the models which sustained both national economies and the EU itself need more than tweaking, they need radically recasting in a way that will lead in time to the resumption of the European project as one intended to benefit Europeans, rather than to admonish, discipline and even punish them.

Of course the United Kingdom and the United States were far from immune to these forces, having been at the centre of the financial crash. The UK government in particular tried to anticipate the pessimism of the bond markets about its ability to service its massive public debt by applying a similar logic to its collective infrastructure; it also urged these measures on its European counterparts. As well as lowering expectations, it enforced harsh conditions around claims for assistance, such as the new tests under which people who had been eligible for payments on grounds of disabilities were reclassified as capable of work.

We will show that the links between the crises in the financial sectors and the government treasuries of the affluent countries and these shifts in social policies and in the role of social work were by no means shadowy and indirect. In many cases they were simply two sides of the same coin, as in the revelation that the bulk of the commercial residential care system in the United Kingdom was financed by 'investment funds' through a massive pyramid of debt.

But we will also aim to prove that none of these developments are inevitable. The crisis was not caused by the profligacy of welfare states but by the contradictions in the global economic system, and by the attempts that governments had made to reconcile them. The intuition of the mass demonstrators against austerity measures – that the many are being penalised for the greed and folly of the few – is right; there are alternative steps by which public policies can steer societies in new directions.

We will also suggest that the processes by which social work is coming to play a front line role in the authoritarian aspects of new regimes are reversible, and that there are opportunities for it to recapture its emancipatory traditions. Such a shift would require a transformation in the institutions of these societies, but it would demand a positive response from professionals also.

Background

The extended crisis from 2008 was the culmination of a 30-year process in which (one by one) the fiscal regimes of the affluent countries required radical overhaul in the face of deficits, debt mountains or both. First the United Kingdom and the United States, then New Zealand, Australia, Italy, the Netherlands, France, Sweden, Finland, Italy (again) and even Germany had to apply for international loans or restructure their public finances, and in each case it was government spending (and specifically expenditure on income transfers and social services) that was blamed for the problems.

But in fact this period saw a transformation of the global economy in which these countries came to play a new role in relation to world production and trade. As industrial mass production was relocated to Asia and Latin America, they became centres for finance, research and high-tech manufacturing; their labour markets were stripped of skilled factory jobs for men and eventually also of administrative and office jobs for women. As a result, the expansion of some well-paid professional and managerial posts was accompanied by a swelling volume of low-paid, part-time and occasional work, mainly in services (Sissons, 2010).

All this involved governments of these countries in new tasks to sustain the living standards of their citizens and protect them from the full impact of global market forces. In one way or another, they were required to bolster the incomes of those households on below-average earnings, as well as maintain a growing proportion of the population excluded from paid employment. Whether through targeted housing benefits and tax credits (as in the United Kingdom and the United States) or through taking large proportions of workers out of the labour market to protect the wage levels of the remainder (as in Germany), these governments found themselves involved in sustaining the subsistence of more of their citizens of working age than ever before (Jordan, 2006).

Furthermore, and partly in reaction to the recognition of this new role, new regimes of 'activation' were adopted in all the different systems in response to fiscal crises, as governments extended their new role in income maintenance into one of official guardian of the work ethic. Insisting on the duty to take available employment, however unpleasant and poorly paid, was the counterpart to the state's supplementation of wages, first manifested in 'workfare' in the United States, but gradually adopted in the United Kingdom and in EU countries in the form of various welfare-to-work schemes (Cox, 1998). Germany was the last country to take these measures (because of its associations with its Nazi past), and finally did so after its own encounter with fiscal difficulties and slow growth at the beginning of the new century.

These innovations created a new kind of public official, the 'advisor' or 'counsellor' to working-age claimants of benefits, a role defined in terms similar to those used in the job descriptions of social workers in the social services, even though professionally trained social workers were seldom employed in this work (Jordan, 1998). As support for those of working age increased, the functions of assessing, training, preparing and placing claimants (including lone parents of ever-younger children and people with long-standing disabilities) for labour market roles were extended, and their obligations to 'reciprocate' for their benefits through work was intensified.

Finally, governments saw their public sectors as in need of rationalisation and modernisation, including the contracting out of services to private firms and the creation of arms'-length quangos to manage agencies. Far from reducing the proportion of employment directly or indirectly relying on funding from taxation, in several countries (such as the United Kingdom under New Labour) it substantially increased it; many 'private' enterprises, including schools and hospitals, ran on contracts from local or central government. In addition, of course, other states expanded public employment under traditional forms of government patronage, as in the southern regions of Italy (Putnam, 1993) and in Greece. All this added a dimension to the involvement of official organisations in collective life and in labour markets.

The dominant rationale behind all these developments was derived from the economic orthodoxy of the time – that governments which had sought to offset the consequences of market distributions and capitalist exploitation in the era of welfare states should instead accommodate themselves and their public sectors to market norms and forces, and make their citizens more ready and willing to accept employment on almost any terms. Especially in the United Kingdom, the language of business came to displace the whole terminology within which issues of health care, education, social housing and social work had been arranged in the previous three decades, and relationships between and within agencies, as well as with government itself, were defined in terms of contracts, targets and unit costs.

All this might seem to imply that governments had assumed a leading role in societies, shaping collective life according to their designs, albeit market-orientated ones; but this was far from being the case. As well as demanding that public services emulate banks and supermarkets in their flexibility and responsiveness to consumers' preferences (DSS, 1998, p.26), government policies actively discouraged citizens' reliance on state benefits and services, except when they were unable to meet their needs from earnings and savings; in the United Kingdom, they promoted 'independence', 'choice' and initiative, portraying good citizenship in terms of self-realisation through homeownership, private insurance and pension arrangements, and responsibility for family members (DSS, 1998, p. 80).

This version of mainstream achievement directed people towards the banks and the financial sector more generally, and away from public agencies, for its realisation. In the United States and the United Kingdom it was this that precipitated the crash of 2008–09, first through sub-prime loans to homebuyers in the former, and then through these and other forms of household credit in the latter, bundled up into various forms of derivatives and sold on markets dealing in risks. When some of these gambles started to be losing ones, the casinos that were Wall Street and the City of London came crashing down, ultimately dragging governments into the levels of debt which brought about the second leg of the crisis in 2010–12.

It might have been expected that the economic model which underpinned public policy in the United Kingdom and the United States, and strongly influenced in all the other affluent countries – the theory of information, incentives and contracts (Macho-Stadler and Pérez Castillo, 2001; Laffont and Martimort, 2002; Bolton and Dewatripont, 2005) – would have been discredited by this chain of events. After all, the World Bank's orthodoxy, and the leading role for financial intermediaries it recommended (Stiglitz and Greenwald, 2003), was an integral feature of the 'light touch' regulation which had facilitated the banking collapse. But instead the interests of the financial sector were adopted as the guiding principles for governments, as much in the second phase of the crisis as the first; it was the risks that these intermediaries were exposed to by their holdings of sovereign debt that determined the austerity conditions imposed by the European Central Bank (ECB) and the International Monetary Fund (IMF) on Ireland, Portugal, Greece and Italy. These terms drove down the incomes of citizens, cut benefits and services and raised unemployment. They also undermined the prospects for growth in all except the agile resilient Irish economy.

Furthermore, the eurozone crisis of 2011 saw power assumed by the Frankfurt Group, a 'politburo' made up of the presidents of Germany and France and various bureaucrats and bankers from the IMF, the ECB and the European Commission. This group laid down the rescue terms and even brought down the prime ministers of Greece and Italy in October–November, 2011, installing bureaucrats and bankers in their own image in their place. As it was German banks which stood to lose most from default on these countries' repayments, and the German treasury was required to supply most of the rescue funds, it was deemed justifiable that the German Chancellor's views on the depth of cuts and restructuring required should take precedence in the rules imposed. It was not considered relevant that Germany had gained most from the creation of the eurozone, and had allowed its trade surplus and its loans to its debtors to grow beyond the realms of prudence or mutual interest.

So the initial response to the second phase of the crisis consolidated the grip of finance capital on government policy, but did so in perverse ways; austerity strangled growth, and with it the prospect of loans being repaid or imbalances corrected. Southern European states became a string of basket cases, and the prosperity of northern European ones (the Hanseatic League, as one wag with a historical memory dubbed them) was dragged down as a result. In the days when the Hanseatic League flourished, Mediterranean city states were richer still (Spruyt, 1994).

Arguably social policy had been made subservient to the quest for competitiveness in the global economy since the 1970s as each of the affluent countries faced fiscal problems, but this was the first time that all of them had explicitly sacrificed the goals of equality, inclusion and social justice to the contradictory demands of bond and equity markets. This was the background to the issues of policy and practice in the public services analysed in this book.

Plan and themes of the book

We will argue that the nature and depth of the crisis represented a disjunction in the history of social policy development, as the era of the West's global dominance (which had extended since the seventeenth century) came to an abrupt end. The spectacle in early November 2011, of the leaders of the eurozone looking to China and the oil-rich Middle Eastern countries to supply the credit for a fund to guarantee the sovereign debts of European countries, symbolised the undignified slide of these states into positions of dependence on the emerging industrial powers and those holding reserves of easily accessible fossil fuels.

Up to this point it had been possible to continue to believe that the forms of welfare states which evolved in the twentieth century would be the models for economic and social development worldwide, and would be the counterparts to the growth of liberal democratic polities and capitalist economies across the globe. Suddenly it was obvious that no such assumption was justifiable, and that all the variations in 'welfare regimes' to emerge in the affluent countries (Esping-Andersen, 1990) were in trouble for one reason or another, and all required radical remedial interventions. In previous crises it had been the habitual response to identify an institutional system which was functioning better than its rival models, and argue that this set the pattern for future success. No such wishful thinking was any longer plausible.

The crisis represented an equal failure of political and economic functioning. Markets and firms which had been resuscitated by injections in government funding in 2008–09 panicked or froze in response to the spectacle of defaulting state treasuries in 2011–12, and the few truly solvent regimes held back from wholehearted participation in concerted action on behalf of the most indebted ones. International corporations and a global elite floated above the chaos and even profited from it; the vast majority of the population were cast into situations of insecurity, and many into one of penury. The young generation leaving education in search of work saw their prospects of incremental careers, earnings and pensions, of homeownership and asset ownership, blighted.

But at the same time as capitalism and democracy seemed equally at sea, an even deeper level of uncertainty also swelled beneath these manifestations of a tipping point in historical processes. The notion of global integration under the aegis of the United States as the sole, unchallenged superpower, and through the adoption of an industrial model derived ultimately from mass production based on fossil fuels, was evidently no longer tenable. Both the hegemony of the West and the productive systems it had exported to the rest of the world were unsustainable, and required radical revision in the immediate future.

The aim of this book is to conduct just such an inquiry in relation to the political, economic and societal underpinnings of social policy and social work. If these foundations have been undermined by the shifts that have accompanied globalisation and the rise of the new industrial giants of Asia and Latin America, what are the prospects for an equitable, sustainable alternative, giving a good quality of life to citizens of developed countries, consistent with the growing prosperity of populations in the rest of the world?

In Chapter 1 we will analyse the implications of the new phase in human development now being entered for work and income in the advanced economies. Under the version which had prevailed since the Industrial Revolution, workers in low-productivity sectors were constantly being drawn into those forms of production susceptible to technological and organisational innovations, which allowed them to be paid higher wages. This dynamic, first recognised by Adam Smith (1776), still applies to countries like China, where a 'floating population' of nearly 250 million citizens of rural provinces have moved across administrative boundaries to work in new manufacturing and construction employments. If newly industrialising countries such as Indonesia are included, over a billion such unskilled workers have shifted from peasant labour to industrial production in the past decade, driving the rapid growth of output and incomes in these economies.

But the corollary of this is that no such dynamic is any longer available to populations in the affluent countries. Technological innovation can certainly still raise earnings, but only those of the relatively small number of employees of companies engaged in producing the high-value goods which allow their owners a niche position in global markets, often based on research into new fields such as biotechnology. Among the affluent economies, only Germany, which achieved productivity growth of 10 per cent and expansion of 9.4 per cent in GDP in 2010, could boast consistent national success in reproducing the dynamic of the previous two centuries. By contrast, Italy, which achieved no growth from 2000 to 2010, had no growth in output per worker either.

More typically, economies like the United Kingdom, the United States, and France had pockets of successful innovation (Silicon Valley in California, the concentration of biotech companies in Cambridge and the aerospace industry in Marseilles) in wider stretches of post-industrial decay or serious distress. In such economic landscapes, resourceful migrants (from Central America and East Asia in the United States, from Central Europe in the United Kingdom, and from North Africa in France) often competed successfully with unskilled indigenous people and with those of longer-term immigrants origins, for low-paid and unpleasant work. With the onset of the crisis, even these jobs became less available, and the young generation were unable to establish a position in the labour market.

The social policy tradition of all types of welfare regime was rooted in the idea that entitlement to a share of the prosperity stemming from this process of development was based on *labour*, specifically the type of employment which created economic growth and hence social progress. All other transfers and services were related to this foundation – health care and education through improving productive potential, social care in allowing participation and so on – and provision which was not directly derived from this justification (such as social assistance for lone parents) carried a stigma in consequence. Historically, groups of workers not connected with the organised labour market, such as subsistence farmers and self-employed craft workers, were the last to be included in social insurance schemes, and these systems notoriously failed to recognise the work done by those who cared for children at home, or for elderly and disabled relatives, as giving access to the same sorts of entitlements.

This chapter examines the implications of the collapse of these principles. We can now recognise that economic growth, even when it has been achieved, does not guarantee rising earnings. It traces these features of the crisis to a particular version of how markets work, and how governments can best harness them for their purposes. This approach had its roots in the 1970s, and its early proponents strongly influenced the neo-liberal regimes of Ronald Reagan and Margaret Thatcher; but the ideas reached their mature expression in the versions which influenced the Third Way governments of Bill Clinton and Tony Blair, and in the global programme of the World Bank (Stiglitz, 2002). These economic theorists insisted that markets (including financial markets) could regulate themselves in the right institutional environment, and that political authorities should focus on creating this environment. But they failed to anticipate the consequences if the recklessness of bankers led to a collapse, and governments had to bail out the whole financial system.

By the time of the crash in 2008–09, these ideas had been incorporated into the public services, especially in the United Kingdom but increasingly across the affluent countries. This meant that social policy no longer offset the workings of the private sector but largely complemented it. We will show how both public services, including social work, have been drawn into the logic of these developments, and how they need to change in order to be part of an alternative direction for these societies.

In Chapter 2, we consider how the crisis has influenced governments' role in income transfers. Because of the shifts in the labour market and in earnings analysed in the first chapter, social insurance benefits, always too low in the United States and the United Kingdom, became inadequate to the tasks of income maintenance for the working-age population in the affluent states, eventually even in the Nordic countries. Since the crisis, the collapse of bank credit has demanded an increased role for government credit, but the big issues concern the forms this will take and the conditions which will be attached to provision.

These developments have gone furthest in the United Kingdom, where the Conservative Party in opposition outlined medium-term plans for reforms to income maintenance for this age group, based on a report by the Centre for Social Justice (CSJ) in 2009. This proposed the partial integration of income taxation and means-tested benefits (including those for housing and disability living costs) into 'Universal Credits'. The aim was to allow a far more seamless and advantageous transition from the role of claimant outside the labour market to part-time wage earner, above all supplying incentives for those (such as lone parents) with other responsibilities or problems to enter employment, perhaps initially for a few hours a week.

In office the Secretary of State for Work and Pensions, Iain Duncan Smith, who had endorsed the CSJ Report's plan, introduced a watered-down version of Universal Credits, together with an extensive new welfare-to-work initiative, the Work Programme, under which large firms contracted to prepare claimants for employment, and to earn fees by placing them in lasting posts. He also pursued a scheme for testing applicants for disability-related benefits, reclassifying a large proportion of them as fit to do some work. Whereas the CSJ emphasised the need to improve incentives, the coalition government introduced its measures to enforce work obligations ahead of the reforms which would make participation more advantageous.

This chapter will examine the complex connections between the state's role as a supplier of credit for consumption (implicitly recognised in the title of the basic building block of the new tax-benefits scheme) and the emergence of new forms of work which will allow full participation rather than full employment. The crisis drew attention to the worldwide phenomenon of a 'precariat', employed in temporary or marginal roles and with poor prospects of gaining security or the status of a incremental career as a member of an occupation (Standing, 2011). This group (or class) could be recognised as the instigators of the 'Arab Spring'; in the affluent countries, members now include many graduates and offspring of middle-class households.

We will argue that the partial integration of the tax-benefit system could represent the first step on a road towards an income maintenance system consistent with the evolution of a mix between paid and unpaid work roles which could support a sustainable and equitable form of collective life in the affluent countries in this century. But this will need to overcome fierce resistance from those interests with a stake in the authoritarian tendencies of policies designed to intensify official pressures on the 'flexible' labour supply that allows workers to be exploited.

Recognising that no mechanism in capitalist development exists to correct such imbalances is the first step towards this new form of income maintenance, to ensure that the many receive some benefit from processes giving dramatic advantages to the few. We review the literature on this proposal and its implications for the established social services.

In Chapter 3, we look at how the public services contribute to the construction of the social order in our societies. The economic model, which sees public services primarily in terms of the 'delivery' of collective goods in cost-effective ways, pays little attention to these issues, which were at the heart of the post-war attempt to create common interests between the classes, and hence to avoid the bitter conflicts of the inter-war years (Judt, 2010, chapter 3). But some such attempt is again required with the breakdown of the contract-based order which characterised Third Way regimes.

Here again, the United Kingdom provides an instructive case study. The riots which took place in the English cities in August 2011 were widely interpreted as signalling some kind of breakdown in the social order – the standards and practices through which the various kinds of bonds and linkages connecting society's members are stitched together into a fabric which enables workable cooperation and harmony.

In a socially diverse liberal democracy, the social order is in part sustained by political and cultural leaderships telling citizens a story about how their society is developing. New Labour's story – of self-respon-sible individuals realising their potential through projects with chosen others, in a modern, flexible economy, adapting better to globalisation than its continental neighbours, and served by modern, businesslike government agencies and services – was tired and discredited by the time of the 2010 election.

Yet the Conservatives' 'Big Society' – a revival of civil society, with power transferred to individuals and communities –remained shadowy and unconvincing to the electorate, and in government its reform agenda was largely postponed in favour of cuts and privatisation. There was little evidence of the promotion of 'collective action' promised in Cameron's pre-election speeches; charities and community groups were conspicuous casualties of the new austerity.

The coalition government's response to the riots relied heavily on puni-tive criminal justice, but ministers also proposed measures to disqualify offenders from benefits payments and even to evict them and their rela-tives from social housing. Later it became clear that social work – in the form of concentrated, focused 'tough love' programmes for 120,000 deprived and deviant families – could become central to the next stage of its strategy. This would install a very particular style of work at the heart of a new regime, intended to construct a very different social order to the one presided over by New Labour, or indeed by any other administration in the United Kingdom since the Second World War. This chapter will review the direction of changes in social programmes and social work, and consider social work's position in the overall configuration of the public services, to analyse what kind of social order is in the process of construction.

The idea that the public services, spearheaded by a new type of correc-tive social work, might be deployed to repair the torn social fabric in the aftermath of austerity and violent reactions to it is clearly most applicable to younger populations in urban areas. In Chapter 4, we turn to the services for health and social care, which deal disproportionately with older people and those with disabilities that keep them outside the spheres most affected by economic change and social conflict.

Here pressures to reduce government spending run up against the technological advance in prolonging life and the associated costs of maintaining an ageing population. The economic model of public service reform and management attempted to deal with this dilemma through the introduction of a business approach to the organisation of these forms of care, along with greater opportunities for individuals needing services to opt for particular hospitals, clinics or social care providers. Austerity makes it more difficult to sustain the second part of this equation; resource constraints limit the scope for improvements in promptness, choice and quality of services available.

The risks of this situation are increasingly borne by those with least visibility and capacity to publicise their plight. In the United Kingdom, scandals about the care of elderly patients in hospitals started to surface before the crisis of 2008, but reports by the Care Quality Commission (2011) and the Patients' Association (2011) suggested that problems such as nutritional neglect, lack of hygienic assistance and undignified routines were far more widespread (in England) than had been suspected.

One source of these problems in the United Kingdom has been the lack of a reliable system for funding social care services. In the Nordic countries these are paid for out of general taxation, and northern European states like Germany and the Netherlands raised social insurance contributions in the 1990s to finance them. Although a report by a committee chaired by Andrew Dilnot (2011) recommended a centrally funded national Care Service for the United Kingdom, no such scheme appears to be in the offing.

But another strand of policy and practice development could, we will argue, focus on the potential for increasing the involvement of older and disabled citizens in the life of their communities. The emphasis on individual choice and the specific competences of professional staff which characterised the Third Way era distracted attention from these issues. Austerity concentrates attention on the attempt to increase economic activity by people with disabilities; we argue that equal attention should be given to social and cultural activity and inclusion as participants in the collective life of communities.

This leads into the subject matter of Chapter 5. Any alternative to the projected societies of the future, dominated by small super-rich elites and with impoverished populations increasingly overworked and under the surveillance of officials, must rely on mobilising local communities to solve local problems. Work in such alternative futures must become a more flexible mix of paid and voluntary activity, self-directed and organised in groups. This must rely on loyalties and solidarities at the level of communities, and not simply on the quest for self-realisation in personal or household projects. It must also be enabled by public services with a community development focus, and not simply those focused on individual welfare.

But local solidarities should not flourish at the expense of wider national and international ones. One of the more alarming features of the crisis was the rise of xenophobic nationalist groups in countries like Finland, Sweden and the Netherlands, and in England the response to the riots took the form of mono-ethnic vigilante groups on the streets of several city districts. Collective action can be exclusive and discriminatory if it is mobilised in an atmosphere of indignation, fear or defensive resentment.

In the United Kingdom, the notion of a Big Society programme to transfer power and resources to local communities was overtaken by austerity policies, which inflicted terrible damage on just those organisations and practices which that approach had promised to nurture. The closure of youth facilities certainly contributed to the riots in the English cities, for example. When the collective action Cameron pledged to promote came about, it took the form of protests and occupations.

However, another legacy of the crisis has been a shift in thinking on the political right in the United Kingdom, which focuses once more on civil society as an important counterbalance to both the state and the market (Norman, 2010). One of the more radical texts to appear in this tradition was Phillip Blond's *Red Tory* manifesto (2010), self-consciously harking back to the writings of liberals and conservatives who championed the cause of peasants and craft workers, who were instinctively suspicious of monopoly capitalism, and who opposed social insurance as an instrument for coercion of workers. This represented a revival of social policy and social work traditions predating welfare states but not in the market-minded, *laissez-faire* mode. We will explore the relevance of these ideas to the post-crisis situation.

This would be the counterpart of the shifts in the organisation of work and the provision of credit analysed in earlier chapters. It would not replace the need for policies requiring national and international solidarities for their funding and political support, but it would complement them in important ways.

But the approach we advocate does not look nostalgically back to past working-class communities, in the manner of Red Toryism, or indeed Blue Labourism (Glasman *et al.*, 2011). It seeks its basis in those groups in society which are still 'classes in the making' in the new economic landscape, the underemployed youth, the 'precariat' and even the 'squeezed middle' (already a social movement of sorts in Greece, and on the way to being one in Spain and Italy). It is from these that a new politics and a new community should emerge.

In Chapter 6, we turn to the issues of intergenerational justice and the family generated by the crisis, and requiring new institutional solutions. The most obvious casualties of the recession and the eurozone sovereign debt debacle were those just reaching adulthood. Transitions to adulthood have been increasingly problematic since Margaret Thatcher's cuts in benefits and allowances for young people in the 1980s, but these have suddenly become much harder still. Austerity programmes in public services affected this generation most adversely; in the United Kingdom they were the first to organise mass protests over having to pay higher fees for university courses and losing maintenance allowances, and as jobs become scarcer and less secure and their career prospects worsen, they are the obvious losers among society's members.

In the United Kingdom, as in other countries, it was the eldest generation who retained the largest proportion of the rights that were created during the welfare state era, in the form of pensions and access to acute medical care. Arguably, this represents a relationship of injustice between the youngest generation and the eldest, with the situation of the middle generation somewhere in between.

One rationale for the 'race to the bottom' on public-sector pensions and the rise in the qualifying age for state retirement pensions was that the young generation would revolt against the privileges enjoyed by the old, as predicted by Thatcher's guru, Friedrich Hayek. This argument was used to justify reduced entitlements during the austerity programme; in fact, young people were more resentful of the huge increases in the pay and bonuses of the elite than the benefits received by their elders. They recognised that the capitalist system's capacity to distribute income to the majority had broken down.

It is therefore the need for a new way to transfer income across the generations which is at stake, rather than a gradual erosion of the rights embodied in welfare state institutions. This chapter will show how the proposal for a basic income for all citizens would meet the requirement for intergenerational justice. We consider how social work can best form part of a new range of policies to improve the well-being of individuals and families, and engage in negotiations about the new relationships appropriate for the post-crisis order.

In Chapter 7, we turn to the analysis of how social policy and social work might be transformed in response to a different perspective on growth, consumption and sustainability. If a diminishing proportion of the population of the affluent countries are directly linked to the financial intermediaries and business corporations which dominate the global economic system, but the new system of universal state credit, Basic Incomes, supplies them with the means for subsistence, how might they organise their activities so as to enjoy the most prosperous and rewarding collective existence compatible with the survival of the planet?

The demand for 'prosperity without growth' (Jackson, 2009) has become increasingly insistent since the crisis, because it is an equal requirement of ecological sustainability and the new diminished role for the affluent states in the world economy. Part of the squaring of this circle lies in new, cleaner modes of production of energy and new forms of fuel-efficient transport, as well as new technologies for the manufacture of everyday commodities. But another part is social – the reordering of relationships between citizens to reduce the vast costs (in terms of inefficiency and waste) of struggles for positional advantage which seem rational for individuals but have very adverse collective effects.

As Frank (2011) has pointed out, a great deal of the consumption expenditure in affluent societies consists in people's attempts to gain positions of higher status (for the social value they confer, or for the sake of the advantages they give to their offspring). These competitive efforts are rational and confer benefits on society as a whole if they allow individuals to move into work which is more productive, or to become innovators (inventors or entrepreneurs). But in a mature affluent society only a tiny number of young people can progress into these roles; the vast majority will increasingly be confined to work in social reproduction, allowing society to move from one generation to the next without losing ground (something the recent cohort of adults failed to do).

It follows that much of the energy and effort put into attempts to improve any individual's position relative to others in such a society will not only be fruitless and increase frustration and personal unhappiness (Layard, 2005; Lane, 2000), it will also contribute to a collective increase in the overall costs to the group of similar people in that society engaged in equally fruitless endeavours. For instance, aspiring parents will drive up the prices of houses in a district with a successful school, and more students achieving postgraduate qualifications will increase the demand for such credentials by employers, even when the work on offer requires no such skills. In both instances the outcome for individuals is no better, and that for the group is increased costs.

Perversely, national income statistics count all such expenditures as gains in GDP, although they are completely unproductive. A state whose whole marketable output was created by 5 per cent of its population, but the rest of whose citizens were required to hold doctorates in the arts of looking after each other, and paid large salaries for this work, would statistically be seen as extremely prosperous; one in which the latter majority were paid small allowances to look after themselves would be recorded as relatively poor.

The process of reducing these costly aspects of the competitive cultural life of affluent societies will take many years, but the crisis has at least served to signal the need for it to begin. Instead of seeking growth, employment and material consumption for their own sake, governments can steer citizens in the direction of forms of well-being derived from cooperation rather than rivalry, and quality of life rather than quantity of possessions.

The crisis also pointed to the importance of developing services to meet human needs in ways that do not rely too heavily on increased state spending or the exclusive expertise of professionals. The argument of the book points towards the evolution of types of collective action which spring from the perceptions, motivations and self-organisation of citizens themselves. These will supply the sense of purposeful involvement in society which is an essential element in well-being.

On our analysis, it is 'social work' in this sense that should expand, not the kind of disciplinary interventions envisaged by austerity programmes. Social work in our sense would indeed become more central to social policy, but not as part of a more coercive regime, focused on disadvantaged individuals and communities.

Even if the world economy does grow continuously – as seems unlikely – affluent societies should become models of how the fundamental contradictions of free market capitalism, which have become so obvious in its mature form, may be resolved through radically transformative new institutions.

Our aim in this book is to use a range of theoretical perspectives – on the economy, democratic politics and social relations as well as public policy and practice in human services – to show how the crisis unfolded, and what might be done to transform the frameworks of ideas and institutions within which social work is conducted in future.

Capitalism in crisis: How did we get into such a mess?

chapter 1

Capitalism and social policy have always been symbiotic; post-war welfare states allowed the affluent countries to experience rapid reconstruction and growth without the class conflicts of the interwar years. Since then social policy has been like a critical junior partner to capitalist interests – one which has had to put up with increasing slurs and indignities over the years since the early 1970s.

In this chapter, we will trace how a certain version of economic analysis came to dominate both politics and the social sciences, subordinating social work and social policy to the logic of markets. Starting as a minority school of thought among a few academics, it went on to become the hegemonic orthodoxy, disseminated by think tanks funded by big business and defence contractors in the United States, and sustained by propaganda in the media (such as *Fox News*) and by the 'shock jocks' of countless local radio stations.

In the face of this dominance, any political forces which might have upheld the values and goals of social policy and social work fragmented into a set of single-issue campaigns over the oppression of specific groups, so a coherent opposition to the forces for privatisation, the extension of consumerist logics into public service organisations and the business model of state agencies failed to materialise. Just as the interests of weapons manufacturers and security services came to direct foreign policies in the United States and the United Kingdom, those of the banks and insurance companies determined economic decisions. When the crash came, there was no alternative set of ideas ready to be mobilised as replacements.

Social policy as an academic discipline had come into existence as governments were experimenting with the first social insurance schemes and public welfare services; it was rooted in progressive liberal principles such as social justice (Hobhouse, 1922). Social work, by contrast, came from an earlier tradition, more individualistic and pious in its moral notions, and hostile to collective state provision. It accommodated itself less critically to capitalism, but eventually allied with the principles that informed public service provision.

The aftermath of the First World War brought huge economic and social instability and insecurity in its wake. Orthodox economists believed this to be a temporary aberration. Left to itself, the market would produce a new equilibrium, free of the artificial constraints and interferences which wartime had brought about. By contrast, John Maynard Keynes (1936) developed an analysis which suggested that instability and uncertainty had come to be inherent in capitalist economies, already moving rapidly into mass production and battles for international markets. Malfunction was, for Keynes, inherent in unregulated capitalism. Left to itself it would always go wrong – producing ever-greater swings between periods of boom and bust.

The answer, for Keynes, was that governments could and should use their powers of intervention and regulation to act *counter-cyclically* – spending money to bolster economies in times of recession, taking money out of economies to prevent overheating during periods of rapid growth. Keynesianism was first successfully implemented in the Roosevelt 'New Deal' in the 1930s United States. It became the prevailing orthodoxy there for the quarter of a century after the Second World War, and was institutionalised in government systems throughout Europe, either by political choice (as in the Attlee Labour government in the United Kingdom) or under the guidance of the American victors (as in Germany, Austria and Italy).

This version of the role of the state in the economy involved the creation of systems like social insurance (Beveridge, 1942), including coverage for health care (though not in the United States), and social services. Social work accepted these developments in economic management and social policy (Bourdillon, 1945), though it largely remained within the voluntary sector, but funded by the state, in Germany in particular.

Even during the period of Keynesian hegemony, however, a very different view continued to be advanced by economists such as Friedrich Von Hayek (1960), who argued that free markets were inherently self-balancing and that state intervention could only ever make things worse. Economically, it led to inefficiencies, inflation and the suppression of enterprise. Socially, it led to the destruction of freedom and the suppression of the individual in the face of an all-powerful state. While Hayek's ideas remained firmly in the policy undergrowth during the 25 years after 1945, they came to new prominence in the troubled 1970s, when oil-price hikes fuelled 'stagflation' – a period of high inflation with slow economic growth.

Since then, these neo-liberal views have become a new hegemony, in which deregulation, small government and a belief in the intrinsic virtues of free markets have dominated. As Hayek would have advocated, it combines both an economic theory and a fundamentally political view of the state. The practical outcomes of market liberation and state retreat were all too apparent in the crash of 2008.

Meanwhile, social policy and social work have been strongly influenced by this ideological shift. Both the organisation and management of the public services and practice itself have been pervaded by principles derived from contract theory and business methods, with the state actively promoting markets and individual choice.

Although the crisis-ridden period which followed the high-water mark of welfare states in the late 1960s caused some commentators of the left (Gough, 1979; O'Connor, 1977; Offe, 1984) and the right (Brittan, 1976; King, 1976) to see social policy as trapped in capitalism's contradictions, the fact that countries seemed to come through their fiscal problems and resume growth paths after restructuring and retrenchment led to the belief that there would always be ways to adapt to each new stage in the development of these economies.

In consequence, neither mainstream social policy analysts nor social work theorists ever had reason to look at the fundamentals of capitalism and ask themselves whether their values and principles could be realised within its dynamic. Although it was clear that the integration of the world economy into a single system and the weakening of all forms of national boundaries against the flow of money, ideas, technology, materials, products and people put enormous strains on states' attempts to protect the living standards of their more vulnerable citizens, globalisation was theorised as a challenge rather than a death knell to welfare state regimes.

In this chapter, we will argue that the assumptions behind this complacency were blown away by the crisis which began in 2008, and that it is therefore now necessary to step back from those events and examine what changed in the dynamics of a global economy which still seemed to be running on the same fundamentals – property rights, money, markets, firms, prices, trade – as when Adam Smith (1776) described how free markets optimised the distribution of resources, in terms of efficiency and equity. Our first task is to suggest reasons for the paradigm shift which meant that (at least in the affluent countries) mechanisms which could bestow reasonably reliable progress towards the prosperity of whole populations suddenly ceased functioning. In retrospect, there was evidence that the supposed benefits of globalisation and the deregulation of these economies had cloaked a gradual decline in the fortunes of those lacking links with large international banks and companies for several decades.

In order to do this, we need to trace the origins of a certain approach to the study of economics which although it was claimed to be fully in accord with the methods and principles developed in earlier traditions of the subject in fact removed it from the human and social sciences (as properly understood) and incorporated several grossly misleading assumptions into its basic theorems. These were adopted from speculations in the natural sciences which turned out to be mistaken, and then grafted onto the use of new electronic technology so as to give enormous power to unaccountable forces in global markets.

In other words, power in the newly integrated world economy passed into the hands of organisations in the grip of a deluded view of how a viable version of capitalism operated, who then consolidated their distorted version into systems largely beyond the reach of regulators or even shareholders. This system served the interests of the power elite of the global economy only as long as governments could be relied upon to bear the costs of its catastrophic failures; but this condition was certain to be realised, because power and wealth had become so concentrated in their hands that governments could not afford to let them lose their vast assets.

Once we have explained how this came about, we will turn to how it impacted upon the economies of the affluent countries, and eventually led to the crisis. We will show that the events of 2008–12 revealed that the mechanisms allowing welfare capitalism to function were broken beyond repair, and how austerity programmes adopted to try to save capitalism from itself caused huge additional damage to the lives of populations. This meant that conventional social policy remedies could not protect people from the impact of global market forces, and entirely new approaches became necessary.

<table>
<tr><td rowspan="2">case study</td><td>

The relevance of the crisis in capitalism for social work and social policy

In the 1970s, when the UK economy experienced its first major crisis of the post-war period, students of social work and social policy were vividly aware of the effects this had on the welfare state, and critical texts on capitalist development were part of the everyday substance of debate. But since then, issues of policy and practice have been reduced to technical discussions about efficiency and effectiveness. Paradoxically, the triumph of market economic thinking has meant that students are insulated from the big questions about the nature and direction of economic change.

This is not so everywhere. For example, a group of radical social workers in Slovenia issued the following statement in support of the Occupy Movement in February 2012:

Direct social work

At Occupy Ljubjana, we have formed Direct Social Work Initiative.

Not to be servants of finance capital, supervisors of expenditures of the poor!

</td></tr>
</table>

To become an advocate for the people, join the movements today.

Social work emerged from working class movements for social justice – and became a mediator between the state and the people. In time, social workers became expropriated, too.

With neo-liberalism, social work has become a global profession – to reduce and repair the harm done.

But social work is also an opportunity for all those who are pushed into the shadow of silence to speak, for those who have become dependent on others to take things into their own hands.

We need to relinquish roles in which we treat people as things, in which paper is more important than deed, and by which we serve disablement and not empowerment.

Enough of the indirect social work, enough of the paperwork, enough of the closed institutions…

150 is an opportunity for social work, an opportunity to become directly responsible to the people.

False assumptions and shaky foundations

To trace the origins of the crisis in capitalism, we need to look back to a crucial set of assumptions which were incorporated into economic theory in the late twentieth century, and which in turn became central to the ruling orthodoxy in political economy (Buchanan and Tullock, 1962). These untested and grandiose notions were deployed in a form of intellectual imperialism (Hirschman, 1981) which allowed economists to dominate political programmes in the affluent countries, and eventually to exert a decisive influence on the restructuring of the economies of the former Soviet Bloc states.

Two central ideas informed this hegemony. The first was that markets were self-ordering because they tended towards equilibrium – the point at which all the forces influencing outcomes were in balance. Although enormous mathematical ingenuity and elegance were used to demonstrate this fundamental principle, it was in fact uncritically imported from a mistaken model of how *nature* ordered itself – the idea of the universe and life on earth as obeying predictable and regular rules, like a machine. This mechanical fallacy was the first step on the road to creating an uncontrollably dysfunctional world economy.

The second ruling idea was the corollary of this – that attempts to steer or regulate these processes of self-ordering were therefore certain to be counterproductive. This implied that politics in general, and democratic politics in particular, would distort the emergence of optimal outcomes in the name of such ethical goals as equality and social justice. On this account, political decisions should aim to clear away impediments to the functioning of free markets; best of all, they should loosen the grip of any human influences on these impersonal, mechanical processes. The ideal global economy would be run by machines – a fantasy which became increasingly plausible with the development of computer technology and the Internet. Indeed, organisations like those trading in currencies and shares began increasingly to install vast banks of computers, conducting electronic trading, as their *modus operandi*.

The first of these false assumptions stemmed from a hubristic attempt to make economics into a natural science, on par with the sciences of the physical and biological orders, and derived from mathematical princi- ples – to escape the stigma and limitations of being a mere *social* science, compromised by its subservience to political folly, and forced to deal in human cultural and contextual contingencies. But this in turn assumed that nature was itself governed by immutable laws that tended to order and equilibrium, a view that was orthodox at the time (the 1950s and 1960s) that economics began to take this turn, but since decisively over- thrown (at least at the scale of human beings and objects observable to their senses) by a very different notion of how nature takes the shapes it does (Al Khalili, 2010).

Since the early 1980s, scientists have increasingly rejected the analogy of a machine for their understanding of how the universe and life have developed, in favour of a model of complexity and unpredictability. Chaos theory showed how small events could trigger huge reactions and alter the course of major natural forces; but this did not imply that nature does not follow self-ordering principles. Rather, it pointed to phenomena like the way huge flocks of starlings fly both apparently randomly and as an ever-changing close formation, or sand dunes constantly shift yet form repeating patterns, or trees grow in recognisa- ble shapes yet are all individually different, to indicate how certain simple rules give rise to an extraordinary irregularity and diversity of phenomena.

Nature, in other words, is not smooth and symmetrical like a geometri- cal diagram or an engineering construction; it is epitomised in clouds, rivers, plants and waves, ever-shifting and taking certain shapes, but often uneven, bent, rough or lumpy. The mathematics of the processes behind these phenomena are now better understood (Mandelbrot, 1982); pattern- ing comes about through feedback loops, leading such things to shape themselves at smaller and smaller scales over and over again. This follows a simple mathematical formula, $z = z^2 + c$; as each shape contains a smaller version of itself, it produces an infinitely complex pattern, as in the branches and twigs, all similarly shaped, which go to make up a tree, or a broccoli plant. In this way, repetitions of a simple process give rise to unpredictable complexity, self-ordering as both the explosive chaos of a storm and the tranquillity of a summer day.

Yet despite the fact that natural science had moved beyond the mechanical paradigm to this organic one, economists continued to develop models in which the self-ordering of market forces produced regular, even and predictable outcomes, under assumptions which bore no relation to the real world. Once it is recognised that in economic development, as in biological evolution and the history of human societies, the principles followed are derived from feedback of the Mandelbrot kind, these models become actively misleading. In particular, the attempt by investment banks to discover mathematical formulae for eliminating risk, developed with disastrous consequences in the 1990s (Tett, 2009), can be seen to have led directly to the crash of 2008. Instead of producing more optimal equilibria at a higher level of income, they contributed to the radical destabilisation of the global financial system.

The second fallacy, that regulation distorted market processes and limited growth, and that human societies were best left to develop through spontaneous interactions, had an equally powerful hold on the elites which gained power in this period, and through even more irrational influences. Whereas the first source of error was the right-wing economists (such as Milton Friedman) who had been influenced by the philosophers of the Austrian School, Hayek (1960) and Von Mises (1966), the second was a more diverse group of 1960s intellectuals, entrepreneurs and eccentrics, who imbibed the libertarian ideas of that era, and then entered positions of power and influence.

case study

The sorts of problems which emerged in financial services in 2008 were not unique. Twenty years earlier, similar issues had been experienced in the Savings and Loans organisations of the United States. S&Ls were 'thrift' organisations, rooted in working class communities, with a social as much as a financial mission. Two acts of Congress, during the Reagan presidency of the 1980s, removed many of the previous safeguards which had surrounded their operation, as part of a wider shift towards 'deregulation'. Now S&Ls were reshaped to maximise profits, rather than to promote responsible saving and borrowing, especially in relation to housing and homeownership. A large number of defaults and bankruptcies followed in which many S&Ls became insolvent. The fact that a federal agency existed with an obligation to repay all depositors whose money was lost highlighted the issue of *moral hazard* in the way in which the system operated. The organisations had been allowed all the trappings and rewards of success when their risk-taking led in that direction, but were protected from the consequences of their own actions when they led to failure.

One of the more extraordinary pathways which was taken by this strand of thought began with the Russian-born American author Ayn Rand whose science fiction novels such as *Atlas Shrugged* (1957) anticipated the invention of interacting computers and the Internet (BBC 2 tv, 2011). Although she had no training in economics, her radical vision of how the power of such machines could free people from the need for government control, regulation and authority attracted a devoted group of followers, enthralled by her vision of personal liberation and a spontaneous global order of societies mechanically coordinated through electronic networks.

One of the leading members of the Rand clique was Allen Greenspan, who went on to head the US Federal Reserve in the 1990s and early 2000s, and whose low-interest policies defied all warnings to create two bubbles in that economy (Fleckenstein and Sheehan, 2008). He helped edit a collection of her essays, published as *Capitalism: The Unknown Ideal* (Rand, Branden and Greenspan, 1966), arguing that free markets enable the only moral social system, and that the mixed economy leads inevitably to 'statism'.

The young entrepreneurs of Silicon Valley were fervent adherents of Rand's message, and called their children after her, and their companies after characters in her novels. They invented a game which could be played by people on computers remote from each other, and one even conducted a social experiment to show that people's actions could be rationally coordinated without any external guidance or direct contact between them.

So the whole tendency of this school of thought was towards transformations which allowed individuals to act from their desires and preferences (as in markets), and their decisions to be related to each other by interactive machines, electronically reconciling them with each other in a single system. Here again the adherents of this model drew an analogy with the living world, in this case a supposed 'balance of nature', through which all the species in any ecology, including predators and prey, were supposed to respond to each other in such a way as to bring the whole system into equilibrium.

There were two things wrong with this analogy. First, observation and research soon showed that there was no such law ensuring that natural species balanced each other in this way; they were quite likely to hunt each other to extinction, to overbreed or to devastate their environments (Botkin, 1990). Second, it ignored the issue of power in human societies. As attempts at egalitarian communes showed, people were able to use conditions of freedom to gain the means to control and exploit others, in the absence of rules restricting such behaviour.

In spite of this, a version of the libertarian fallacy has been the ruling global ideology since the 1980s, with different variants supplying the basis for the Washington Consensus (the free market orthodoxy imposed on the developing countries through the International Monetary Fund (IMF), and then on the former Soviet Bloc after the collapse of state socialism) and the Third Way (Jordan, 2008, 2010). Financial markets were deregulated and governments retreated; as gullible customers of the banks, whose strategists claimed to have eliminated risk, people enjoyed the opportunity to borrow more than they could afford. Power had not disappeared from the global economy; it had become concentrated in the hands of a plutocratic elite.

In the final incarnation of the orthodoxy, the theory of information, incentives and contracts (Laffont and Martimort, 2002; Bolton and Dewatripont, 2005), the aim was to improve the efficiency of government agencies as much as the functioning of markets, by contracting for public services in ways that minimised 'asymmetric information', thus dealing with issues of moral hazard. The theory also installed banks at the centre of their economic model as the best-informed agencies in the economy, and hence the most capable of steering investment to its most productive uses (Stiglitz and Greenwald, 2003).

One part of this was the chance for firms to take over aspects of the collective provision of states, gaining opportunities to develop themselves into international suppliers, for instance, of schools, hospitals and social care facilities worldwide. Using the opportunities created by the World Trade Organisation's General Agreement on Trade in Services, these companies extended their reach into the developing world, at the same time winning contracts from governments in the affluent countries convinced by the case for improved efficiency and choice advanced by these interests.

The other part was the constant growth of banking and insurance companies as part of this orthodoxy. Particularly in the United States and the United Kingdom, public policy favoured the expansion of the financial sector as much as the penetration of private firms into the government's functions – for instance, Bill Clinton abolished the laws forbidding banks from conducting both retail lending and borrowing and speculative investment, thus allowing them to gamble with their private customers' savings. Between 1997 and 2007, over 80 per cent of investment in the United Kingdom was in financial products and mortgages.

Deploying sophisticated mathematical modelling and devising increasingly complex financial products, these giant banks then bundled up various loans (including sub-prime mortgages) and sold them to each other, fully confident that they had eliminated the risks of a collapse in their value (Tett, 2011). The size of the financial sector had grown tenfold in a generation since the liberalisation of the 1980s, and the interconnectedness of its institutions added to its vulnerability. Contrary to the strategists' model's predictions, diversity at the level of individual banks' products actually meant uniformity in the system as a whole, and no attempt had been made to calculate the hazard to this total system. It was a pair of biologists, writing in *Nature*, who pointed out that the excessive size and interconnectivity of the banks made them into super-spreaders of infection once loans started to go bad; the promiscuity of their links made one outbreak of insolvency spread like an epidemic to the rest (Haldane and May, 2011). The financial sector generated chaos for the global economy, not the spontaneous order promised by economic theorists.

research box 1.1

In the aftermath of the 2008 crisis, the Bank of England's executive director for financial security, Andrew Haldane, and Robert May, formerly the UK government's Chief Scientist, set out to answer the question, 'Are big banks less prone to failure?' Drawing on research and evidence from the natural sciences – and especially epidemiology, ecology and genetics – they concluded that they were not. Conventional economics had suggested that big banks would be able to survive crises because they could spread their risks across a wide range of different activities. In fact, the authors concluded, complex systems tended to increase risk, rather than reduce it, because of extra chances of cross-contamination. When a big bank goes wrong, it acts as a 'super-spreader, infecting other parts of the financial system. As Haldane and May point out, 'When Lehman Brothers failed, it spread financial infection on a global scale.'

The last element of the orthodoxy's contribution to the crisis was its trust in the technology of computerised networks. By linking together high-powered machines in areas as large as three football pitches, large, wealthy firms were able in the later 2000s to conduct trades in shares, bonds and currencies in about 30 millionths of a second (i.e., 400,000 transactions a second). Programmed with algorithms allowing them to do this automatically in response to very small movements in prices, this enabled these companies to harvest large profits – one was reckoned to have netted US$21 billion from high-frequency trading in a single year (BBC Radio 4, 2009).

Quite apart from the dubious fairness of these methods, which make prices opaque to those who cannot afford such technologies, the capacities of huge trading floors to cause panics and pick off currencies, companies and countries perceived as vulnerable are magnified and accelerated by these technologies. Far from presiding benevolently over a rationally ordered global economy, such machines, in the hands of a few immensely wealthy corporations, perpetually threaten to destabilise it; far from being impeded in their work of optimising outcomes by interfering governments, they brought many governments and their citizens to their knees during the crisis.

Taken together, this combination of theoretical delusions and real-world shifts put the whole global system beyond the reach of any remedial measures available within the orthodox economic paradigm. Markets simply followed their instinctive blood lust to hunt down the weakest members of the sovereign pack; governments responded with self-defeating austerity measures designed to distract these predators, but which added to the supplies of potential victims; and the rich grew richer in the certainty that the organisations in which their wealth was concentrated could never be allowed to fail.

Obviously, economists were forced to reappraise their discipline in the light of this catastrophe, but their search for an alternative approach led backwards into the disputes between Keynes (state economic management) and Hayek (free markets), because they were unable to move forward from an intellectual prison of their own making. According to the former, government spending on initiatives like infrastructure projects (as launched by President Obama in the United States) was the only way to break out of a vicious circle of failing demand and consequent deflation. According to the latter, this risked inflation and did nothing to address structural distortions in the economy or uncompetitive wage rates. The solution required the pain of letting the banks with bad debts go bust, unprofitable businesses to fail, public services to shrink and wages to fall – anything else was just postponing a worse outcome.

So the pessimistic prognostications of the two schools of economic thought which had dominated the twentieth century were danced out between the protagonists at conferences of the G8, the G20 and the European Union (EU) during the autumn of 2011, with no decisive outcomes. Even within these groupings, there were divisions of opinion about the least worst options. For instance, when Angela Merkel of Germany met David Cameron in Berlin on 18 November, she wanted a pan-European Tobin tax on financial transactions to help pay for the bailout of insolvent eurozone states, whose enforced austerity programmes she was overseeing; he resisted this, claiming that 85 per cent of it would have to be paid by the speculative financial intermediaries of the City of London. Even as Greece and Italy were installing technocratic governments to do the bidding of their richer European masters, those austerity hawks were squabbling about how best to administer the corrective remedies.

Financial transactions tax

Originally named after the American economist James Tobin, and today more often known as a Robin Hood Tax, a financial transactions tax (FTT) would be a very small tax (of 0.05 per cent) levied on transactions such as stocks, bonds, foreign currency and trading in derivatives. It is strongly supported by a wide range of economists, regulators and some senior figures in the business world. It was the proposal to introduce a EU-wide FTT which led to the United Kingdom veto being exercised in December 2011. Those who advocate a Robin Hood tax do both because of the very large sums of money which could be raised, by taxing all such transactions by a very small amount (some estimates, for example, put the global figure at around £250 billion annually), and also because such a tax would help reduce the volume of the sort of financial gambling which helped trigger the 2008 crisis. Such a tax would not only be socially just, but economically effective.

In the next section we will turn to how the version of capitalism created by the discredited economic orthodoxies of the pre-crash period had subverted the processes by which the incomes of mainstream citizens, as well as poorer ones, were sustained.

Why are earnings falling?

The origins of the crisis traced in the previous section explain how governments got suckered into swallowing up the debts of the banks, and hence became vulnerable to the predation of global bond markets. But these factors do not of themselves account for the stagnation of earnings growth and the increase in income inequality in most of the affluent countries – a trend compensated by in-work benefits in many cases – and why median wages have been falling for several decades in the United States and Australia (Luttwak, 1999; Pusey, 2003), even when their economies were expanding at quite acceptable rates.

To see how this was happening, it is necessary to analyse the model of growth, rising productivity and increased equality which prevailed in the affluent countries in the two decades after the Second World War. We will argue that it was interpreted as a generalisable model of how capitalism operated, but was in fact a special case. Even though the conditions for its effectiveness now exist in parts of the developing world which are far more populous than those countries which benefited from the post-war boom, this simply indicates that the model can work on a far larger scale than it ever had previously. But just as the rapid growth in Europe, North America, Japan and Australasia relied on 'uneven development' – the exploitation of the less developed countries of Africa, Asia and Latin

America, and in many cases their impoverishment – so the present wave of growth in the global economy need not benefit those parts of the world in which these special conditions do not hold.

The virtuous circle which existed in the post-war period, most notably in Western Europe, allowed a plentiful supply of mobile labour power, consisting in the European case of refugees from the east of the continent as well as rural populations in search of urban opportunities, to find employment in new centres of industrial production, deploying new technologies and organisational systems to increase their output (Kindleberger, 1967). The post-war situation had two additional features which were special: in Europe and Japan, the devastation caused by bombing meant that obsolete and redundant buildings and machinery had already been written off; and there was a supply of capital for reconstruction in the form of loans from the United States, which had political motives for supporting the emergence of a new prosperity, as a bastion against the spread of Soviet-style state socialism (Judt, 2010, chs 3 and 8).

All this provided conditions almost perfectly replicating the version of capitalist development set out in economics textbooks (Lewis, 1954). If it could be assumed that there could continuously be improvements in the output per worker in the expanding sectors of an economy which was attracting additional labour power from a less productive sector, and that investment in these new facilities would also continue to flow, then the social consequences would be reliably benign. Better still, if the organisations representing labour are willing to negotiate smooth and steady increases in their pay (as they were in most of these countries, as a result of the institutions for cooperation between employers, unions and the state established after the war), then a prosperous middle class and a contented skilled industrial workforce could develop at the centre of a new type of democratic polity, as happened in this period.

The same dynamic has been achieved in China since the reform programme of the early 1980s, but by means of less benevolent political instruments. Imitating post-war Japan and the Tiger economies of some smaller Southeast Asian states, the Chinese authorities launched a giant project for exporting manufactured goods to the West, developing its coastal regions and drawing in unskilled workers from the rural north and west of the country. These migrants were paid better than they had been in their home provinces, but enjoyed few social rights and little employment security. Without democratic political constraints, the regime was able to control migration flows, to keep its currency undervalued, to attract investment from international firms and eventually to sustain rates of growth by lending vast sums to the United States in particular, to fund its consumers' increasing reliance on products imported from Chinese factories.

Meanwhile, none of these conditions held any longer in the affluent countries; all of them lost industrial employment with the rise of China and the other new manufacturing giants. The expansion in well-paid financial, professional and business service work, in research and development and in managerial occupations was accompanied by a growth of low-paid, insecure, part-time employment in retail, hospitality and personal services, leaving an hour-glass-shaped labour market, with office and routine administration work also outsourced to developing countries. The stripping out of jobs paying around median earnings left an emaciated upper working and lower middle class, reversing some of the structural changes of the previous three decades; it also created greater inequality of earnings.

The Third Way was an attempt to combat these trends in the United States and the United Kingdom, which was imitated in Europe. It used the expansion of public sector employment to fill up the gaps at the centre of the earnings range, and developed the notion of tax credits for those households with below-average pay, started under the Reagan administration in the United States, to supplement low wages (Newman, 2002). In the northeast of England, for instance, a majority of the jobs created under New Labour were in the public sector, and tax credit schemes were consolidated as key features of the income maintenance system nationally.

research box 1.2

Researchers in Manchester University have looked at the sorts of jobs which were created during the late 1990s and 2000s in the UK economy. They reported on the growth of public sector employment which, during the New Labour period, was one of the main ways in which the dividend of economic growth was distributed. By 2007, before the downturn began, the official count of those employed in the state sector had grown to 5.8 million, or 22 per cent of the total workforce. However, researchers also argued that some 1.7 million of those officially categorised as working in the private sector were, in reality, employed wholly on the basis of state funding. Thus, a teacher at a private school or a nurse at a private hospital appeared in the figures as a private sector employee. Yet, the research demonstrated, thousands and thousands of these jobs only existed because the state paid for National Health Service (NHS) treatment to be provided in the private sector, or pupils to be educated in private schools. Far from being private sector jobs, the authors argue, this is 'para-public' employment. Taken together, they conclude, fully 57 per cent of all new jobs created

> in the 15 years to 2007 were a combination of state-direct and para-state employment, with the latter category a major driver behind what appeared in official statistics to be a growth in private employment and thus masking the continuing failure of the private sector to generate and distribute jobs.
>
> *Source*: http://www.cresc.ac.uk/sites/default/files/wp%2075.pdf.

Obviously such strategies could only work if at least one sector of the economy was being successful in global markets, earning enough to support a larger role for the state in the labour market and in subsidising earnings. In the case of the United Kingdom, the New Labour government convinced itself that its financial sector was the world leader, and could be relied upon to sustain the continued growth of national income, and also to enable public borrowing to be increased. This was not so much a miscalculation as a piece of systematic self-deception; Gordon Brown in particular swallowed the orthodoxy of the financial speculators and the World Bank hook, line and sinker, boasting of 'no more boom and bust' and insisting on a 'light touch and a limited touch' in his regulation of the City of London. Later Brown wrote:

> " According to pre-crisis assumptions, if there was diversification of risk across the financial system, then the leveraging of financial institutions was less a systemwide threat than a matter of risk management in the individual institutions. ... It wasn't until later that we saw what none of us had bargained for: the sheer scale of the shadow banking system that would create a race to the bottom and co-opt mainstream banks to their practices. They had not, in fact, diversified much risk, and their entanglements threatened all financial institutions. (Brown, 2010, pp. 20–1)

What was really happening was that national prosperity had come to depend on the success of a few international companies, and particularly the financial sector. The free market experiment launched by Margaret Thatcher in the 1980s had demanded the sacrifice of citizens' economic security for the sake of the United Kingdom's competitiveness in global markets. The boom of the New Labour period had been an illusion, generated by financial trickery which fuelled household debt. When the government bailed out the banks, its fiscal crisis indicated the failure of the free market model.

Between late 2008 and the end of 2011, the world economy grew by 20 per cent, based on increased productive activity in every continent except Europe and North America. The rise in the value of stocks on leading markets in London, Wall Street and Tokyo was far higher than this. The companies making up the FTSE 100 in the United Kingdom were gaining 70 per cent of their profits abroad. But most of the population was essentially surplus to the requirements of capital.

The share of national income going to labour had fallen from a peak of 65 per cent in the early 1970s to little over 50 per cent; earnings failed to rise in real terms during the 11 per cent expansion of the economy in the five years before the crash, and the median wage has been failing to keep up with overall productivity increases since 1980. The earnings of those in the middle range have been moving away from those with the lowest wages, while those of the top three per cent have soared away from the rest. This matched trends in the United States (BBC Radio 4, 2012). It represents a huge challenge for public policy.

Hence the eurozone crisis of 2011–12 was not simply a question of fixing a broken currency union; it was an existential crisis for a set of economic, political and social arrangements for social harmony and cohesion, the European Social Model. After the Second World War, almost all the countries of Western Europe had, somewhat miraculously, adopted institutions for incorporating labour organisations into the management of their economies, the political processes of democracy and the sharing out of national income among their citizens (Judt, 2010, chs 3 and 8). The only exceptions were Spain, Portugal and Greece, where fascism and military suppression continued until the 1970s, a fact which helps to explain both their vulnerability to the crisis and their populations' resentment of austerity enforcement.

But beneath the apparent similarities in these arrangements lay a deep legacy of differences in the way internal cleavages and conflicts were managed, and the processes (and side-payments) through which the most intractable problems were defused – the relationship between the Italian North and South being an obvious example of an enduring set of issues. The EU project, and more strikingly the currency union, were attempts to smooth over all the disparities and inconsistencies between these systems and policies, which could function in good times but which produces cracks and fissures during the crisis. Above all, it exposed disparities between the competitiveness of member states, and imbalances in their trading relationships.

The net effect of all these factors was that the Southern European countries were forced to cut public services and benefits to raise taxes, and also either to suffer pay cuts of up to 20 per cent in the next decade or to endure far higher unemployment and increased casualisation of their employment arrangements (or some combination of the two). Spain had, by the time the bond markets were charging it almost seven per cent for its government loans in mid-November 2011, already reached a level of 45 per cent unemployment among its 18–24-year-olds, and over 20 per cent for its whole workforce.

The crisis in the eurozone affects social work and social policy directly, not only through the cuts in benefits and public services which have been made, but also because the programmes for managing unemployment in all these countries except Ireland are staffed by social workers. Organising work and training, especially for young people, and deciding about their eligibility for assistance, are deeply political issues, and should raise ethical dilemmas for all practitioners. In the United Kingdom, of course, these tasks have been contracted out to firms like A4e; but this in turn has illustrated the links between the crisis in capitalism and the moral basis for social policy in this field. In February 2012, the founder of A4e, Emma Harrison, resigned from her post as a government advisor and from the firm because of charges of fraud in the organisation, and a group of leading retail firms forced the government to drop the threat of benefits withdrawal hanging over participants in its work experience programme for young claimants, because they were under pressure from anti-capitalist protesters.

In the next section, we will turn to the dilemmas over how to sustain incomes and demand that these developments caused for governments.

The paradox of austerity

As the twin crises of sovereign and bank debt unfolded in Europe, governments – even solvent ones – were frozen in uncertainty about how to respond. Fear of the bond markets indicated that a posture of austerity was the only safe option, and this was how the coalition administration in the United Kingdom reacted. But the United States, with nothing to fear from markets despite its $15 trillion debt mountain and $1.5 trillion fiscal deficit, had taken a different course, and adopted a programme of public works spending to try to boost employment and earnings. Yet in spite of this, growth remained extremely sluggish and unemployment high; this gave ammunition to the Republican majority in the House of Representatives, fuelled by Tea Party fundamentalism, in its refusal to countenance tax increases.

For those in the eurozone looking anxiously across the Atlantic for signals of a rescue mission in the autumn of 2011, this was deeply discouraging. But our analysis would suggest that it was neither more nor less than could have been expected from the evidence of how the capitalist dynamic of the affluent countries had come to operate. Since the growth of the previous decade had turned out to be the illusory effect of gambles on borrowed funds, and even this had not led to higher earnings, but only to greater household debt, it was not surprising that the stimulus package failed to boost wages or consumption. These outcomes gave little comfort to Keynesians elsewhere.

In the United Kingdom, the government faced another set of problems. In addition to its cuts in public services, it had also picked a fight with the trade unions in that sector over their pension contributions and entitlements. It did not want to be seen to exert downward pressure on wages in the private sector, but its quantitative easing (QE) programmes were feeding inflation at around 5 per cent throughout 2011, leaving the majority of workers with a real-terms pay cut, at a time when chief executives of large companies were making gains of 49 per cent a year and bankers' bonuses remained eye-watering.

One trouble for the government was that the inflation rate triggered proportional rises in benefits for people out of work. In consequence, incentives to take work at wages whose real value was shrinking were further diminished. QE and inflation did have the effect of reducing the value of debt repayments, but they failed to improve output or employment. The government put increasing faith, therefore, in its reforms of the benefits system, designed to make the transition from claiming to taking small numbers of hours of work smoother, while making eligibility rules for incapacity benefit (renamed Employment and Support Allowance) far tighter; and in its Work Programme, which offered incentives to private companies to prepare claimants for the labour market and find them lasting employment.

The details of these schemes and their shortcomings and perversities will be analysed in the next chapter. For now, the point increasingly made, at first half-jokingly and then as a serious policy proposal, was that if the government really wanted to get the economy moving, to create growth and jobs, it would do far better to stop the QE injections, the bank rescues and the technical adjustments to the benefits system, and simply give each citizen a handout of several thousand pounds. Simon Jenkins in *The Guardian* (28 September 2011, p.27) pointed out that the money printed through the QE programme amounted to some £200 billion, yet 'it cannot explain where the money has gone'. In his column, he recommended several times since the beginning of the crisis that it would be better to distribute this sum as a payment to each citizen, which by November 2011 would amount to £3,000 (Jenkins, 2011b).

Much the same argument was advanced by the Australian economist Steve Keen, one of the few to have predicted the crash. On his analysis, during a bubble speculators borrow money to fund investments, gambling that they will be able to pay back what they owe from the rising value of their assets. In essence this was what the disgraced financier Bernie Madoff did in the United States for many years – a giant Ponzi scheme, in which each cohort of lenders is paid off in turn by the takings from a new cohort. In that country, by the middle of the first decade of the century private debt was 300 per cent of the gross domestic product (GDP). In the United Kingdom, households borrowed £300 billion during the boom (Keen, 2011, a and b).

Bernie Madoff, for decades a fabulously rich and highly respected New York stockbroker, in fact operated a scheme in which cash from new customers or investors was used to pay returns to existing investors. It depended on a constant stream of new investors to fund the payouts. He made it look as if he was investing in blue-chip stocks and options, but actually money was simply being recycled from new investors to pay dividends to old ones. New investors were attracted by the high rate of return which could be generated in this way. However, new clients began to dry up once the credit crunch took hold. When people began to want to withdraw their cash, it turned out that there was none there. It was, he told his family, 'all just one big lie'. Arrested, he pleaded guilty to having profited from some £38 billion of his clients' money. He was sentenced to 150 years imprisonment in 2009.

All this debt reflected the risky lending by banks which led to the crash, but as people started to pay it off, QE was supposed to boost demand by making the banks more willing to lend again, as well as driving down interest on government bonds. But this part of the UK government's strategy failed to stimulate production or spending, especially in the small business sector, where firms found it difficult to get credit. Speaking in London, Keen recommended that giving cash to every citizen would kick-start investment, because the extra spending this would enable would encourage large companies to spend the cash they had been hoarding (*The Guardian*, 21 November 2011, pp. 22–3).

This was one of the few examples of an economist 'thinking the unthinkable' during a crisis, yet it was a fairly obvious response to the Catch 22 of austerity policies. The problem of the stage of capitalist development reached in the affluent countries had for some time been one of rises in GDP not being reflected in rising earnings. This was hardly surprising, given that much of the income earned by global corporations came from productive activities in the developing world, or services bought in those economies. Hence the income from these gains went to the managements and owners of the firms, and a few highly skilled employees. Most of the workforce in the advanced economies was engaged in supplying services to each other, and the productivity gains required to justify increased earnings were difficult to make in these occupations (Baumol, 1967; Baumol *et al*, 1985).

Indeed, the alternative account of the origins of the crisis was that governments in the affluent countries, desperate to achieve growth in citizens' incomes and seeing that earnings and employment were not increasing, either encouraged the reckless lending that finally triggered the crash or themselves borrowed excessively to create more work and pay, or both. Even a country like Germany, with its fiscal prudence, high savings ratio and success in world markets for manufactured goods, could only achieve buoyant employment and earnings by sponsoring a monetary union in which its banks lent billions of euros to its customers – a kind of reverse Ponzi scheme – allowing consumers to borrow to afford its products.

The final irony came on 23 November 2011, when the German government failed to sell 40 per cent of a bond issue in global markets. So the one copper-bottomed, fiscally sound regime in the eurozone had failed where even Greece, Italy and Spain in their worst hours had (with a bit of help from the European Central Bank (ECB)) managed to offload their tainted issues. The reason for this reversal in fortunes was, of course, that for all its rectitude – some would say sanctimonious rigidity – Germany's treasury and banks were compromised by involvement in the stricken currency, and the going interest rate on its debt gave a minimal return to its bondholders. If anyone was going to hold a stake in risky loans to sovereigns, they might just as well enjoy the high rates from the bonds of impecunious member countries. Only the day before, a feature about the German Chancellor, Angela Merkel, had proclaimed her 'the most powerful person in the world' (*The Guardian,* G2, 22 November 2011). *Sic transit gloria mundi.*

This Alice-in-Wonderland logic epitomised the fact that finance capitalism and the real world of production and earnings had become parallel universes; the tasks of reconciling them were well beyond the powers of governments, enfeebled as they were first from their willing retreat from regulation, and then from their unwilling rescue of the financial system. All this explains why a fundamental transformation in these relationships is required.

Conclusions

The prolonged crisis which began in 2008 gradually dissolved the pretensions of politicians in the affluent countries to exert any control over the impersonal forces of capitalism or the personal greed of its plutocracy. As protest occupations of strategic squares spread to 1,500 cities worldwide, one common slogan, directed to the elites in all these countries, was 'You've Run Out of Ideas'.

Events had demonstrated that, in all the circumstances of that time, none of the basic assumptions of abstract economic theory held. Individuals could not make rational decisions to further their own interests if the world's holders of capital could lay a whole country's economy low within a matter of days, because it was profitable to bet on its failure at some future date. Governments could not supply the level of public goods needed for the proper functioning of these economies if their decisions were aimed at avoiding the fate of such victims. Firms could not invest to increase production if government austerity measures choked off demand.

And the whole system could spiral into recession if every individual, every government and every firm responded to these threats by further reductions in their outlays.

But – as we have shown in this chapter – none of these traps and paradoxes was susceptible to a simple set of Keynesian remedies, because of far more deep-seated and long-term malfunctioning of the capitalist machine. Employment was failing to distribute rising incomes to workers as a class, even when the economy seemed to be growing; instead, the banks distributed an expensive form of credit, which could quickly turn to unaffordable debt. Work was being intensified, but welfare and well-being were declining.

In the absence of real gains from all this extra effort, interactions between members of the populations of the affluent countries became dominated by struggles for positional advantage – the attempt to improve status in relation to others, or to gain strategic advantage over them. Even when such action appeared individually rational – as in the competition between parents for places at schools with good examination results – they summed together as collectively unproductive and costly. These phenomena had been recognisable for decades (Jordan, 1996).

The crisis made any surviving credibility of the modified versions of welfare states which prevailed in these countries threadbare. The situation demanded a set of coordinated responses from governments, but also a new approach to policies at the level of societies. Increasingly, political and social theorists turned their attention to ideas about work, property and income which had been influential some hundred or more years earlier, but had been largely forgotten since; they also began to take seriously ideas about state action for redistribution which had been seen as utopian. It is to these notions that we will turn in the next chapter.

main points

■ The pre-1945 relationship between social policy, capitalism and welfare services was symbiotic, but came under increasing strain, from the mid-1970s onwards. It finally broke down as the 2008 crisis exposed the way in which its foundations had been eaten away by neo-conservative economic orthodoxies.

■ Deregulated free markets failed to create the spontaneous order which their supporters claimed. Instead, it produced inherent inequality and instability on a massive scale.

■ In the process, the share of national wealth taken by workers, and those without work, has fallen, as have their real incomes. The gap in purchasing power has been filled by debt, based on belief that this could be covered by the ever-rising value of assets such as housing. These issues lie at the heart of the wider eurozone crisis.

■ Faced with this difficulty, the 'austerity' programmes of right-wing governments across Europe have simply intensified the difficulty – soaking effective demand out of economies, including draconian cuts to welfare services and benefits. Against this background, some analysts have turned again to look at different ways in which incomes might be redistributed and welfare of whole populations produced and protected.

taking it further

■ Lanchester, J. (2010) *Whoops*, London: Allen Lane.
■ Jordan, B. (2010) *Why the Third Way Failed: Economics, Morality and the Origins of the 'Big Society'*, Bristol: Policy Press.
■ Reid, H. and Lawson, N. (eds) (2011) *PLAN B – A Good Economy for a Good Society*, London, Compass. Available at: http://clients.squareeye.net/uploads/compass/documents/Compass_Plan_B_web.pdf.

2 Secure flexibility? The search for work-friendly welfare

In the history of both social policy and social work, issues of how the state seeks to support household incomes have been pivotal. Social work, first as a voluntary activity and then as a profession, came into existence as a charitable or church-sponsored activity, focused on those who, because they lacked the security of full membership of their communities or the support of family members, had insufficient means for subsistence – it was a way of giving alms in a compassionate and organised way. But it also sought to rescue respectable but unfortunate people from the stigma of the often punitive methods with which political authorities dealt with poverty, disability, widowhood, homelessness and the frailties of old age.

This was because, both at the local level and among the emerging nation states of Europe in the late middle ages, these authorities were trying to deal with the social consequences of economic change and the first manifestations of market relationships (de Swaan, 1988). Whereas feudal societies tied individuals into roles based on the status (noble, squire, wife, peasant, villain, serf, etc.) into which they were born, markets allowed them to become disconnected from these roles, giving them the freedom to move and acquire possessions, but also putting them at risk of penury. First in England, where markets in land were established earlier than in the rest of Europe (Macfarlane, 1978), and gradually all over the continent, the fear of wandering gangs of beggars and the distress of displaced vulnerable individuals led to laws which controlled those seen as a threat to society (often putting them to work in degrading tasks, or violently punishing them), and giving the latter assistance on terms that were stigmatising and that often blighted their future prospects.

Today's fundamental dilemmas of social policy were present from the start of these interventions, known as the Poor Laws. If the authorities were relatively generous and kind, giving assistance to people in distress without harsh conditions or public disgrace, then the numbers of inactive 'dependent' individuals claiming support rose over time. If they imposed punitive work regimes which were stigmatising, as in the English workhouses of the nineteenth century, there was little prospect that inmates would ever again enter society as functioning members.

In the nineteenth century, working people organised themselves into savings clubs and mutual associations to reduce the risk of destitution, and from these other traditions for assistance, with a more collective basis, developed. For people unable to afford membership of such groups, or who had run out of resources to pay their dues, social work tried to find ways of substituting personal counselling for official sanctions in the financial support of the most deserving cases, aiming to restore their 'independence' by strengthening their moral fibre and their social ties.

case study

Octavia Hill was a leading nineteenth-century philanthropist and an early advocate of a particular form of social work. Her work was carried out mostly in London, and centred around the provision of housing for families who, in her judgement, were capable of improving their circumstances through personal determination and sustained effort. Strongly individualistic in her thinking, Octavia Hill was firmly opposed to state help of almost any sort, believing that it served to undermine the moral integrity of its recipients. Instead, she believed that the well-off had an obligation to assist those who could demonstrate that they were deserving of help. The *Charity Organisation Society* which she and other like-minded colleagues founded was, in most ways, a product of the Victorian period in which it operated. Nevertheless, her emphasis on the importance of close personal relationships between those who provided help and those who received it – founded, she said, on 'perfect nearness and respect' – has make her influence upon social work an enduring one. As long ago as 1984, Malpass (1984: 31) concluded that 'the political and intellectual climate is today more sympathetic to the kinds of ideas promoted by Octavia Hill than at any time for at least a generation', a conclusion which holds good today.

So, by the late nineteenth and early twentieth centuries, there was a demand for new ways to counter poverty and ensure security. At this time, the socialist ideas of Karl Marx (1867) gained mass support in working-class organisations, especially in Germany, prompting the conservative Imperial Chancellor, Prince Otto Von Bismarck, who was equally opposed to liberal democratic demands and to socialist ones, to create the first social insurance schemes for industrial injury, widowhood, sickness, retirement and eventually unemployment (Rimlinger, 1971). It was Bismarck's approach that came to be adopted by the governments of the most industrialised countries, while a version supposed to be based on Marx's principles was used to expropriate private property and eliminate the nobility and upper middle class in Russia, then still a largely agricultural economy with many feudal features.

It would be surprising if social insurance, a principle devised well over a 100 years ago and adopted in liberal democracies in the first half of the twentieth century, was still an effective way to provide income security to populations today. Its success lay in its ability to combine elements of self-insurance by workers against loss of income with employers' contributions for the sake of a healthy and reliable source of labour power, under the aegis of state-sponsored, inclusive national risk-pooling and solidarity. Well suited to the needs of workers in an age of industrial mass production, it had come to cover a dwindling proportion of citizens in all the affluent countries (except the Nordic ones) by the time of the crash of 2008.

As a growing number of employees came to be working in low-paid, part-time or casual posts, and numbers of those outside the labour market to need targeted means-tested support, the expansion of systems targeted at people on low incomes revived all the issues associated with Poor Law regimes (Jordan, 1973, 1974), including the poverty and unemployment traps (Jordan *et al.*, 1991), conditionality and work enforcement, and stigma. So the pressure for a fundamental rethink, from those concerned both with the technicalities of benefits administration (Centre for Social Justice, 2009) and with principles of political and social theory (Van Parijs, 1995) began to grow. After 2008, the crisis made this *the* urgent question for social policy.

It was also one to engage the attention of those, like the mass protesters occupying squares, streets and parks near the financial centres of New York, London, Frankfurt, Madrid, Rome and other cities, who were drawing attention to capitalism's failure to sustain the earnings of its workers or the many who were surplus to its operations. How did the rich so easily evade taxation? How were corporate leaders able to reward themselves so lavishly? Why were the banks immune from the consequences of their greed and folly? And – above all – how could freedom and security of income be better combined in some future system?

Several features of the income maintenance systems adopted by the affluent countries in the embryonic phase of welfare states began to come under question. Why was it income, and not property, that was to be redistributed by the state? After all, in many postcolonial situations, huge tracts of land, formerly owned by colonialists, were redistributed, giving a strong basis in the ownership of small property for economic development in societies as diverse as Ireland and the former French colonies of Southeast Asia. These questions became more pressing as it was increasingly apparent that homeownership, the classic feature of the 'property-owning democracy' espoused by Margaret Thatcher, was actually waning in the United Kingdom, where the age of first-time buyers had risen to 37 by 2011, as housing assets became more concentrated in the hands of the older and better off.

The idea of trying to give every citizen a capital sum as a basis for saving and property ownership had been explored in the United States (Ackerman and Alstott, 1990) and the United Kingdom (Nissan and Le Grand, 2000). New Labour introduced a first step in this direction with the Child Trust Funds, but these were abolished by the coalition government in its first round of cuts.

Of equally questionable relevance in the context of the new economic landscape was the rigid division between paid and unpaid activity, and the problems of combining the two. This made sense in the days when productive work could be seen as 'labour' for a large-scale employer, and when the organisations defending workers' living standards were known as the 'labour movement' (Standing, 2009). But if work was to become more self-directed and creative, to involve more small-scale services and fewer mass processes, and to allow collective action by a diversity of groups, neither social insurance nor targeted systems adequately enabled the flexibility and complexity of working lives that was increasingly required.

In this chapter we will address all these questions in the context of recent policy dilemmas and developments in the affluent states.

stop and think

- For able-bodied people of working age, help from the state has always depended upon a willingness to do paid labour, whenever that became available. Does that make sense in an era of mechanisation? Is the problem today one of a shortage of work, rather than a shortage of workers? Do the boundaries between 'work' and 'welfare' need to be eroded, if a system is to be created which matches contemporary social and economic conditions?

Enabling the transformation of work

The question of how to discover a new principle to replace both social insurance and means-testing in income maintenance systems arises as much from the need to transform work itself as from the traps, perversities and disincentives of the established systems. During the crisis, and especially as the eurozone was threatened with collapse, the notion that all the affluent states must become more like Germany was touted as the panacea for every economic woe. But it was obvious that not all countries (in Europe, for example) could be net exporters, and particularly that all could not be net exporters of high-tech machinery. Even the more modest goal of the UK government to 'rebalance' its economy in favour of manufacturing activity had proved impossible to realise, despite painful cuts in public services, aimed at enabling private-sector expansion (BBC Radio 4, 29 November 2011).

So a more realistic way to frame the question was in terms of the forms of sustainable work and earning which might be enabled by a different approach to state redistribution of income for people of working age; and this directed attention to a body of literature which had been neglected since the establishment of social insurance-based welfare states in the post-war period. In this section, we will consider the relevance of a group of theorists, the Guild Socialists, Distributists, Social Crediters and Anthroposophists, who opposed social insurance because it would enforce factory labour which was alienating and degrading, and some of whom proposed an alternative principle for income maintenance. This will lead into our analysis of the renewed relevance of that principle, which is being trialled all over the world in very diverse societies, and embryonic signs of which are already evident in some of the thinking behind the reforms being carried out under austerity in the United Kingdom.

The distinctive feature of the half-forgotten debates of the first three decades of the twentieth century was that these critical voices were concerned with the *quality* of work, its meaning to workers, and the moral principles which should govern how income and property were distributed, as well as the forms of economic and political organisation which would promote them. They deplored the way in which workers were being turned into extensions of machines in dehumanised production processes, and were losing any sense of involvement in decisions over output or in the finished product itself. Both capitalism and the new state socialism being established in the Soviet Union were accused of robbing people of the sources of well-being by imposing these mechanical forms of work and ways of life.

One reason why these views are recovering some relevance (in the affluent countries, but not in the new industrialising giants of the world economy) is that the newest technology favours decentralisation and small scale rather than mass production, leading to the possibility that the overwhelming tendencies of the past century towards concentration of capital and large-scale organisation might be reversed. For example, the Internet, new forms of electronic imaging and the microgeneration of power all make work in dispersed units, and with an ethos of craft or artisan quality, much more feasible. In turn, the ownership of land, buildings and relatively inexpensive machinery therefore become significant considerations for the future of work, and it implies that a larger proportion of the population might be able to organise their own working lives, individually or collectively, given a redistribution of property and credit.

The schools of thought that contributed to this approach in the original debates on these topics were:

1. **Guild Socialism**: This movement argued for self-government in industry, whereby workers controlled production in a democratic process; the abolition of the wage system and the commodification of labour; and the replacement of central state power by decentralised democracy. Its central value was fraternity. An early influence was William Morris, and its best-known advocate G.D.H. Cole (1920, 1921).
2. **Distributism**: This group proposed that property should be reallocated in favour of small producers (farmers, artisans and cooperatives), and that credit and interest related to unproductive uses should be outlawed. The best-known authors advocating these ideas were Hilaire Belloc (1912, 1924) and G.K. Chesterton (1926).
3. **Social Credit**: In the immediate aftermath of the First World War, Major C.H. Douglas (1919, 1920, 1931) argued for Producers' Banks under the supervision of a central clearing house, to replace the commercial banking system. These would enable production for 'sufficiency', and the common ownership of productive resources would allow satisfying work, better wages and unconditional 'dividends for all'.
4. **Anthroposophy**: Rudolf Steiner (1923) proposed that society should be divided between three spheres, that of rights (the political), in which the principle of equality should be paramount; that of the economy, where fraternity and cooperation should have priority; and that of culture (civil society), where freedom and the creative imagination should hold sway.

All these ideas and movements had several features in common. They were even-handed in their criticisms of capitalism and the bureaucratic, centralised socialism of the British Fabians, of markets and states, and of class-based politics; they all favoured redistribution of power and resources from the banks, large corporations and the state to individuals and communities; they all argued for forms of production which allowed people's creativity to find better expression; and they all saw the financial sector's role in the capitalist economy as violating all defensible moral principles.

In the United Kingdom, the separate strands of this critique came together in articles in the *Daily Herald*, and essays in the *New Age*, a journal edited by the Guild Socialist A.R. Orage, who took up Douglas's Social Credit ideas from their first appearance, and probably wrote several pieces with him (Hutchinson and Burkitt, 1997). Belloc and Chesterton were also regular contributors.

Earlier, Cole, Orage and Chesterton had united behind Belloc's attack on the first National Insurance Scheme in *The Servile State* (1912). Although he was a Liberal Member of Parliament from 1906, Belloc saw Lloyd George's measure as a means for delivering working people to industrialists as factory fodder, in exchange for limited sufficiency and security of income. Born in France, he admired the independence of peasant producers. Similarly, Chesterton (1904, p.82) opposed the labour colonies for the unemployed supported by Liberals and Fabian Socialists alike; he also deplored the removal of old age pension rights from citizens deemed to have been work-shy or found guilty of minor criminal offences (Canovan, 1977, p. 44).

Because by then the path of economic development had moved decisively towards large-scale industry and state intervention in the United Kingdom and Germany, they appealed to examples in other countries – the Guild Socialists to French syndicates, the Distributists to Ireland (Chesterton, 1919) and Southern Europe (Belloc, 1924), Social Credit supporters to local projects in various cities in Europe, and Steiner to small-scale experiments of their own. Their warnings about the trajectory of finance and industrial capitalism and their relation to state income maintenance – that the dehumanising, mechanical, intensified exploitation of workers in the former would be increasingly enforced by the latter – have again become timely in the age of austerity, as the prospects of prosperity for the working people recede.

These ideas were in wide circulation during the interwar period, but failed to make it across the great gulf created by the 1939–45 war. While never disappearing completely, they were debated only at the margins of politics and policymaking during the era of flourishing welfare states and rapid economic growth in the affluent countries.

But they were surprisingly injected into UK politics after the crash with the publication of a series of articles and a book by the self-proclaimed 'Red Tory', Phillip Blond (2009a,b and c, 2010). A lecturer in Theology at the University of Cumbria, Blond was quickly taken up by David Cameron, and installed at the head of a new think tank in London. Not only was he one of the key influences on the 'Big Society' theme of the Conservatives' election campaign of 2010, he also evoked an echo in the Labour Party, where Maurice Glasman, a lecturer at London Metropolitan University, was elevated to the peerage and became a leading speech writer for Ed Miliband, the party's new leader. Glasman took up many of Blond's themes, and called his approach 'Blue Labour', also appealing to working-class collective action in the period before the beginnings of the welfare state (*Prospect Magazine*, 2010).

In the next section we will show how these themes fed into the concerns in the Conservative Party about work incentives in the benefits system and the social fabric of deprived districts before the 2010 election in the

United Kingdom, and how this influenced plans for radical reform of the tax and benefits system, as it affected lower-paid workers.

The 'Big Society', 'Broken Britain' and 'Universal Credits'

The crash of 2008–09 cast a cloud over the New Labour government of Gordon Brown, who was justifiably seen as having been far too gullible about the claims of the financial sector to have eliminated systemic risks during his period as Chancellor of the Exchequer. What was surprising for commentators was that the Conservative Party came to the general election of May 2010, with a programme largely focused on the revival of civil society, and appealing to many of the ideas which had been widely canvassed by Phillip Blond. In the event, as we shall show, these proposals were considerably watered down by the tide of austerity measures released by the coalition government, but they did constitute a potential shift away from the kind of economic model embraced by New Labour under Blair and Brown, and indeed from the market-driven hegemony launched by Margaret Thatcher.

Blond had argued that monopoly capitalism, as much as the power of the centralising state, had been responsible for a damaging weakening of civil society in the United Kingdom (Blond, 2010, p.3). Drawing on the writings of radical Tories from Burke and Cobbett to Carlyle and Ruskin, but referring especially to the dissident Liberals Belloc and Chesterton, he claimed the Distributists as the inspiration for his critique of monopoly ownership of land and capital, the dispossession of the populace and the enslavement of workers (p. 30), on the way even giving an approving nod to the Social Credit proposals for a universal National Dividend for all citizens (p. 32).

In an implicit recognition of the work of Cole and his movement, Blond recommended a wide range of measures to 'moralise the market', including combating monopoly by the formation of 'free guilds or professional associations' (pp. 192–3) and 'mutualist structures of ownership and reward' (pp. 197–9), to 'create popular prosperity', through local and regional banks, distributing investment vouchers to poorer citizens, transferring council-owned property to local communities, creating community land trusts and community development financial institutions (pp. 205–24), and transforming the public sector into a 'civil state' through employee ownership, active participation and public engagement (chapter 10).

All this implied a transformative shift in resources and power, with the growth of social enterprises and cooperatives and local financial institutions at the expense of big corporations and banks. In its election manifesto, the Conservative Party (2010, pp. 25–7 and 35–7) gestured towards a programme inspired by these principles, largely abandoned in office. But, as we will now show, the whole approach also implied a transformation of the tax and benefits system, to enable these new forms of cooperative work and mutual association.

The stream of research and thought leading to the specific proposals for these reforms began when the former party leader, Iain Duncan Smith, set up the Centre for Social Justice (CSJ), a think tank specifically for the analysis of 'Broken Britain'. This idea was linked to the perception that New Labour's economic model of society was individualistic and contractual; it had weakened social bonds, community and mutuality (all themes in Blond also), excluded a poor minority and led to the political alienation of the young generation. This thesis was advanced in a series of reports by the CSJ, documenting the rise of socially problematic behaviour in deprived neighbourhoods. But the crucial step which potentially linked this diagnosis to the debates about the future of work and collective action at the local level was the claim that the existing benefits system trapped claimants, and that to expect them to work without adequate additional reward was hypocritical –an assertion made in his preface to the Centre's report on tax-benefit reform by Duncan Smith (2009, p. ii).

The moral basis for the CSJ report was that marriage and saving should be rewarded, that people doing small amounts of paid work should gain from it and that taxes and benefits withdrawals should not negatively affect the incomes of the lowest earners. It argued that New Labour's programme had intensified the moral hazard in the system, and failed to reduce poverty, the number of workless households and the number of young people not in education, employment or training (NEETS) (CSJ, 2009, pp. 20–22).

case study

Why should we expect people out of work to behave differently to those in work?...when it comes to the unemployed, Government lazily assumes people will take work out of a sense of obligation – enforced or voluntary. That is why Government has, over a number of years, produced a complex system which, rather than moving people to financial independence, instead entrenches economic dependency and ensures claimants remain

> net receivers in society rather than contributors...Our reforms will remove the financial roadblocks to entering and sustaining work. They will also steadily move benefit recipients towards their full employment potential...unless we put the system right now, we run the risk of increasing the number of residually unemployed, only this time it will manifest itself as large numbers of younger people permanently excluded from gainful employment. That is why we simply cannot go on talking about the importance of getting people into work while we persist in creating disincentives for the very people we say should be in work. Our existing complex and inefficient benefits system should finally be laid to rest; otherwise all the talk about improving the number of people going back to work will be just another form of empty rhetoric.
>
> *Source*: Iain Duncan Smith M.P. (2009) *Breaking the Dependency Cycle*, Centre for Social Justice, preface.

The bulk of the report was highly technical. It recommended that the assessment process for all of working age should be reduced to just two elements. Eligibility for 'universal work credits' (which would replace Job Seekers' Allowance, Income Support, Incapacity Benefit and Employment and Support Allowance) would combine all these elements related to being outside the labour market in the existing benefits system. 'Universal life credits' would replace Housing Benefit, Council Tax Benefit, Disability Living Allowance, Working Tax Credit and Child Tax Benefit, thus combining all those elements relating to living costs. The effect would be to create one payment acting as a combined benefit and tax credit, the first part of which would be withdrawn as people moved from very low amounts of work to higher, and the second from those on slightly higher earnings, with the effect of the withdrawal being at the same rate right up the scale. All benefits were to be paid by a single agency, regardless of whether someone was at work or not, and withdrawn through the Pay As You Earn (PAYE) income tax system.

The report claimed that these changes and simplifications would make the reform pay for itself, if there was a new, more generous disregard of earnings, allowing claimants to keep their benefits for the first few hours of the week they worked. The effect would have been an even 55 per cent withdrawal rate for their subsequent earnings (across the board, post-tax), and to reduce penalties for couples, mortgage-holders and low-income savers (CSJ, 2009, p. 25).

The authors claimed this would have given five million households an extra £1,000 a year, and taken 800,000 of them out of poverty. They estimated that employment would have increased by 600,000 and GNP to rise by £4.7 billion, making the reforms revenue-neutral in the medium term. The report made almost no mention of measures to induce claimants to take available work, instead focusing on improved incentives for employment, family formation, saving and home ownership.

Two implications of these proposals stood out, in the context of the attempt to revive civil society and collective action, and to transform work. The first was that these proposals would have ended the rigid distinction between employees and benefits claimants. By integrating the income tax and means-tested income maintenance systems at the lowest level of earnings, the reform would have abolished the pretence that the subsidies going to those earning low wages were quite different from the benefits received by claimants outside the labour market. This shift would have enabled people to combine paid and unpaid work roles in far more flexible ways, as well as reducing some of the stigma of claiming. This would have been consistent with the ideas of the Big Society approach.

The second was that it could have represented the first step in the direction of a universal, unconditional payment – a Basic or Citizens' Income – distributed without tests of work or household status, of a kind which had been recommended by Major Douglas in the 1920s and 1930s, and since advocated by a range of economists (Meade, 1989; Parker, 1989; Brittan, 1995; Standing, 1999, 2009), social policy analysts (Jordan, 1973, 1985, 1996; Fitzpatrick, 1999) and political philosophers (Van Parijs, 1995; Barry, 1998; Pateman, 2004). The CSJ scheme was to be for households rather than individuals, and was more of a negative income tax than a Basic Income, but it could have been the first step in the direction of a transformative shift.

stop and think

- In what ways do Tax Credits (as introduced by the New Labour government of 1997–2010) and Universal Credit (as proposed by the coalition government) differ? Do Universal Credits have the potential to break down the distinction between work and welfare? How would that policy objective be achieved through a Basic Income system?

research box 2.1

Basic income

The idea of integrating the tax and benefits system into a single system, which would give every individual an unconditional guaranteed sum, which would ideally be sufficient for subsistence, irrespective of their work or household status, has a long history. It can be traced to leading figures in the movement for American independence from Britain, Thomas Jefferson and Tom Paine, to French socialist thinkers, and to both Guild Socialist G.D.H. Cole and Social Credit theorist C.H. Douglas.

It was revived in the post-war era by social movements for poor people (Jordan, 1973), and by economists (Parker, 1989, Meade, 1989, Standing, 1989); but the most influential expression of arguments in its favour was the work of moral and political philosopher Philippe Van Parijs (1995).

Opponents of the idea say that it would give 'something for nothing', and that any viable benefits system must not only stipulate but also enforce the duty to take any paid employment available. But the complexity and perverse incentives in means-tested systems of benefits have led more policy analysts to recognise that it would be a more work-friendly approach to income maintenance than these schemes (Fitzpatrick, 1999).

The failures of capitalism highlighted by the crisis have made more commentators recognise that it would be a better approach to sustaining incomes and the economy than supplying taxpayers' money to the banks. If the earnings of a large proportion of households are to be 'squeezed' for the next five or more years (Resolution Foundation, 2012; Institute for Fiscal Studies, 2012) while an elite continues to get richer, it makes sense to give people an income as an entitlement of citizenship, rather than to make them jump through hoops to qualify, and then to tax their earnings as these rise above a certain level.

It would be impossible to move to this system in a single jump, but the CSJ scheme for partial integration of income tax and benefits might have represented a first step in this direction. It might then have been eventually followed by something like a Participation Income scheme, paid to those in activities such as student and carer as well as workers and unemployed people (Atkinson, 1995).

In the event, although the evocative term Universal Credits was retained from the report by Duncan Smith when he took office as Secretary of State for Work and Pensions, his reform package was far less radical. Not all the means-tested benefits were included in the new credit, some cuts and caps were imposed and the withdrawal rate was higher at 65 per cent. The Conservative Party in parliament was more concerned about the rate of taxation on the highest earners (50 per cent) than the effective rate on poor people.

But far more significantly, the enforcement of work conditions was strengthened, ahead of the introduction of the scheme; in other words, the hypocrisy which Duncan Smith had identified, of applying sanctions before improving incentives, was implemented in full measure, and at a time when employment opportunities were shrinking rapidly due to the austerity programme. As a result, the universal credit scheme could become (like tax credits) a rationale for forcing claimants into low-paid 'entry' jobs in which they then get stuck, or a succession of precarious short-term contracts. The major beneficiaries of the reform would then be employers in cleaning, hospitality, care and other occupations at the bottom of the hollowed-out labour market.

Furthermore, a far stricter regime of testing the work capabilities of claimants with disabilities and illnesses was introduced at the same time, with the explicit goal of returning 1.5 million of these to the jobseekers roll. Anyone who could do any kind of work for any duration was to be counted as fit enough to be transferred. An investigation revealed that among claimants of Employment and Support Allowances appeals against disqualification were up from 70,000 a year in 2009–10 to an estimated 240,000 in 2011–12, the cost of the latter being £80 million. People being assessed as fit to do some work were being reinstated on appeal, only to be refused again immediately on reapplication, indicating that the company conducting the tests was operating quite different standards from the appeal tribunal (Channel 4 TV *News*, 21 November, 2011).

The coalition government justified these actions, which had provoked protests by organisations of people with disabilities, by insisting that its new Work Programme, contracted to large corporations and giving them incentives to train, prepare and place claimants in long-term employment, was established precisely to deal with 'hard-to-place' jobseekers, including ones such as these. (In fact, few of those diverted from Employment and Support claims were feeding through to the programme, because of the appeals merry-go-round.) But equally disturbing was evidence that young jobseekers were being placed in 'work experience' which effectively supplied big retail companies with unpaid labour.

case study

A report in *The Guardian* (17 November, 2011, p.49) documented a scheme to send such claimants to supermarkets and budget stores for up to two months without pay. They were required to work for up to 30 hours a week, and be available from 9 a.m. to 10 pm; having begun to participate in the experience, they could after one week lose their benefits if they dropped out. Claimants interviewed by the paper said they had little or no 'training', and were simply left to get on with the work; a young woman graduate said that she was threatened with disqualification from her Jobseeker's Allowance when she questioned the value of the scheme for someone like her with extensive retail experience. The Minister at the Department for Work and Pensions said the scheme was a success, as half of the participants left benefits after the experience; lawyers for some claimants were considering a case against the department, arguing that it represented slavery under the Human Rights Act.

After mounting pressure from protesters outside leading supermarkets and the withdrawal of several leading companies from the scheme, the government met with major employers on 29 February 2012, and (despite ministers' repeated statements that sanctions against young claimants who dropped out of the work experience programme were justified) it was forced to make participation completely voluntary. But the coercive element in the scheme for older long-term claimants remained in place (*The Guardian,* 1 March, 2012, p. 1).

Such examples indicate that Universal Credits, when they were fully introduced, would bear little relation to the design envisaged in the CSJ report. Far from trusting to improved incentives, the government has reverted to relying on coercion and threats to enforce low-paid work on often overqualified claimants. In other words, this is more of a return to the Poor Laws, and specifically the Roundsman system (Checkland and Checkland, 1974; Jordan, 1973), under which those getting parish support were forced to work for local farmers in exchange, while those in normal employment received income supplements to top up their wages as in the Speenhamland system, than a step towards an unconditional Basic Income. Yet the fact that the CSJ recognised all the dilemmas that had come back to haunt the tax-benefit system, and had come up with a scheme which moved in the latter direction, represented a glimmer of hope for medium-term developments in these systems.

In the next section we will consider whether a shift towards a Basic Income approach might enable a sustainable transformation of work which would be appropriate for the role of affluent countries in a global economy increasingly dominated by emerging industrial powers – not just Brazil, Russia, India and China (the BRICs), but also a second cohort of Colombia, Indonesia, Venezuela, Egypt, Turkey and South Africa (the CIVETS).

Transforming work

Although the compulsion involved in welfare-to-work schemes like the Work Programme should be unacceptable in a liberal democratic country, because it violates the freedom to choose one's employment, this is not the only, or indeed perhaps the most important objection in the long term to such public policies, which have been adopted all over the affluent world (Cox, 1998). The fact that so-called 'activation' distorts the labour market and thus the whole economy of these countries is more damaging to the human development of society as a whole, and means that the decline of the affluent part of the global economy in relation to the fast-growing industrialising ones will be more marked and faster than necessary.

During the Industrial Revolution, the United Kingdom experienced a social upheaval, accompanied by considerable political turmoil, from which both free-market capitalism and liberal democracy emerged as the dominant economic forms, but only after considerable conflict and struggle (Polanyi, 1944). The wealthiest and most powerful forces, the landed aristocracy, were no supporters of Adam Smith's (1776) prescription for prosperity and harmony; they saw the rise of the industrial bourgeoisie, and the migration of workers from their fields into the cities, as threats to the order in which they held sway. Polanyi argues that their use of the Poor Laws both to subsidise low agricultural wages and to enforce work on their land and in their villages under the Roundsman and Speenhamland systems was designed to slow or halt the processes through which a market-driven society was developing. After a near-revolution in the countryside in 1830, the aristocracy finally accepted parliamentary reforms which enfranchised the middle classes, allowing a new politics of urbanisation and industrialisation to appear (Thompson, 1968); under this regime, both allowances to the working poor and systems of enforced work in the rural economy were abolished under the Poor Law Amendment Act of 1834.

Although the reformed system, which intentionally stigmatised those claiming assistance by consigning them to workhouses, was in many ways more cruel than the old Poor Law, it did end a systematic distortion of the labour market which subsidised low-productivity agriculture and held potentially higher-earning workers in backward rural districts. All the suffering of the slum-dwellers and casual workers of the Victorian cities so vividly captured by Dickens (and by Marx) followed from the shifts which took place in the early 1830s, but so did 40 years of unprecedented economic growth, the emergence of a new class politics and the organised labour movement.

Without those reforms, all this would have been impossible, and another power would have used different means – almost certainly more authoritarian and less democratic if that power had been Germany – to gain the edge in manufacturing and trade worldwide. It should not be forgotten that the United Kingdom, despite its earlier record in the slave trade and later in colonial exploitation, did also take the lead in the abolition of slavery, and in some of the more enlightened practices of colonialism (compared, for example, with Belgium in the Congo, or Portugal in Mozambique or Germany in Namibia).

So it was a significant moment, which did not go unrecognised at the time (Jordan, 1973), when the UK government of Edward Heath revived a Speenhamland-style subsidisation of low wages in the Family Income

Supplements – a scheme which was vastly extended by both Conservative and Labour governments as tax credits in the following four decades to embrace a high proportion of households with less than median earnings. The similarities with the old Poor Law were intensified, of course, when welfare-to-work programmes began to enforce low-paid employment in the 1980s, and these too have been extended and intensified ever since. We will argue that the transformation of work required to adapt to this country's position in the new global economy can never happen under such a regime.

stop and think

- The modern welfare system remains based on the Beveridge Report, and the legislation which flowed from it during the 1945–51 Labour government. It would have been unthinkable to Beveridge that an individual could be, at one and the same time, well-off enough to pay tax and poor enough to receive state benefits. The world of work and of income maintenance were entirely separate – administratively, practically and conceptually. What factors do you think might have led the Heath government to break down that distinction for the first time? What might have been the impact of women joining the labour force in greater numbers? What was the impact of Family Income Supplement on families with low incomes? Who benefited the most from such a scheme: The government? Employers? Families themselves?

Just as the old Poor Law tied workers into low-productivity tasks in employments which did nothing to advance the processes of economic development, so the combination of tax credits and welfare-to-work 'activation' promoted exactly those sectors of the labour market – routine work like shelf-stacking in supermarkets and menial tasks in the public infrastructure like street-cleaning – which least allowed the expansion of innovative, creative, socially constructive work, and least enabled people to improve the quality of their lives, either individually or collectively. Indeed, involvement in such schemes was likely to induce a sense of alienation from mainstream society and mistrust in fellow citizens. A study in Sweden, a country with among the highest levels of trust in others in the world, found that although retirement pensioners trusted their fellow Swedes almost as much as those in full-time employment did, those on welfare-to-work activation schemes had levels of trust only two thirds of the rate of mainstream citizens, and closer to the average for Turkey or Brazil than for a Scandinavian country (Rothstein and Stolle, 2002).

This is why policies such as the Work Programme were counterproductive in the post-crash economic environment. On the one hand, the money created by the government through its programme of 'quantitative easing' was being absorbed by the banks to cover their bad debts from the pre-crash period, and not lent to firms for expansion. Just as it would have been far better for businesses if government had given money to citizens in the form of Basic Incomes than to pump it into zombie banks which soaked it up as 'credit sponges', so it would have been far better to allow those without jobs to organise their own activities, with the support of local advisors and the opportunity to join community initiatives which were self-directing. Just as almost every business would rather have more customers buying its products than have to ask a bank for a loan, so most claimants would rather have the chance to plan and carry through their own way of earning a living and building a career than be sent into a monotonous, dead-end job. And the Work Programme was both vastly expensive and largely ineffective. The National Audit Office (2012) reckoned that the proportion of claimants it would place in jobs was more like 25 per cent than the 40 per cent estimated by government (i.e., around the numbers who would have found work anyway).

case study

The work programme and A4e

A storm gathered over A4e, the company which had won the largest government contract to supply the Work Programme for unemployed claimants, in late February 2012. Under pressure to find employment for the growing numbers on its books, in order to earn large incentive payments, several employees were under investigation for alleged fraud. The firm had been forced to repay public money on five occasions (*The Guardian*, 23 February 2012, p.6). Its staff had also compelled claimants to clean the company's own offices under a work experience scheme (*The Guardian*, 23 February 2012, p. 1). Finally, its founder, Emma Harrison, resigned, first as a government advisor on families and employment, and then as chair of the firm, amid growing media criticism (*The Guardian*, 25 February 2012, p.2).

At the time when the Guild Socialists and Distributists advocated the redistribution of property and a return to the ethos and structures of guilds and crafts, this seemed a somewhat backward-looking programme. In the present age, when information technology, the Internet and microprocesses of all kinds have made a radical decentralisation of economic activity, including industrial production, a reality and a potential source for economic progress, the transformation of work demands the dismantling of the power of officials (or commercial companies under contract to the state) to coerce those needing assistance, while preserving the positive, enabling features of the public service ethos (for instance, in the best traditions of social work).

In most of the affluent countries, welfare-to-work schemes are staffed by social workers or their equivalents. So, in Italy, Spain and Greece, for example, these programmes would require such professionally trained workers to ration benefits and enforce conditions on the growing millions who are unemployed as austerity measures bite. In the United Kingdom, first New Labour policy and then the privatisation of these schemes meant that specially trained staff were used for this work (Jordan with Jordan, 2000); but essentially the tasks of 'personal advisors' to claimants are the same, and people whose job descriptions sound like those of social workers are at the front line of this coercion.

stop and think

- Social workers have long resisted attempts to make them responsible for administering parts of the social assistance system (as they are in most other countries). Why do you think that would be the case? Are social workers not ideally placed to know and understand the income maintenance needs of individuals and families with whom they work? What tensions might arise if social workers were to be responsible for making decisions about benefits? What would be lost in the process?

If Universal Credits were decoupled from this machinery, they might – especially if they were combined with some of the other redistributive measures advocated by Blond – supply the first step towards making an unconditional income available to all citizens, and hence to a new kind of labour market and economy

Conclusions

These ideas about the future of income maintenance policy might be dismissed as utopian dreams, were it not for the fact that a few countries are already implementing versions of the idea of unconditional state payments for all their citizens. A local scheme has been tried out in Sao Paolo, the largest city in Brazil; but the other economic environments in which the approach has been pioneered are more surprising.

On the one hand, the state of Alaska (hardly a stronghold of progressive principles, and boasting Sarah Palin as a former governor) has for almost 30 years paid everyone resident within its borders an annual sum, now well over $1,000, simply for living there. Far more recently, an area of Namibia has tried out a Basic Income scheme, with encouraging social consequences. And in 2010–11, the Mongolian government announced that it too was about to introduce such a scheme (*BIEN Newsflash*, December 2010 and November 2011).

What all these have in common is that their economies comprise enormous mineral wealth, side by side with subsistence nomadic pastoralism, hunting and gathering among their indigenous populations. In other words, their economies are divided between a small but hugely wealthy sector, producing commodities which are traded in global markets, and employing workers who are paid high salaries, and far larger sectors of small producers and petty traders, in addition to that rural subsistence sector, which do not sell abroad, and where wages are far lower (or non-existent). The problem of extreme inequality and the rising prices associated with the affluence of the few has been addressed by the payment of an income to all citizens as an indication of their equal status as well as a way of sustaining their living standards.

case study

Sovereign wealth funds and basic income

Throughout the world, 41 countries now have 'sovereign wealth funds', accumulated out of taxation or earnings from abroad, in order to invest for the future or to support their populations. The best-known of these are China's and those of the oil-rich Middle Eastern states, used to buy land and infrastructural facilities (such as ports) in countries which supply them with food and raw materials. But Norway, too, has a large sovereign wealth fund, derived from its oil revenues.

The example of Mongolia shows that sovereign wealth funds could be another source for Basic Income payments. But in the United Kingdom there has been long-term resistance to the obvious source for such a fund, a tax on land. The land holdings of some of the largest aristocratic owners are not even recorded by the Land Registry – but all of them, including the Queen and Prince Charles, claim their Rural Payments under the EU's farm subsidy scheme.

The fiscal crisis has revived interest in a land tax, and one leading economist who recommends both, Samuel Brittan, has come out in his *Financial Times* column (23 February 2012) recommending them.

We have argued that, although the situation is very different in the affluent countries, the failure of capitalist mechanisms to distribute rising salaries to the majority of the population indicates a far more complex instance of the same problem – as signalled by the protests by the '99 per cent'. Indeed, since almost 30 years before the crash, median earnings had been declining in the United States; in the United Kingdom, the

Institute for Fiscal Studies reported on 30 November 2011 that it was predicting a decline of median disposable household incomes of 4.7 per cent between 2009 and 2012, by far the largest fall in a three-year period since the Second World War. Extrapolating from the Chancellor's Autumn Statement of the previous day, it was also predicting that UK citizens would be on average no better off in 2015 than they had been in 2001.

research box 2.2

So what has happened to living standards in the United Kingdom over the last thirty years? In absolute terms, UK earnings growth was strong from 1977 to 2003 but from 2003 to 2008 – before the 2008–09 recession, and despite GDP growth of 11 percent in the period – wages in the bottom half flat-lined. There is emerging evidence that wage growth has fallen behind growth in labour productivity. After a sharp fall as the result of the downturn, wages are now set to recover only very slowly. Based on current government forecasts, we expect that average wages will be no higher in 2015 than they were in 2001. In relative terms too, the position of the United Kingdom's 11 million people living on low to middle incomes has deteriorated. The stark increases in inequality that took place in the 1980s and 1990s have now levelled off – *but only within the bottom half of the distribution*. The earnings of those at the top have continued to move away from those in the middle, while the wage characteristics of the bottom half have coalesced.

A system of tax credits has been created to boost incomes, particularly targeted at low- to middle-income people in work and with children. This has raised living standards, but has also meant higher marginal tax rates, with many people on low to middle incomes now taking home less of every additional pound they earn.

Growth Without Gain? The faltering living standards of people on low to middle incomes, James Plunkett (2011) Report for the Resolution Foundation, Commission on Living Standards

In the United States, the share of national income that goes to workers as wages rather than to investors as profit and interest has fallen to its lowest level since records began after the Second World War (now at 58 per cent). 'If wages as a share of national income were at the post-war average, each US worker would be $5000 better off' (Harding, 2011). This is part of the reason why incomes at the top – which tend to be earned from capital – have risen so much. If wages were at their post-war average share of 63 per cent, workers would earn an extra $740 billion a year. 'This so called labour share has been in gentle decline in most industrial economies, but especially Anglo Saxon economies, for the past couple of decades. In this recovery, however, something strange and unprecedented is going on…Historically, the labour share tends to rise during recessions as companies hold on to workers and sacrifice profits, then falls back during a recovery. But during the 2008 recession, the labour share did the opposite: it fell, and when the recovery began it kept falling' (*ibid.*).

Remarkably, the share of profits in the US economy has risen by about 25–30 per cent during the recession. The decline in the labour share, along with a shift of labour income towards higher earners, may be an important part of why the US economic recovery is sluggish. Workers on lower wages consume much of their income, while higher-wage earners and those with capital income are more likely to save. That does not affect local demand if savers lend to those who want to consume or invest in buildings and start-ups, but investment has been slow to recover in the wake of the recession.

How can this phenomenon of the post-2008 period be explained? The massive increase in the global labour supply from rural migrants into cities in the developing world means a lower price for labour, relative to capital. A second part of the explanation is the impact of technological change. As the pace of this quickens, so technology both replaces workers and accelerates labour turnover – reducing the bargaining power of workers. But there has also been a marked change in firms' strategic responses to the downturn, with top executives seeking to maximise share prices rather than market share, at least partly to secure the largest gains in their own rewards.

We have shown that targeted benefits systems recreated all the dilemmas of the Poor Law administration over five centuries, and these were exacerbated by the stagflation of the crisis period. Being forced to raise benefits by 5.2 per cent as price inflation peaked in September 2011, the coalition government was left with the additional headache of trying to spring the poverty trap that stemmed from rising state payments and falling wages. As the long trend of subsidising earnings involved the public purse in ever-growing outlays, the system itself defeated reforming intentions.

This was in part because a large proportion of employers – in many cases the least efficient and productive – had come to rely on the supplementation of the wages they paid through tax credits and housing benefits. The only way of creating a level playing field for enterprises would be to give *all* employees, indeed all citizens, a payment. This would mean that extra subsidies were not given to those paying least; it would give all the same incentives to improve productivity and efficiency, for instance, by automation of processes.

By requiring less efficient employers to use labour power to better effect in order to be able to compete, the Basic Income might actually reduce the total number of hours spent in employment in the economy as a whole. But we have argued that this would promote a new approach to work, both paid and unpaid, which would link it better to real improvements in well-being and the quality of individual and collective life.

stop and think

- In an era where there is a shortage of work, but not of workers, do we need to rethink the traditional approach to redistribution? As well as redistributing income and wealth, do we also need to think about a redistribution of work? If so, how do we create a mechanism which allows people who are sharing the available work also to have a fairer share of available income? What are the advantages and disadvantages of Basic Income programmes as a way of achieving that new balance? How might social work service users be affected?

Neither the replacement of social insurance and means-testing by Basic Income nor the transformation of work could be quickly or painlessly accomplished. Established rights and a culture of expectations would have to be changed; this would involve struggles and conflicts in the political arena and the workplace. But – as we have seen in this chapter – there is no smooth or trouble-free pathway to the future under a policy programme of tinkering to existing forms and institutions. Capitalism in the affluent countries has ceased to offer the prospect of better lives to the majority, and it outrages the sense of social justice and democratic equality by rewarding a plutocratic elite with huge wealth and golden opportunities. It is not only the disparity between the fortunes of Namibian diamond miners and their subsistence-hunting fellow citizens, or Mongolian gold traders and their neighbouring yak-herders, which demands redress; the same reproaches to fundamental moral and political values have become evident, and provoked protest, in Wall Street and the City of London.

In the 1930s, the relationship between what Marx and Engels (1848) called a 'rentier' class of those who lived from interest on wealth, dividends from shares and rent on property and those who earned wages and salaries was depicted in political cartoons by drawings of stout elderly men in top hats lording it over huddled impoverished masses. Although this caricature might seem no longer to apply to our societies, there is strong evidence of a return to something like this situation; whether or not one owns wealth is becoming a key determinant of one's position in economy and society.

A television documentary called 'Money: Who Wants to be a Millionaire?' (BBC2 tv, 29 November 2011) showed how 'wealth gurus', offering expensive courses on the ways in which ordinary working people could reach a position of being able to live on 'passive income', mainly from rent on houses and flats, were themselves gaining large returns. Mass gatherings of aspiring rentiers cheered the most noted consultant in this field, Robert Kiyosaki, bought his book, rehearsed his axioms and posted notes to themselves around their houses about how to get rich. Some borrowed substantial sums to attend these meetings, or to engage wealth coaches. Speaking about the morality of becoming part of the new class of rentiers, successful property owners argued that the 'balance' of society required there to be some people like themselves, and others who claimed benefits to support their affluence.

We would argue that this emerging pattern of economic and social forces means that social work and social policy cannot be neutral about the future distribution of property, income and work. They will serve the interests of the elite, often in routine and invisible ways, or they should challenge and seek to change them. In subsequent chapters we will show how these issues work out in the major spheres of social policy and social work.

main points

- In an age of industrial mass production, social insurance provided an effective means of protection against a wide range of social ills. As patterns of work fragmented into low-paid, part-time and casual employment, so the social contract on which social insurance was based gave way to conditionality, work enforcement and stigma. The malign consequences of such shifts has given rise to calls for a more fundamental reappraisal of ways in which fairness, freedom and security for all citizens can be secured in the post-2008 world.

- There is a long, if neglected, history of ideas which aim to recalibrate the relationship between income and work, a debate which has re-emerged in recent times. On the income side, in its original formulation proposals for a Universal Credit aimed to erode the distinction between employees and benefit claimants, allowing for more flexible combinations of paid and unpaid work. The debate has also brought renewed attention to the case for a Basic Income, paid as-of-right to all citizens.

- Reformulating the relationship between income and work also breaks the cycle in which people without work are coerced into taking pointless, dead-end, make-work jobs, in order to qualify for benefits. In its place, existing activity, such as 'care work' would be better recognised, and new opportunities would be created for local, collaborative energies to be released for common purposes.

taking it further

- Blond, P. (2010) *Red Tory*, London: Faber and Faber.
- Resolution Foundation (2012) *The Essential Guide to Squeezed Britain*, London: Resolution Foundation.
- Trade Union Congress (2011) *Unfair to Middling: How Middle Britain's Shrinking Wages Fuelled the Crash and Threaten Recovery,* London, TUC. Available at: http://www.tuc.org.uk/extras/unfairtomiddling.pdf
- A wide range of papers on Basic Income developments across the globe can be found at the website of the Basic Income Earth Network (BIEN) http://www.basicincome.org/bien/

3 The public services and the social order

One of the defining features of the Age of Austerity has been the programme of cuts in public services. As soon as the crisis began to destabilise public finances, depleted by the rescue of financial intermediaries in all the affluent countries, the knee-jerk reaction was for governments to prune expenditure on the collective infrastructure of social provision. In response, public service staff rallied in protest against redundancies, effective cuts in pay, and (in the United Kingdom as well as Greece and Ireland) raised ages for retirement and increased pensions contributions, as well as reductions in provision for citizens.

So the largest and most visible signal of resistance against austerity came from those taking mass action to protect this sector's jobs, pay, conditions and the services they produced. There were also protests by citizens against the closure of libraries and swimming pools. This contrasted with the political protests which made up the Arab Spring, where mainly young citizens took to the streets to express disgust over their oppression, impoverishment and exclusion, but above all against the corruption and abuse of power of their rulers. Yet both might be seen as evidence of the breakdown of the gears linking economic processes with particular forms of social order. In the Arab dictatorships, the secret police were the hated upholders of the old order; but in the affluent countries, public servants had come to see themselves (and over the years be seen by most citizens who actually used them) as creating these links in ways which supplied moral legitimacy to the political authorities in terms of their commitment to social justice.

Yet in English cities in early August 2011, there was also another type of mass protest, and one which in some ways more resembled the scenes in North Africa and the Middle East that year. The riots and violent disorder that followed the killing of a young black man, Mark Duggan, in Tottenham represented some kind of breakdown of the social order in those (mainly deprived) districts where they occurred, and caused the public services, the political authorities and academics to ponder on the origins of such an outbreak of lawless disaffection (Newburn *et al.*, 2011).

Professor Tim Newburn, head of the Social Policy department at LSE, who led the research team, said:

> This is a pathbreaking study of the August riots in England. It reveals the anger and frustration felt by those who were involved in the disorder, in part a product of the unfair and discourteous treatment they feel they suffer at the hands of the police, but also reflecting the disillusionment many feel at the social and economic changes which leave them increasingly disconnected from mainstream society.

Rioters identified a range of political grievances, but at the heart of their complaints was a pervasive sense of injustice. For some this was economic – the lack of money, jobs or opportunity. For others it was more broadly social – how they felt they were treated compared with others.

Many rioters conceded their involvement in looting was simply down to opportunism, saying that a perceived suspension of normal rules presented them with an opportunity to acquire goods and luxury items they could not ordinarily afford.

Gangs behaved in an entirely atypical manner for the duration of the riots, temporarily suspending hostilities with their postcode rivals. However on the whole, the role of gangs in the riots has been significantly overstated by the government.

Contrary to widespread speculation that social media was used by rioters to organise and share information, sites such as Facebook and Twitter were not used in any significant way. However, BlackBerry phones – and the free messaging service known as BBM – was used extensively.

Although mainly young and male, those involved in the riots came from a cross section of local communities. Just under half of those interviewed in the study were students. Of those who were not in education and were of working age, 59 per cent were unemployed. Although half of those interviewed were black, people who took part in the disorder did not consider these race riots.

Source: Reading the Riots (2011)

Sociologists pointed out that two factors made these phenomena somewhat predictable. On the one hand, the population of young people had been increasing more rapidly than that of older age groups in these areas, always a sign that disorder could break out. On the other, the very *announcement* of redundancies and cuts in public spending (along with the damaging impact on families of some, such as the reduction in the non-dependent element in housing benefit, already implemented) had been a known factor precipitating riots in previous periods of austerity (Ponticelli and Voth, *The Guardian*, 17 August 2011, p. 26).

In this chapter, we will analyse the contribution of the public services to the social order – the standards and practices through which the relationships between members of a community are sustained, creating the bonds that form the fabric of society – and how these came to be disrupted by the crisis. We will argue that the particular version of this order which had been established during the two decades before the crash can never be rebuilt in its previous form, in the United Kingdom any more than in Italy, Spain or Portugal. Even though there will continue to be many parts of the United Kingdom, especially in the north of England, in Scotland, Wales and Northern Ireland, where public sector and government-financed jobs will continue to supply the main source of employment, the strategy used to increase growth and jobs in such regions during the boom years will not be an option in future. Work-sharing can be a way of avoiding redundancies, and this and other new strategies by citizens will be needed to offset the effects of austerity.

Those who looted high-value electronic goods and gangster-chic sportswear from smashed high street stores were acting out the fantasies encouraged by advertisements and by the ideology of governments. The economic model of society maintained that markets were the fundamental institutions of a spontaneous order, reproduced by earning and shopping, in which contracts defined relationships among the wider population. People were supposed to respond to the incentives of a consumer lifestyle, complying willingly to the rules of the capitalist game because they desired the rewards it delivered, and adopted identities in the images of its models and celebrities.

Faced with the destructive force of the riots, government ministers fell back on the discourses of morality and the law. David Cameron spoke of a 'moral collapse' in some districts, and Justice Secretary Kenneth Clarke blamed a 'feral underclass' for the disorder (*The Guardian*, 6 September 2011). The coalition's response relied heavily on punitive criminal justice sanctions, but Cameron and Iain Duncan Smith also promised measures to disqualify offenders from benefit payments and even to evict their families from social housing (*The Guardian*, 8 September 2011).

There were also strong hints that social work – in the form of concentrated, focused 'tough love' programmes for 120,000 deprived and deviant families – could become central to the next stage of the response. The model was said to be based on a project carried out in the City of Westminster, where such a programme spending £20,000 on each intervention in such a family was reckoned to have paid for itself in three years, given that six months in a young offender's institution cost £40,000, and a year in care £50,000 per child in London (*The Guardian*, 16 August 2011, p. 5).

case study

A team of 25 officials was formed to look after 150 problem families. Officials had access to police databases, council rent logs, immigration records, medical histories and benefits agency files. The families were visited four times a week. They would have to comply with officials' orders: clean yourselves up, take your pills and stop beating the wife. For Westminster, it worked ... A year before the 'family recovery' squad was set up, the taxpayer faced an annual bill of £60,000 per family. A year after it was £20,000 ... that is a saving of £2 for every £1 spent. (Ramesh, 2011, p. 32)

The question for this chapter, and indeed for the whole book, is how social work is to be deployed in this initiative, and how it should respond. We are not suggesting that the fact that what David Cameron calls the 'social recovery' programme, aiming to cure the 'responsibility deficit', is explicitly aimed at dealing with the aftermath of the riots means that it will necessarily use methods that are unacceptably authoritarian. There are better and worse ways to undertake work with 'chaotic families', as Cameron calls them (*The Guardian*, 15 December 2011). Social work over the decades has had a long and honourable tradition of family casework. Our concerns focus on the ideological rhetoric and the policy framework in which this initiative is cast.

On the government's own account, 'the typical profile of the rioter is 35 per cent out of work or on benefits, 42 per cent on free school meals, 66 per cent with special educational needs, only 11 per cent with 5+ GCSEs and 70 per cent living in the 30 per cent most deprived post codes, with 36 per cent excluded from school'. This paints a clear picture of a group experiencing poverty, social exclusion and a lack of links into the mainstream social order. It calls for an approach which attempts to reconnect this group with the standards and aspirations of that mainstream through access to a whole range of experiences and interactions, for the sake of social justice as well as the prevention of disorder.

Instead, the argument used by Cameron for setting up local authority teams to identify these families and appoint a caseworker for each was that they currently cost the taxpayer £8 billion, and that the programme could save a large proportion of this outlay. The initiative was to be overseen by Louise Casey, former New Labour 'Respect Czar', with a reputation for toughness, and would concentrate on making them understand their obligations.

This approach would install a very particular style of social work practice at the heart of a new regime, intended to construct a new, more authoritarian social order, of a kind not seen since the Second World War in the United Kingdom, or anywhere else in Europe, but reminiscent of the urban villages created by Hitler for 'problem families' in need of reso-cialisation, one of which can still be seen in the Neustadt district of Bremen.

There is a connection between the prospect of this kind of approach and the structural changes in the economy, labour market and income distribution patterns analysed in the previous chapter. If the majority of the population in the United Kingdom (and indeed in many other afflu-ent countries, including the United States and most Western European states) is to be excluded from the dividends of growth in the global economy, to what extent will the public services, as instruments of the government, become disciplinary, tutelary and surveillance forces, upholding an order based on control rather than freedom?

In this chapter, we will investigate the nature of the social order, and criticise the model of how the public services were positioned to uphold it under neo-liberal and Third Way regimes. We will go on to review whether changes already recognisable in social programmes and social work practice provide clues to this possible direction in policy. We will also consider which traditions in social work might embrace or oppose them.

Constructing the social order

It is tempting to see the history of human societies as an evolution from small hunter-gatherer tribes to large, complex states, in which individuals became increasingly differentiated from the collective. On this account, the former were units in which members shared a single mind and will, founded in a common (mythical) cosmological understanding of their origins and place in the world of nature; whereas the latter enable a diver-sity of social roles, of expertise, of knowledge and beliefs about society itself, and about the material universe and human beings' significance in it. This implies that in complex societies, individuals have distinctive identities and institutional means of realising their projects through actions and strategies, which did not exist in simple ones.

In reality, even the earliest human groupings seem to have contained culturally established ways in which members could resist collective pres-sures. They could invoke ancestors or gods to justify making their own decisions, even when these deviated from group norms, or they could simply leave the group, with or without others, for a time or permanently (Sahlins, 1974; Hirschman, 1981, p.252). They also had familiar processes for challenging any attempts to impose leadership on the collective, as much by ridicule as by threats to anyone claiming such authority. Even in these tribes, group action had to be negotiated; there were no ready-made cultural prescriptions for specific contingencies, and every situation demanded interpretation of the group's norms and beliefs.

But by the same token, present-day affluent societies involve a plethora of ritual practices, unchallengeable assumptions and uncriticised group think; individualism (of the kind which forms the dominant social environment in the United States and the United Kingdom) is itself a culture, which is sustained in everyday interactions by what Mary Douglas (1987) calls a cult of the self. As Durkheim (1898) commented, this involves giving constant obeisance to the 'little gods' of others' self-esteem, and avoiding giving offence by failing to respect their conventional projects of self-realisation. Indeed, as Goffman (1967) pointed out, everyday interaction ritual consists of claiming and giving 'face', that is, the social value we and others demand in the accounts and performances we give of ourselves, and thereby creating a social world experienced by each of us as external and morally binding. This *is* in fact our social order, socially constructed and collectively inescapable (Jordan, 2008).

stop and think

■ How should we best understand how social order is created and maintained? Is it something spontaneous? Is it rooted in deeply held, shared norms which bind people together? Or is it something more provisional and manufactured through ways in which people come together for particular purposes and at particular moments in time? Think about how good heads of homes create a culture of mutual support among residents, or how a team ethos is built among social work staff in a district office.

The most obvious representations of the current order are the celebrity gossip and lifestyle images in our media, the advertisements and fashion pages which define the latest must-have items of clothing and footwear, the tide of new gadgets and gizmos which keeps washing into our shops, and the impractically enormous vehicles seen driving around the streets of all our towns and cities. But there are also many ways in which we signal our membership of occupational or faith groups in our appearance and behaviour, showing that individualism based on consumption and its display is not the only kind of cultural standard shaping behaviour in affluent societies.

In general, however, the social order in the United Kingdom and the United States – as a result of our history and traditions, but intensified by neo-liberal ideology and economic restructuring since the advent of Margaret Thatcher and Ronald Reagan – relies less on standards we derive from membership of *groups*, or from our place in a *grid* segmenting our societies in terms of age, sex and status (Douglas, 1970, p.57), and more on our interactions with other citizens. In what Douglas calls 'low-group, low-grid' cultures, which existed even among some forest tribes, individuals are competitive and unconstrained by social boundaries, groups are provisional and temporary and status is negotiable. Power is exerted by gaining 'followings' of clients or customers, through the achievement of reputation, and celebrity, and through brand images.

The question for social policy and social work in such societies is always therefore whether law, provision and practice should reinforce such features of the social order, or to offset them by introducing other principles and sources of social value. The experience of wartime solidarity and equal sacrifice created a cultural environment in which the post-war Labour government was able to build on these new standards in creating the National Health Service, the social security system, universal secondary education and the local authority social services. The aim was explicitly to introduce institutions which would consolidate equality of citizenship and social justice through everyday interactions with the staff of these services, as well as in new entitlements (Cole, 1945, p. 29).

The fiscal crises of the 1970s shifted the direction of policy, and eventually of practice also. Although cuts in public expenditure and a new emphasis on choice introduced managerialism, cost efficiency and mobility between options for service users, there was also a greater recognition of diversity. Post-war services were culturally insensitive and discriminatory in terms of ethnicity and sexual orientation, excluding minorities and often also many people with disabilities from participation on terms of equality. But policy and practice built on legislation of the 1970s to change the culture of these institutions in important ways. They also became more responsive to the distinctive claims of women for recognition and support.

But by the time the New Labour government was elected in 1997, the individualistic basis for the collective infrastructure had been uncritically adopted, as part of the new economic orthodoxy for public finance. Tony Blair and Gordon Brown were convinced that – following the example of Bill Clinton in the United States – they could rely on the self-regulating mechanisms of markets to ensure stability and prosperity. Mainstream citizens were directed towards the banks to borrow what they needed to construct their projects for self-development, on mortgages and credit cards. The social services were increasingly reserved for the minority who could not achieve 'independence' of this kind (DSS, 1998, p. 80).

As we now know, this economic strategy implicitly relied on the banks (and later the government itself) borrowing huge sums from Japan, China and the Middle East, in order to lend to citizens who were spending well beyond their means, on the strength of the inflated value of their houses. The City of London grew far faster than the rest of the economy, as financial speculation came to be the only form of economic activity in which the United Kingdom claimed competitive advantage (Ertürk *et al.*, 2011). This was also enabled by low interest rates, especially in the United States, which were possible because of the sheer volume of Chinese and Japanese savings available for such loans, and the ever-lower prices of manufactured goods from the former country. So the whole model on which the strategy was based was sold to the public as a story (for businesses to repeat in their commercials, and citizens to recount to each other in their offices and pubs) about the scope for ever-increasing consumption of lifestyle products in a world with no more boom and bust. This version came to be woven into the fabric of a social order through these communications.

At the same time, the New Labour leadership insisted that the revival of the United Kingdom as a leading player on the world stage depended on the reform and modernisation of a public sector that would occupy a different role in that social order. These services would be restructured and realigned to be part of a new businesslike orientation of the state ('UKplc', as it was increasingly referred to by government officials of all kinds), to be implemented as much in schools and clinics as in the Immigration Service or the Department for Trade and Industry (DoH, 1998).

This view of the role of the social services validated the New Public Management (Clarke and Newman, 1997), which emphasised the need to price each unit of provision, to contract between units in the sector as well as contracting out certain tasks to private firms and the voluntary sector, and to target, plan and develop services on the basis of research into specific outcomes. It led to an approach to practice which was task-orientated and quantified, both focused on specific outcomes and quality standards and constantly measured and assessed through checklists and tick-boxes, feeding statistical information, inspections and league tables.

The legacy of New Labour

case study

The language of business management infiltrated the whole of social work in the New Labour period of government, and this continued after it left office. Consider the following opening paragraph of a letter from the Chair of the Social Work Reform Board to the other members of the Board, in September 2011.

> I am pleased to enclose the information about the suite of recommendations and related products recently agreed by the Social Work Reform Board (SWRB) for improving the quality and consistency of social work initial qualifying courses ... These reforms have been agreed by all members of the Board, including HPC, GSCC, JUCSWEC and the College of Social Work.

In part, the emphasis on recording, planning and reviewing in social work was a response to shoddy standards of practice which had been revealed by the enquiries into child abuse scandals since Maria Colwell in the mid-1970s. This was justified; there was no past 'golden age', with stable teams of social workers, all committed to high standards of professional practice. The issue was that ideas about consistency and quality were linked with business-style management and the prescription of practice responses to every situation.

So, instead of seeking to modify a market order by introducing practices of equal citizenship, collective solidarity, risk-sharing and cooperation, the new orthodoxy in government aimed to promote the same business values as prevailed in the wider economy; and instead of cultivating relationships of support and mutuality, the new culture laid stress on choice, mobility between providers and a consumer-style culture of 'personalisation'. In all this, Blair and his colleagues were supported by sociologists such as Anthony Giddens (1991, 1998), who wrote of a new, post-traditional order of reflexive individuals pursuing 'projects of self', no longer constrained by the limiting rules and roles of gender and class – people could now construct and revise their own life narratives, free from the dead weight of inherited moralities.

Government policy was based on confidence in the market and in this new type of identity. The social order it sought to enable was competitive and acquisitive; the information made available to the public helped the best-informed and most resourceful gain access to the most advantageous positions in the classrooms and the hospitals, as well as the labour and housing markets. In the absence of rising earnings or opportunities for better-quality employment, the positional struggle led to a culture which was insecure, edgy and defensive, as well as self-indulgent; without social mobility, people were less trusting and less willing to attend to each other's needs. One research project after another blamed flat-lining figures on subjective well-being (overall assessments of life quality) on 'excessive individualism' (Layard, 2005; Unwin, 2009, p. 4; Layard and Dunn, 2009, p.9).

research box 3.2

In 2009 Professor Richard Layard and Judy Dunn produced a research report for the Children's Society called *A Good Childhood*. They concluded that children's lives had become more difficult than in the past, and they traced this to excessive individualism. In their analysis, this produces more family discord and conflict; more pressure to own things; excessive competition in schools and unacceptable income inequality. The authors argued that excessive individualism needs to be replaced by a value system where people seek satisfaction more from helping others rather than pursuing private advantage. Their findings included:

- The proportion of children experiencing significant emotional or behavioural difficulties rose from 8 per cent in 1974 to 16 per cent in 1999, and has remained at that level.
- Some 70 per cent of children agree 'parents getting on well is one of the most important factors in raising happy children'. By contrast only 30 per cent of parents agree with the statement – a significant difference of perspective.
- Children with step-parents or a single parent are, on average, 50 per cent more likely to suffer short-term problems with academic achievement, self-esteem, behaviour, depression or anxiety.
- Only a quarter of the children who are seriously disturbed by mental health difficulties get any kind of specialist help.
- Increased exposure to TV and Internet increases materialistic desires and reduces mental health.
- Children who spend 18 hours taking a Resilience Programme, which teaches children to manage their own feelings and how to understand and care for others, are half as likely to experience depression over the next three years and also do better academically.
- Britain and the United States are more unequal than other advanced countries and have lower average well-being among their children. In Sweden 8 per cent of children live at below 60 per cent of median income. In Britain the number is 22 per cent.

In the next section we will focus on the effects of these aspects of the public culture on the experiences of those using the social services.

Shortcomings of the contractual model

It was not only the economic crash, highlighting the regulatory failures of Gordon Brown as Chancellor, which brought about the defeat of New Labour at the 2010 UK general election. In opposition, David Cameron gambled that the additional spending by that government on public services would not have increased its popularity proportionately, because of the very technocratic approach to provision for human needs which had been adopted. New Labour ministers had also been continuously critical of the performance of the public services, so that when they did claim successes (such as falling rates of crime) these were discounted by the public. Insisting that 'we are the radicals now', Cameron (2010) outlined an alternative set of priorities which seemed to put professional expertise and empathy before cost efficiency, and to encourage citizens to act together in pursuit of local improvements in their quality of life. Even though the electorate was unconvinced by his Big Society ideas, there was some resonance with his critique of the Third Way model.

The contractual model – derived from the economic theory of information, incentives and contracts – postulated a solution to the problems of 'asymmetric information' and 'moral hazard' in relationships between economic agents. Especially in human services, it was impossible for managers to monitor how their staff performed their everyday tasks. The solution, according to the theory, was to stipulate performance requirements that they would then 'internalise' as standards for their practice (Macho-Stadler and Pérez-Castrillo, pp. 3–10). This led to the attempt to prescribe precise responses and required outcomes for each of a huge range of complex situations and problems, both for practitioners and for companies to whom services were contracted out. It led to the micromanagement of the work, and a loss of the critical judgement required in these occupations.

Long before the election, evidence had begun to accumulate of failures in the services, reflecting a reliance on rules and systems rather than direct communication and professional judgement in the work of the front-line services. Although there was nothing new about scandals in the child protection system, involving health care staff and police as well as social workers, there was something about the Baby Peter case in Haringey which played into this view of how these services had come to operate. The fact that the family in question had been in contact with the services on more than 60 occasions during his short life, including after he received the injuries from which he finally died, without arousing urgent concern for his safety, suggested that a procedural, mechanistic form of practice, lacking a feel for the real dangers faced by the child, had afflicted the practitioners involved. (These issues will be further discussed in Chapter 4.)

Other news stories seemed to convey a picture of official agencies proving ineffective in the face of a disturbing level of collective abuse, directed against vulnerable adults in deprived districts. The suicide in Leicestershire of Fiona Pilkington and the death with her of her daughter, who had a learning disability, and the death of David Askew, an older man with learning disabilities who was baited and badgered to death by youths in Greater Manchester, had followed after years of unproductive call-outs and interventions by the police. Again, it was not that no resources had been devoted to these cases, but that staff time and effort had been expended without any tangible improvements in situations which ended in tragedy.

But more disturbing than these individual cases was the revelation of prolonged failures in the treatment and care given to patients admitted in emergency to the Mid-Staffordshire Hospital Trust in a period from 2004 to 2009. Here, despite repeated complaints by ex-patients and relatives, and despite the avoidable deaths of at least 400 people, the authorities failed to act to address appalling shortcomings and – as if to confirm that these failings were directly related to the government's system of incentives, inspections and funding – had actually been awarded prestigious and lucrative Foundation status during this period. Several subsequent reports on this scandal confirmed that there was obvious daily evidence of neglect of patients' safety, hygiene and dignity, as the management sought to promote the hospital's chances of this recognition by achieving various paper targets, at the expense of its duties of care. That all this should have happened in a facility of the National Health Service, the most valued institution in the country (still highly esteemed by the majority of the public, including those who had recently received treatment), and after major improvements, including dramatic reductions in waiting times for most elective surgery, was very disturbing to the public.

The picture emerging from all these news stories from the period in the run-up to the 2010 election was of a society in which a minority of citizens abused and persecuted those least able to defend themselves, and even some of the best-resourced public services lacked basic humanity in their responses to those in greatest need of their care. New Labour undoubtedly paid a price for these failures in its social policies; but it was far from clear that the coalition which succeeded it in government had rejected the model on which its reforms of these services had been based. Above all, it had not replaced the idea of contractual relationships between parts of these services, with the government itself, and with service users, or the business analogy with their management and functioning. The coalition instead embarked on a new set of organisational reforms of the health service and education, making gestures at changing the way that staff related to service users only in response to the Munro Report (2010) on child protection practice.

research box 3.3

Professor Eileen Munro was commissioned, by the incoming coalition government, to prepare a report on child welfare services. It was published in 2011. Below is an extract from her recommendations.

The full Report was published as:

Munro, Eileen (2011) The Munro review of child protection: final report: a child-centred system (PDF). [Norwich]: The Stationery Office (TSO).

It can be found at:

https://www.education.gov.uk/publications/eOrderingDownload/Cm%208062.pdf

The Government's response was published in July 2011 as:

Department for Education (DfE) (2011) *A child-centred system: the government's response to the Munro review of child protection (PDF)*. [London]: Department for Education (DfE).

It can be found at:

http://www.education.gov.uk/munroreview/downloads/GovernmentResponsetoMunro.pdf

All recommendations refer only to England.

Recommendation 13: Local authorities and their partners should start an ongoing process to review and redesign the ways in which child and family social work is delivered, drawing on evidence of effectiveness of helping methods where appropriate and supporting practice that can implement evidence-based ways of working with children and families.

Recommendation 14: Local authorities should designate a Principal Child and Family Social Worker, who is a senior manager with lead responsibility for practice in the local authority and who is still actively involved in front line practice and who can report the views and experiences of the front line to all levels of management.

Recommendation 15: A Chief Social Worker should be created in Government, whose duties should include advising the Government on social work practice and informing the Secretary of State's annual report to Parliament on the working of the Children Act 1989.

It was therefore not surprising that a series of reports and exposés revealed failures in services which were far more extensive and deep-seated in the following year. Inspections by the Care Quality Commission for England (2011) showed that 50 per cent of wards for elderly patients failed to meet adequate standards in nutrition, in basic hygiene and in human dignity, and that 20 per cent failed to meet standards of safety. Another report by the Patient' Association for England (2011) reached broadly similar conclusions. And an investigation by a BBC1 tv *Panorama* programme (2011) found that at the Winterbourne View Hospital, a private facility for patients with learning disabilities and autistic conditions, contracted to the NHS, staff were routinely abusing them. Finally a report by the inspectors of social care services in England (2011) found that these were failing a high proportion of the most vulnerable recipients of domiciliary services (see Chapter 4).

What seemed to be happening in all these fields was that staff had lost sight of the central purpose of their work (or had it obscured from them by management systems and government targets and procedures) – to relate to service users in human, supportive and respectful ways, which gave them value as fellow citizens despite their afflictions. Instead, at best they were treating them as objects in need of technical fixes, and at worst as subhuman creatures to be ignored or hurt on a whim. The reports painted a picture of staff performing tasks without engaging in any contact or communication, or being too rushed to finish the most basic of helping work properly or of failing to respond to cries of distress. In other words, far from constructing a social order in which bonds between practitioners and service users were sustained despite the latter's illnesses or disabilities, they were left without the comfort of being recognised as members of society of any worth and dignity.

stop and think

■ Had something fundamental altered in the nature of public services once ideas of marketisation and competition had been imported into them from the economic sphere? Are mutuality, reciprocity and trust possible within relationships which have become essentially commercial in character? What are the implications for social work services, in particular, of such a shift?

The riots in the English cities in August 2011 added several layers of concern about how public agencies were upholding the social order, and whether in fact this order was viable. They contained a cocktail of all the elements discussed in this chapter – resentment by the excluded, opportunistic consumerism and the ineffectiveness of the police's response to the initial outbreak of disorder. These and other aspects of the events will be analysed in the next section.

A moral and cultural collapse

The Prime Minister's immediate response to the English riots claimed that the disorder stemmed from a collapse of moral and cultural regulation in deprived districts. But the understanding of these processes conveyed in his pronouncements was crude. He and the other ministers who spoke in the immediate aftermath of the violence, looting and burning implied that it represented failures in the self-discipline of the participants, who had allowed themselves to take advantage of a mass breakdown in compliance with the law and standards of acceptable behaviour, because they had a tenuous and unreliable sense of right and wrong. This in turn suggested that they needed individual resocialisation, perhaps by means of the kinds of programmes of intervention developed by the City of Westminster.

The view of the social order we have outlined above indicates a different approach to the analysis of the riots. It focuses attention on the ways in which ideas and actions which are potentially antagonistic to the authorities representing government and mainstream society can be generated in groups which perceive themselves as excluded, stigmatised and oppressed. Whereas the majority of citizens use parts of official ideology and the policy aims of the regime to make sense of the social world and steer their course through it, these groups may adopt other cultural resources, available in music, the alternative media or in local folklore, to weave together a very different version of how their society works.

On this account, morality is not a set of unchanging, abstract rules that children learn from parents and teachers, but a cobbled-together guide to action which is assembled from all sorts of experiences and interactions, and can be deployed to produce and justify a variety of responses to situations. Which sort of reaction is chosen depends on whom one is with, and how events and circumstances are perceived. Even mainstream citizens with conventional ideas about the virtue of hard work and property ownership may behave in deviant ways if they are away from the company and social institutions which sustain these ideas, and with others who are moved by different interpretations.

Since the Brixton and Toxteth riots of 1981, minority ethnic citizens have made great strides in terms of access to many of the advantages and opportunities of UK society. Organisations, particularly in the public sector, have a far healthier culture of diversity and equality, partly as a result of the report on those riots (Scarman, 1981), which accounted in large part for resentment in the communities affected in terms of racism and exclusion. But because the official version of the social order since this time has been individualistic and contractual, these gains have been concentrated on a minority able to escape from deprived communities through education and successful careers. As the murder of Stephen Lawrence demonstrated, racism and discrimination persist in those districts, in the official responses to black citizens as well as on the streets.

stop and think

■ Do we all commit offences against morality and, indeed, against the law? Is behaviour situation-specific, so that we all behave in different ways in different circumstances? Does crime really reduce as we get older, or does it just change in nature? Young people commit their offences in public; older people commit theirs in the privacy of the car, the office and the home. One is easily visible; the other is not.

In the justification given by the founders of post-war welfare states for their creation, the social services were supposed to supply institutional means for citizens to experience themselves as equal in value and status as citizens, and interactions with staff who would communicate this in concrete ways to them. So it was not merely that social policy and a new kind of social work would redistribute income, improve education and health, and supply the services for social support; they would also allow even materially disadvantaged people to perceive themselves as sharing in the advantages of membership.

The success of this contribution to moral and cultural regulation by governments was revealed by the researches of Wilkinson and Pickett (2009), who found that more equal societies had lower levels of crime and disorder and better physical and mental health, and their citizens were better educated and lived longer. We would argue that these findings show as much about how the greater equality of self-esteem, the sense of membership and trust in others achieved by such institutions (which give people credible cultural resources for narratives of inclusion and belonging) as about the material effects of income redistribution or specific services.

research box 3.4

The work of Richard Wilkinson and Kate Pickett is easily available through the website of the Equality Trust. The extract below sets out the key claims made through the research. The detailed evidence on which the conclusions are reached can be found at:

http://www.equalitytrust.org.uk/why/evidence

Why more equality?

Evidence shows that:

1. In rich countries, a *smaller gap between rich and poor* means a happier, successful population. In fact, there is no relation between income per head and social well-being in rich countries.
2. *If the UK were more equal,* we'd be better off as a population. For example, the evidence suggests that if we halved inequality here:

   – Murder rates could halve – Mental illness could reduce by two-thirds – Obesity could halve – Imprisonment could reduce by 80 per cent – Teen births could reduce by 80 per cent – Levels of trust could increase by 85 per cent

So it is important to see the riots in a context of how young men in those districts understood their place in the social order, and their relation to representatives of the state. In particular, as the trigger for the riots was the shooting dead by police of a young black man, Mark Duggan, who was alleged to have been carrying a gun as a passenger in a car, we need to analyse the significance of this event for the young black men who were prominent in the protest that followed, and then in the disturbances themselves.

Among the early reports and statistics released since the riots, some suggested that the participants were mainly people with criminal convictions – disorder was therefore an extension of a pattern of unlawful activity. However, this was misleading in at least two ways. First, in the trawl of CCTV footage and witness statements after the disorder, it was far easier for the police to identify those who had been previously prosecuted than those with whom they had had no statutory contact. Second, in such districts a very high proportion of the population have been in police custody. One study conducted at the turn of the century found that, among Class V males in the United Kingdom born in 1970, 45 per cent had been arrested by age 30 (Bynner and Parsons, 2003).

A more thorough investigation, published the following December, found that those interviewed after participating in rioting and looting accounted for their actions as much in terms of their experiences with the police as of the opportunities presented by a temporary collapse of public authority. It should be borne in mind that young black men are 26 times more likely than their white counterparts to be stopped and searched, as well as more likely to be imprisoned if convicted. This report discovered that participants said their anger at the police, expressed in their actions, was more about *how* the police conducted these operations than the actions themselves. They described the officers' behaviour as hostile and aggressive, sometimes even violent, and considered this a partial justification for their involvement (Newburn *et al.*, 2011).

Seen from the police's perspective, the sequence of events was very difficult to handle. The death of Mark Duggan put them on the defensive, because it raised questions about the legitimate use of firearms in making an arrest, and provoked an angry protest from his community. The way the police held back as the riots started could have been related to fears about stirring justifiable grievances by heavy-handed tactics, especially if the mob was perceived as a collective of the very young men who were routinely being individually stopped and searched on the streets. This hesitancy was perceived as a surrender by the rioters; because they had come to see themselves as at war with an authority that was antagonistic towards them, they went on to escalate the mayhem in a kind of orgy of celebration of their temporary power.

All this illustrates how fragile the fabric of the social order can be, especially where social relations are potentially volatile because they rely on the interpretation of postures and actions rather than direct communications. In everyday interactions, people cooperate to repair tears in the fabric, such as a misunderstanding or an unintended slur, or even someone's failure to give a morally adequate account of themselves (Jordan *et al.*, 1991). Moral regulation takes place through these barely noticed processes, by which people maintain normal appearances, even in exceptional situations. When public services are working with the grain of normalisation, staff help people to make sense of emergencies and crises, and absorb them into the everyday routines of their lives. Between the rioters and the police, no such exchanges were possible.

In the next section we will consider how a transformation of the public services might affect the construction of the social order.

Accountability and community

One feature of the model of public services developed under New Labour was that accountability was interpreted as consisting in the justification of expenditure to taxpayers. This involved demonstrating 'value for money', by showing how each unit of service achieved the greatest effect, according to the stated policy goals and target outcomes. It included the contracting out of those activities which could more efficiently be performed by commercial companies or voluntary bodies.

In essence this was a business accountancy model, with taxpayers, both national and local, cast as remote shareholders. Although policy documents paid lip service to participation by service users, their role was to choose and consume what was provided, not to play an active part in planning or creating it.

Austerity potentially changed this, because the funding of services became so problematic. What was lost through the cuts might be compensated by a shift towards more active engagement of communities in meeting the needs of their members. It was understandable that the first reaction of staff of these agencies was resistance to redundancies and reductions in provision, but there were also opportunities for new developments.

The Conservative Party election manifesto (2010, p. 35) pledged to train 10,000 new 'community organisers' to help identify ways of improving their physical and social environment, and mobilise them for action. The tide of community development had been on the ebb in England since the early 1970s; it had been largely dropped from the curriculum for social work education. But in Scotland there were still many projects, and in Bob Holman (2002) the tradition had a notable standard bearer, whose approach attracted the attention of Iain Duncan Smith, and influenced the framing of the Big Society programme.

On 12 November 2010 Bob Holman published a reflection on this experience at Easterhouse and of working with the now-Secretary of State at the Department of Work and Pensions, Iain Duncan Smith. This is an extract from it:

Poverty. In 2003 Duncan Smith said: 'I want to be the party for the poor.' He bravely spoke at a 2005 Labour party conference fringe meeting, saying Labour's definition of poverty was too limited: it is 'not just about a lack of basics but a lack of sufficient resources to participate in the life of the community'. What has happened now? At a time of rising food prices, the freezing of benefits and tax credits makes the poor even poorer. The new system of local housing allowances will mean 774,000 households losing an average of £9 a week.

Communities. Duncan Smith has said again and again that stable communities and families are the core of a good society. And yet the cap on housing benefits will force thousands of families to move to cheaper areas. Simultaneously, deprived communities to which they are drafted will find it difficult to accept more pressure. One of Duncan Smith's great achievements has been to highlight the capacity of locally run community groups to improve local life. He promised his party would legislate to ensure that 'public money would flow to more diverse, innovative and locally based projects'. But the cuts imposed by the coalition government on councils have resulted in grants to many local groups being axed; and many are closing down entirely.

My long experience in deprived areas tells me that the number who make a rational decision to live on benefits is tiny. I know others who cannot face working: those with mental health problems, for instance, or severe behavioural difficulties. These are the very people that the small voluntary projects, highlighted by the Centre for Social Justice, can help. But this involves building relationships and providing support, not compulsion.

The implications of these ideas will be more fully investigated in Chapter 5. For the purposes of this chapter, the important point is that the idea of breaking down barriers between the roles of paid staff and community activists is that accountability becomes direct. Instead of supplying services like a company contracted to organise a concert or to supply an insurance policy, this approach would lead the members of a community to identify what it required and to join together to bring this about.

In this way, they would be constructing their own social order, according to their own standards and aspirations. Whereas there is always a danger that the contractual version of services is experienced as being imposed by an external authority – as indeed happens in parts of societies which are so disadvantaged that they do not identify with the mainstream, participation by members should ensure that they are seen to be woven into the fabric of community life. Professional expertise is valued as a contribution to members' own efforts to organise themselves, and is accountable to the goals and values of activists and service users. Yet it is not simply technical, because it is linked to those goals, and into the substance of the local order through cooperative work.

The coalition government made a gesture in this direction with the 'free schools', which were supposed to enable parents and teachers to set up educational establishments in response to local needs. Unfortunately, this initiative was seen from the start as part of the struggle for positional advantage in education (allowing better educated and resourced parents to give their children a head start over others), and also part of the thrust towards losing schools from the control of local authorities. The danger was that, as in Sweden, most of these would in fact be set up by commercial companies, and not be genuinely the product of local cooperative effort. The reform of the NHS, which is supposed to facilitate patients' access to the best services by empowering GPs to commission them on their behalf, also risks turning into a bonanza for commercial companies (see Chapter 4).

The free schools and NHS initiatives illustrate some of the hazards of introducing new organisational principles into an established system; they can always be co-opted for purposes which serve the interests of some group involved in a struggle for power within that system (and indeed in this case many felt this was the intention behind these experiments). It shows that transformative change requires trust and commitment, if not of all the participants then at least of key people involved in accomplishing change.

The crisis has created conditions in which a major shift is clearly needed if services are to be sustained at an acceptable level. But this is far more likely to be adopted by staff and service users if it takes place in a political and social environment where there is a shared vision of a better future. This to a remarkable extent existed when welfare states were being built; it would be a great advantage if such conditions were to come about again, though preferably not as a result of a world war.

Conclusions

By the time of the UK general election of 2010, the version of the social order which had fuelled the Third Way model of public sector reform had lost its credibility. The Labour Party programme looked threadbare, and government ministers bereft of new ideas. Because it rested on an unrealistically optimistic view of the self-ordering powers of markets, and especially financial markets, the model could no longer supply a viable basis for the ways people lived their lives together as citizens.

The Conservative Party's programme at that election was in many ways a direct riposte to the Third Way. Its emphasis on civil society and local collective action was also a new direction for the party of Margaret Thatcher. The electorate's response was guarded; it is unlikely that the Big Society proposals won many votes. In the event, the coalition's policy programme was derived far more from the economic orthodoxy of George Osborne as a Chancellor of the Exchequer dedicated to restoring fiscal prudence than to David Cameron's speculations about a potential new social order.

Cuts in spending spawned resistance by public service unions, but it was the riots in English cities that provoked a national debate about morality and culture as the basis for a diverse society in the United Kingdom. Under New Labour, the term 'culture' (in the context of the social order) was almost always used to characterise a feature to be deplored and, if possible, replaced by something more businesslike and contractual. In the public services, the 'old passive culture of the welfare state' (DSS, 1998, p. 26) was to be changed into a regime of flexibility and responsiveness to individual needs, with banks and supermarkets explicitly given as model organisations. In society at large, phenomena like 'dependency culture', 'gang culture' and 'gun culture' signalled social evils to be rooted out by anti-social behaviour orders, parenting contracts and behavioural programmes, aimed at turning atavistic, group-orientated denizens of deprived districts into mainstream consumers with projects for independence and self-realisation.

We have argued that the social order cannot be sustainably constructed out of quasi-economic relations and individual aspirations; it is inescapably a web of moral and cultural commitments, maintained through formal and informal institutions, and acting on individuals through their communications with each other. People may adopt aspects of an economic orthodoxy in the way they make sense of their place in the wider world, but what they cobble together out of these and all the other cultural resources at their disposal – from their ethnicity, faith, associational and community membership and all their other affiliations, as well as their occupational identity and political commitment – will form the basis for their relationships with their fellow citizens. In this sense, the official ideology of governments, including market-minded ones, is just one element within a process of moral and cultural regulation that is the social order of that society.

Despite the Big Society rhetoric, little really changed with New Labour's ejection from office, except that the public services' role in sustaining that order was considerably reduced. In the case of certain key aspects, such as the drastic cuts in youth services in England, this was a key element in a new insecurity and drift, which could result in public disorder.

The abolition of Connexions and the Careers Service, and the rise of youth unemployment

On 17 December, *The Guardian* reported that the coalition was to make an announcement on the future of the youth service before Christmas, in a new strategy for teenagers. It would make it clear that there would be no ring fencing for youth services or protection for youth clubs. Instead, the strategy would emphasise the part to be played by businesses and charities. Labour reported that of 74 councils in England which had cut youth services in 2010, only 11 were Labour controlled. The deepest cuts were in Liberal Democrat-controlled Sutton, where the youth service budget had been reduced from £7.5 million to £3.4 million.

Furthermore, such changes in social relations as did occur were the result of a dawning realisation that the old order of consumerist individualism was unsustainable, that people were going to have to look to each other more for solutions to problems and that action at a local level could make a difference. There were countless examples of unsung heroes and heroines taking up the challenges of a neglected social infrastructure, for instance, by providing activities for bored and frustrated young people whose youth centres had been closed.

In this situation, it is the class of property owners which is best able to defend its interests, and it expects the government to act in its support; it is therefore important that those other interests excluded from power in the big decisions do not cease struggling for the cause of the overwhelming majority of citizens, especially at a turning point in the economic basis for the social order. The collapse of what looked like an enduring adaptation to globalisation under the Third Way regime should spur the search for new and more effective policies to redistribute wealth and power for the benefit of all, and a role for social work which is emancipatory rather than authoritarian. Our aim is to contribute to such a search in the rest of this book.

- Austerity policies have exacerbated existing inequalities and led to protests across the globe. In England, the response of government has been to increase the social surveillance of the most deprived and deviant families, with social work deployed as a vehicle for doing so.

- From 1979 onwards, social work has been organised on the principles of New Public Management, with its mechanistic focus on outcomes and standards measured through checklists and tick-boxes and reinforced through inspection and league tables. Trust, as the basis for social work relationships, has been replaced by confidence in marketisation.

- The shortcomings of the contractual model have been apparent in a series of scandals in child welfare and care of older people, in which dignity, care and a sense of human worth have been in very short supply, in what were once known as the *personal* social services.

- A different possibility exists for the future of social work, one which is rooted in a sense of equal value and status between citizens and dedicated to constructing new social relationship based on the positive pursuit of greater equality and characterised by mutuality, reciprocity and trust.

taking it further

- Butler, I. and Drakeford, M. (2005), 'Trusting in Social Work', *British Journal of Social Work*, 35:5, 639–653
- Rowson, J., Mezey, M.K., and Dellot, B. (2012), *Beyond the Big Society: Psychological Foundations of Active Citizenship*, London: RSA.
- Smith, C. (2001) 'Trust and Confidence: Possibilities for Social Work in 'High Modernity'', *British Journal of Social Work*, 31:2, 287–305.

Health and social care: A loss of compassion?

chapter 4

In this chapter we look more closely at the way in which the ideas examined so far can be seen working their way out in health and social care services.

We have traced the ways in which the processes of commercialisation and profit maximisation came to be applied, in new ways, to the business world in general, and to financial services in particular. Over the past 40 years, a particular view of the best way to organise social and economic life has exercised a hegemonic grip over the Anglo-Saxon world, with determined efforts – through institutions such as the World Bank and the IMF – to export this model around the world.

Successive abandonment of controls and regulation allowed capital to move rapidly around the globe, searching for new places where cheap labour could maximise profits. But it also allowed firms in the affluent countries to enter the fields of education, health and social care services, and to export these to developing states. This had three main consequences.

First, in an effort to extract value from remaining economic activity, areas previously conducted by the state as part of the profit-free public service became increasingly colonised by profit-hungry, market actors, with the citizen cast in the role of serial shopper, forever exercising 'choice' in pursuit of 'personalisation' and the extraction of maximum personal advantage from encounters with service providers. Ownership, we were assured, did not matter to users. Today's citizens were interested only in the quality of service, not its origins. The 'any willing provider' mantra of health reforms in England as pursued by the coalition administration is presented by its supporters as just a statement of agnosticism about ownership – because ownership doesn't matter. The duty of the state is simply to secure the best service, at the best price – an outcome which markets is bound to produce – but only for those promoting the deeply flawed reasoning outlined in Chapter 2.

Second, as we have seen, a realignment took place in the shares to be taken from economic growth. In the United Kingdom, by 2011 the share of national income distributed to workers stood at its lowest post-war point since 1945, at 53 per cent, while that going to shareholders and senior executives stood at 57 per cent (TUC 2011). In the process the real value of wages stagnated.

Third, if jobs were being exported elsewhere, and real term wages and salaries were stagnant, a new way of creating effective demand for goods and services had to be brought into being. In the United Kingdom and the United States, the answer was to borrow money. The magic dust of newly freed-up financial services meant that individuals were encouraged to spend today, and pay tomorrow – and in an apparently pain-free way, as today's consumption could be met through the exorable rise in property prices. It was, of course, when so many of these properties turned out not to have a real value that the collapse in the US sub-prime market triggered the exposure of the whole pyramid-selling scam on which a debt-fuelled economy operated.

In the post-2008 period a new dimension of this same phenomenon emerged. Now whole sovereign nations turned out to have lived beyond their means, with no discernible prospect of returning to balance. Now, two quite different solutions were attempted. In the United States, a recognisably Keynesian policy has been pursued, in which government spending has gradually re-injected demand into the economy, promoting growth and looking to pay down debt with the proceeds. In the United Kingdom and, with Chancellor Osborne as cheerleader, the opposite course is being pursued. Here, the anorexic patient has been placed on a starvation diet. Austerity will shrink economies to the stage where activity is so reduced that nations will be obliged to live within their means again, and this will be achieved mainly by reducing the share of national resources going to the public services.

stop and think

■ Can you set out some of the key ways in which governments have come to think about the organisation of social and economic life, over the past 40 years? What have been the main consequences of this underlying approach for public services?

From the perspective of this book, our interest lies in the impact of these economic policies on the public services. In earlier chapters we have suggested that, for such services, a parallel set of developments have taken place in which the pursuit of trust-based, cooperative relationships has been replaced by competition and a reliance on the techniques of new public management (Clarke and Newman, 2004). In this chapter, we shall see how each of these developments has worked its way into health and social care services in the United Kingdom, and in England, in particular. Two extended case studies will be used to demonstrate the operation of these forces in hitherto unsuspected areas. In tracing and analysing the collapse of the Southern Cross care home company the chapter will focus on the impact of marketisation, enforced inequality and debt on the residential care of older people. Thereafter, an account of the scandal at Mid Staffordshire NHS Trust will concentrate on issues of governance and the quality of face-to-face contact between providers and users of public services in contemporary Britain.

These examples show how the economic logic applied to the provision of health and social care led to a crisis in the quality of those services for their most vulnerable users, and especially for frail elderly citizens. This became recognisable even before the financial crash, and these services are now required to face major challenges in improving the ways their staff interact with service users against a background of austerity in their funding.

Southern Cross

Early in the summer of 2011 rumours which had been circulating for some time about the financial difficulties of the Southern Cross care home provider came into the open, when the company attempted to bounce its creditors into a three-month 'restructuring' exercise. The attempt failed when those to whom Southern Cross now owed substantial sums of money declined to cooperate. Within six months, the company had gone out of existence.

The background to the difficulties in residential care services for older people is one which, while relatively brief in time, has been continuously turbulent. The story begins, essentially, with the 1990 Community Care Act. It contained a Faustian bargain at its heart. On the one hand, it provided the vehicle through which a set of essential Thatcherite ambitions were to be achieved. 'Monopoly' welfare services were to be broken up and transferred out of the public sector, while previously free services (provided in the NHS) were to become 'fee' services, by being shifted into the means-tested social care sector. On the other hand, the vehicle through which these transformatory changes were to be brought about was the local authorities, seen as standard bearers for the 'enemy within' by Margaret Thatcher. The compromise was to transfer budgets for these services to local councils, but to make it a condition that 90 per cent of such funds had to be spent on contracting for services, rather than providing them in-house. The first of the fundamental changes set out at the start of this chapter – marketisation – was thus firmly on the agenda almost a quarter of a century ago.

Against that background, it is hardly surprising that a boom followed in the private care home market, attracted by the guaranteed demand provided by an ageing population, matched by what appeared to be a guaranteed stream of government funding. In the process, what had been a near-monopoly of public sector care homes was transformed into a monopoly of the private sector. Johnson *et al.* (2010, p. 236) conclude that 'between 1980 and 2001, the proportion of long-term places in the independent sector rose from 18 to 85%. By 2005, 90% of all residential care home places were in the private sector.'

Over the 20 years which followed the 1990 act, the nature of provision altered radically. The former pattern of small-scale, family-run homes virtually disappeared, bought up by far fewer, but far larger companies. It was at the start of the last decade, however, that the market moved to even greater consolidation, with what the *Financial Times*, in 2004, called 'frenzied private equity activity in the sector'. In September 2004, the New York-based equity giant, Blackstone, acquired Darlington-based, New Zealand-originated company, Southern Cross Healthcare, for £162 million. Southern Cross had been in the hands of another private equity owner, West Private Equity, for barely two years. Blackstone thus became the owner of 160 residential care homes, providing 8,200 beds (see Drakeford 2006; Scourfield 2007, for extended accounts of these developments).

In a little-noticed market manoeuvre, at the time, Blackstone then sold off the freeholds of the homes it had so acquired, in order to obtain funds to finance further care home acquisitions. From now onwards, the company would have to pay rent to the freeholders for the sites which it occupied, and the care homes which it ran. Three months after buying Southern Cross it purchased the second largest UK-based owner of private nursing homes, Surrey-based NHP, in a cash deal of £564 million. NHP owned more than 350 care homes with 17,400 beds throughout the United Kingdom. It also managed a further 165 homes through its subsidiary, Highfield Care.

It is important to be clear that such equity buyouts are motivated by one thing only – the prospect of rapid and rising profits. Blackstone was not an organisation driven by an interest in social welfare. Later in the same week that it acquired NHP, it also bought a French cinema group, a German chemicals company and the Dutch telephone directory supplier VNU. Residential care was simply another commodity from which profit might be extracted, only this time with the added advantage that such profits were being supplied by the public purse.

By the time the equity acquisitions of 2004 were completed, the public sector monopoly of 30 years earlier had, essentially, been replaced by a monopoly of the private sector. Mrs. Thatcher's Hayekian-derived promise of a highly competitive market, in which a plethora of small suppliers would strive for business by providing highly cost-effective, relentlessly customer-focused services, had given way to a very different world in which a small number of dominant suppliers would provide large-scale warehousing of older people, with very little choice for either purchaser or user.

How was it, then, that the heady days of assured profits of 2004 turned into the crisis of 2011?

At the start of the year Southern Cross owned 750 residential homes across Britain, employing 44,000 workers and offering care to 31,000 residents. Some 70 per cent of those living at Southern Care properties had their fees paid by local authorities. In parts of the country, it was, to all intents and purposes, a near-monopoly supplier. In the northeast of England, for example, they were a dominant force, providing 30 per cent of all care home beds (House of Commons Public Accounts Committee, 2011).

Then, as the post-2008 crisis depressed economic activity everywhere, a major flaw in the Southern Cross operating model began to become clear. In 2004, the height of its debt-fuelled dash for growth, those responsible for the conduct of the company's affairs decided to sell off the freeholds of the care homes already in its possession, in order to raise the cash to make further acquisitions. Now, in this sale-and-lease back arrangement[1] Southern Cross would go on providing the care of both residents and care home fabric, but the land on which they stood (and often the buildings themselves) would be owned by someone else. In the blithe belief that trading conditions could only go on getting better, the land and buildings were now rented back by Southern Cross, under legally binding agreements which, in many cases ran for 25 years and were subject to yearly upwards-only rent reviews. Research by the union representing the bulk of workers at Southern Cross homes, the GMB, suggested that over the four years to 2011, rents paid by the company had gone up by 18.6 per cent at a time when property values were falling. By 2011, the cost of meeting these rent rises amounted to £60 each week for every care home bed in the company's possession. In 2010, the union estimated, the company already paid an average rent of £6,444 per bed to landlords (GMB 2011a).

By the time the crisis struck, the company was paying some £250 million annually to 80 different landlords, including the publicly owned Royal Bank of Scotland and Lloyds Banking Group. When it posted half-year losses of £311 million in May 2011, it warned that, without change,

---

[1] According to the Financial Times (6 June 2011) Southern Cross was far from the first company to go to the wall because of such sale-and-lease-back arrangements. It suggested that the demise of the high street store, Woolworths, was very largely explained by the way in which 'they did sale and lease backs on virtually everything' – and then could not afford the built-in escalator to such costs, as markets' rents fell.

it did not have enough cash to survive beyond the end of the following month. On 1 June, Southern Cross had announced what amounted to a unilateral decision to cut the rents it paid by 30 per cent for a four-month period. Within hours of the announcement, however, one of its major landlords, the suitably named Bondcare poured cold water on the announcement. All major creditors followed. Within weeks, the company was at an end.

The Southern Cross story illustrates each of the developments outlined at the start of this chapter, and discussed in more detail in the first part of this book.

Marketisation

Somewhere in the Reagan/Thatcher era, the neo-conservative way of thinking had become so established that, when profit-hungry capital looked for new ways of extracting value from those services which could not be exported elsewhere, the state was able to position residential care services for vulnerable older people as a sector where privatisation could legitimately be pursued. By turning care homes into a market, all the familiar claims could be rolled out. Gone would be the old take-it-or-leave-it, lowest-common-denominator drabness of public services. Instead, here was a sector in which the consumer would, once more, be king – choosing just the right service from a plethora of competing providers, pursuing quality and economy from the best, and in which only the nimble, responsive and customer-focused would survive and thrive.

In fact, as we have seen, the sector was very rapidly infested with those whose overriding interest was to extract maximum profit from a field where the taxpayer was the major contributor. Any pretence to a Hayekian free market, in which many providers competed for business, was quickly shouldered aside, as the monopolistic ambitions of major players reached for a position where they would be 'too big to fail'.

Given that the explicit programme of the coalition government involves large-scale transfer of services and responsibilities out of the public sector and into the hands of 'Big Society' organisations, it is hardly surprising that a substantial campaign has been mounted to portray Southern Cross as an exceptional case, both idiosyncratic and unusual. The whole business of sale-and-leaseback, splitting a business into a service component and a property component (each with its own obscure opco–propco nomenclature), is presented not simply as a conventional device to extract maximum value by profit-hungry, asset-stripping, equity buyout companies, but as something strange and exceptional – certainly not the way that business would normally be conducted.

Of course, if the problems of the company are simply *sui generis* then there are no general lessons to be drawn for the general principle of providing care through companies motivated by profit rather than public service. In fact, as discussed below, the most remarkable thing about Southern Cross is just how typical the problems it highlights turn out to be.

Inequality

As noted earlier, Southern Cross sold off the freehold of its homes, in order to leverage more debt, and so purchase further care homes. The largest freeholder of Southern Cross homes, at the time of its demise, was the Qatari Investment Authority[2] (QIA) which effectively owned 300 of them. To most members of the public, the 70 per cent of fees received by Southern Cross which came from public funds was paid over in order to provide care for residents. In fact, those funds were being skimmed to pay the interest on £1,100 million bonds raised by the QIA when they bought the care home buildings from a private equity company in 2006. Moreover, the Authority continued, throughout, to channel the rents it received via an Isle of Man headquarters to an offshore tax haven, a company incorporated and registered in the Cayman Islands, in order to avoid making tax contributions itself, in the United Kingdom.

All this stands in sharp contrast to the fate of the 10,000 GMB members employed by Southern Cross to staff their care homes. Before the crisis struck, the majority of these staff were paid the National Minimum Wage (NMW) and the majority had had their pay frozen. On 8 June 2011, as it became clear that the company was fighting for survival it wrote to the Union with proposals to cut labour costs by at least £20 million, including 3,000 job losses, wholesale changes to terms and conditions of employment and new work patterns.

This was not, of course , the first example of wages and workers being exploited to the advantage of companies and their shareholders. As early as 2002, the *Daily Mirror* had undertaken a detailed investigation of the employment practices of the Highclear Group[3] which, it alleged, employed nurses from overseas in a 'slave' regime at its residential care homes. Here, workers were oppressed by being forced to hand over documents such as birth certificates and certificates of professional qualification. They were employed in conditions which prevented them from seeking registration with UK professional bodies, and were charged £3,500 each as a 'fee' for

---

[2] Qatari Investment Authority was established in 2000 with $40 billion. A decade later its wealth had risen to around $60 billion, although extreme secrecy about its operation means that this can only be an estimate. The QIA is controlled by Sheikh Hamad bin Jassim bin Jabr al Thani, the Prime Minister of Qatar.

[3] In 2004, as part of the great consolidation, Highclear was bought by another care home conglomerate, Ashbourne, which in turn was acquired by Southern Cross in 2005.

obtaining work in the first instance (see Craig, 2010, for a wider account of slavery in the contemporary British economy).

Nor were workers the only group to be left picking up the tab for Southern Cross' failure. As has been extensively argued elsewhere (see, for example, Drakeford 2000), marketisation of public services inherently involves a privatisation of profit, but a socialisation of risk. When a company of the size of Southern Cross goes out of business, then the public purse is left to pick up the bill for failure. The deal through which the company ceased to trade at the end of October 2011 included a strand in which the government (or the taxpayer, to use the term which its apologists would usually prefer) is to defray or defer a £20 million tax bill which the company had left unpaid as it slid into oblivion.

Debt and the aftermath

By Christmas 2011, the company had finally transferred its few remaining care homes to new owners, and its formal wind up was completed. Some 30 different operators were now responsible for the care previously provided by Southern Cross. The largest was a new company, HC-One, formed by Chai Patel and Southern Cross's largest landlord NHP. Almost exactly nine years earlier Dr. Patel had been chief executive of Westminster Healthcare when residents of one of its homes, Lynde House, had been neglected and mistreated. On 1 October 2002, the London Evening Standard quoted Vince Cable on the campaign which exposed the scandal.

> 'Without Gillian Ward and her brave group of relatives, none of this would have come to light,' says MP Vincent Cable. 'They have done us a major public service. The climate of denial they faced was ferocious.' 'When I first raised the issue with Chai Patel, he totally poohpoohed it. All he had to do was to care enough to acknowledge their complaints, deal with them and apologise. But he chose to deny it and that led to it becoming a national public campaign.'

The next largest acquisition was made by what the GMB described as the 'debt-soaked' Four Seasons Healthcare, which became responsible for 145 homes formerly run by Southern Cross.

The House of Commons Public Accounts Committee reported on oversight of the social care market in December 2011 (Public Accounts Committee 2011). It looked in detail at the background to Four Seasons, which it described as one of the first alternative health care providers to come forward offering to take over Southern Cross homes. It found a similarly troubling history. In 2009, as Southern Cross's difficulties deepened, the Qatar Investment Authority divested itself of its investment in Four Seasons.

A remaining group of lenders exchanged half of the £1.5 billion owed to them for shares in the business as way of saving it from going under. As a result Four Seasons is currently 40 per cent owned by the Royal Bank of Scotland, itself 80 per cent owed by the public pursue. The remaining £780 million debt (against assets of only £326 million which the company possesses) is due to be repaid to shareholders in September 2012. While the underlying financial health of the company is not easy to establish because of its complex group structure and tax avoidance activities, an ADASS-commissioned analysis in 2011 concluded that 'it is impossible to say that the care home operation could be extracted as a profitable standalone operation'. What is clear, however, is that the only source of income which Four Seasons possesses is the fees paid for residents at its care homes. In other words, once again, money which taxpayers provide for care purposes will be skimmed to service the £780 million debt with which the company is saddled, and to repay that debt when it falls due in 2012.

An indication of the scale of profit-taking from care home activity can be found in the annual accounts of Four Seasons, published in October 2011. It showed the company making an annual £8,408[4] for every bed occupied according to a GMB analysis (GMB 2011b).This is £161.69 per week. The turnover per occupied bed was £31,800 per year, which was £611 per week. Earnings amount to 26.4 per cent of turnover.

This account of Southern Cross has focused on the way in which economic developments, set out in earlier chapters, can be seen operating within services which, hitherto, have been regarded as motivated by provision of care, rather than pursuit of profit. It is against this background that the vexed question of funding for social care has been debated in the United Kingdom.

Whereas other European countries, such as Germany and the Netherlands, went through the difficult process of establishing national systems for pooling the risks and costs associated with frailties in old age by paying for care through their social insurance contributions, the United Kingdom chose to let market forces dominate this sector. Now, in addition to the crisis over the quality and supply of this care, there is also one over how those who need it can afford to pay.

stop and think

- In what ways can privatisation and marketisation policies be seen at work in the Southern Cross story? Who were the main winners and losers in the failure of Southern Cross? Are public policy lessons from Southern Cross being learned?

---

[4] These are earnings before interest, taxation, depreciation, amortisation, rent and management costs.

The Dilnot Commission (2011) recommended that there should, in effect, be a National Care Service, with fair rules on eligibility applied across the country, to fund individual citizens needing these services. The resources allowed for qualification for means-tested support should be raised from £23,250 to £100,000, and once any citizen had spent a maximum of £35,000 from their own income and savings they should receive free care. Those entering adulthood with a need for such care should qualify for this immediately.

Part of the justification for such a scheme lay in the failure of financial markets for insurance against the need for care. The Financial Services Authority investigation of mis-selling of bonds (FSA 2011) for that purpose by HSBC, Britain's largest bank, concluded that older people had been misled into gambling large sums of money (an average of £110,000 by each individual, making £285 million, altogether) on financial products which, in 87 per cent of cases were unsuitable for their claimed purpose – paying for long-term care. The average age of investors was 83. The bonds were designed for a five-year investment period. Early withdrawal incurred high penalty charges. The violations, said the FSA, were 'particularly serious' and 'systematic'. A record fine of £10.5 million was levied on the bank, although this was less than the profits which had already been made from products which had been so intentionally designed to deceive.

If this is an example of the impact which the new economic order produced upon vulnerable individuals, it is, sadly, not difficult to assemble recent evidence of parallel deficiencies in the operation of social policies and services in the care of older people. Indeed, 2011 was dominated by such stories, for example as that generated by the Panorama programme expose of abuse at Winterbourne View care home in Bristol, and the report of the Equality and Human Rights Commission (EHRC 2011) into flagrant disregard of the most basic human decencies in provision of care to older people in their own homes. Similar conclusions were drawn in the report of the Care Quality Commission, published in September 2011 (CQC 2011), which concluded that almost half of care homes in England that provided nursing care failed to meet required standards in care and welfare of residents. More than three out of ten homes were not up to standard for safety and suitability of premises; four out of ten failed on management of medicines, and 29 per cent were failing to meet the nutritional needs of users.

So the crisis of social care concerns the quality of provision as much as its costs. The commercial competition and business ethos that was supposed to drive up standards has instead produced a system lacking compassion as well as organisational stability. It is difficult to avoid the conclusion that the business model of social care has failed to supply an environment in which empathy and support are reliably available for our most vulnerable citizens. In future, policy and practice will be required to address both sides of this failure.

We turn now to an exploration of issues of health care provision through a different case study – that of Mid Staffordshire NHS Trust. The focus in this section will be on issues of governance and direct delivery of care. Of course, just as it would have been possible to have discussed these issues in relation to Southern Cross, so it is possible to identify many of the same economic questions in play in the case of Mid Staffs.

Mid Staffordshire NHS Trust

When, in 2007, the scandal broke over the quality of care provided at the Mid Staffs NHS Trust, it was very soon apparent that, at the root of what had gone wrong, was a crisis of finance. Under huge pressure to balance its books, a pressure exacerbated by its decision to seek Foundation Trust status, Mid Staffs had lowered its staff ratios and cut costs, especially in its facilities to treat patients admitted in emergencies, in a quest for this potentially lucrative and prestigious recognition of excellence.

In an earlier chapter, we discussed the ways in which, as other forms of economic activity have been removed from the United Kingdom, so corporations have sought new ways to expand capital accumulation within the domestic economy. Prising open public services for that purpose has been a project which has lasted for over 30 years. In the health field, especially, the Private Finance Initiative provided what Ruane (2010: 520) calls 'a vast space' for such involvement. Under PFI the building and running of new public buildings such as hospitals and schools was undertaken by the private sector, in exchange for a long-term guarantee of annual revenue repayments from the public purse. The capital costs were removed from the public sector balance sheet, but, over the long term, the sums of money involved in repayment are very substantial. Liebe and Pollock (2009) calculated that £12.3 billion invested in health service capital projects would, over the life time of the agreements involved, generate £41.14 billion in repayment for the buildings, and a further £29.1 billion for management services such as maintenance and cleaning.

Tudor Hart (2006:50) discusses the National Audit Office's 2006 review of one of the first PFI schemes which produced the new Norfolk and Norwich University Hospital. Opening in 2001, the hospital was contracted through Octagon Healthcare, a consortium of banks and property developers, for a minimum of 30 years. Following changes in interest rates, it was refinanced by Octagon in 2003 at a windfall profit of £115 million, of which it returned £34 million to the NHS Trust, keeping £81 million in private profit. The rate of return for shareholders rose from 16 per cent to 60 per cent of their original investment, and the contact period rose from 30 years to 39 years.

Shortly before Christmas 2011, Freedom of Information requests showed that the long-term cost of PFI projects with a capital value of £59 billion had risen to £229 billion in ongoing revenue payments. Much of the additional spending goes on expensive maintenance contracts. Newspapers (see, for example, the *Daily Telegraph*, 23 December 2011) highlighted a series of such examples. The North Cumbria University Hospitals NHS Trust had been charged £466 to replace a light fitting and £75 for an air freshener. A Trust in Salisbury had paid £15,000 to 'install a laundry door following a feasibility study', while a Trust in Leeds had paid £962 to supply and fix a notice board. Mid Staffs' neighbouring Trust, at North Staffordshire, had been charged £242 to supply a padlock. In the process very large amounts of public funds are transferred from the public pursue into the balance sheets of private corporations – just as Southern Cross, Four Seasons and other privatised providers of residential care services rely on public funding to generate profits for global shareholders and owners.

Nor should PFI be understood simply as a set of financial transactions. Ruane (2010: 521) traces the way in which it 'has brought personnel from corporate boards into the heart of the state'. The rationale for such a development has been set out in earlier chapters. It rests on the belief that the private sector possess qualities of creativity, innovation and managerial grip and that these qualities are not to be found in public services. Both of these contentions are highly open to challenge, but, in the 'target and terror' (see Mays 2011)) culture of the English NHS in the New Labour period they formed a commercialising hegemonic grip on the way that services were provided.

Care

The scandal which was to break over Mid Staffordshire NHS Trust began in the summer and autumn of 2007 when the then-regulator, the Healthcare Commission, became aware of what it called 'apparently high mortality rates for specific conditions or operations at the Trust' (Healthcare Commission 2009: 3). The Commission was dissatisfied with the response of the Trust to this 'alert', because it believed that much of the Trust's effort had been put 'into attempting to establish whether the high rate was a consequence of poor recording of clinical information' (Healthcare Commission 2009:10). This, and concerns expressed locally about the quality of care provided at the Trust, led the Commission to launch a full investigation, which it carried out between March and October 2008.

During the summer and autumn of 2007, the Healthcare Commission became aware, through its programme of analysis of mortality rates at English hospitals, of unusually high mortality rates for a number of specific conditions or operations at the Trust. A specific investigation followed which identified consistently high mortality rates for patients admitted as emergencies, which the Trust was unable to explain. For the three years from 2005–06 to 2007–08, the Trust's Standard Mortality Rates for patients admitted as emergencies aged 18 and over varied between 127 and 145 – where 100 represents 'average' performance. Standardised mortality was found to be high across a range of conditions including those involving the heart, blood vessels, nervous system, lungs, blood and infectious diseases. The Trust set up a group to look at the issue, but the Commission was further concerned that much of the group's effort was devoted to establishing whether the high rate was a consequence of poor recording of clinical information, rather than focusing on clinical standards and performance.

From the outset, patients and relatives expressed major concerns about poor standards of nursing care. Indeed, the Healthcare Commission's own 2007 survey of inpatients placed the Trust in the worst 20% of all English hospitals for overall standards of care and whether patients felt that they were treated with respect and dignity in the hospital. Much of this concern focused around the Accident and Emergency Department where the Inquiry concluded that nurses were too few in number and the Department staffed after 9 o'clock at night by inexperienced and junior doctors. It confirmed accounts, provided by patients, that initial assessment at A&E was routinely carried out by receptionists with no clinical training. Thereafter decision-making was often driven by the need to avoid breaches of the target that all patients were to be seen, and moved on from A&E, within four hours. The results, it concluded, were 'frequently chaotic' (Healthcare Commission, 2009: 5).

Amongst a catalogue of clinical failures at virtually every stage of emergency care the Inquiry found problems with resuscitation procedures, including problems with the bleep system for the management of cardiac arrests. Records showed a number of cases where patients had developed clots in the deep veins of their legs or pelvis and died from these clots breaking off and blocking the blood flow to their lungs. The care of post-operative patients was poor, such that signs of deterioration were missed or ignored until a late stage. The result, the Commission concluded, was avoidable death for some patients who, otherwise, might have been expected to make a full recovery from their condition at the time of admission.

Yet, despite the regular findings of clinical failings, patients, families and relatives were more concerned with basic standards of care. The Commission summarised it in this way:

> The care of patients was unacceptable. For example, patients and relatives told us that when patients rang the call bell because they were in pain or needed to go to the toilet, it was often not

> answered, or not answered in time. Families claimed that tablets or nutritional supplements were not given on time, if at all, and doses of medication were missed. Some relatives claimed that patients were left, sometimes for hours, in wet or soiled sheets, putting them at increased risk of infection and pressure sores. Wards, bathrooms and commodes were not always clean. (Healthcare Commission, 2009:6)

In all of this, governance arrangements at the Trust were found to be deeply unsatisfactory, from ward level to the Trust Board, which it described as 'insulated from the reality of poor care for emergency patients' (p. 7). It was focused, very largely, in dealing with a projected deficit in the Trust's budget, a problem which it addressed through a loss of 150 posts, including a significant reduction in the number of nurses, and a reduction of more than 100 beds over a three-year period.

Part of the pressure to address budget issues was tied up in the Trust's decision to pursue Foundation status, a course of action which the Inquiry concluded led the Board to become 'focused on promoting itself as an organisation, with considerable attention given to marketing and public relations' (p. 10). In the process 'it appears to have lost sight of its real priorities' (p. 11).

As a result of the Healthcare Commission's report, the then-Health Secretary, Andy Burnham, set up a further independent Inquiry into patient experience at Mid Staffs. It endorsed and extended the concerns which had already been identified.

In this account, we focus on the failures of basic care which the Inquiry identified. Indeed, the Report itself concentrates on what its chair described as 'the almost overwhelming number of complaints I have received about the lack of basic nursing care' (p. 44). Yet it is important to note that it also found a very similar picture to that uncovered by the Healthcare Commission in other aspects. In relation to clinical standards at A&E, for example, it concluded that the drive to meet the waiting time target had a detrimental effect on staff and on the standard of care delivered. There was persuasive evidence that this even led to attempts to fabricate records (p. 17). In governance terms, there was a fatalistic distrust in management amongst the consultant body, with low staff morale reinforced by cuts. The Trust Board conducted large parts of its business in private session and in isolation from the wider NHS community. When it came to responding to complaints from patients and relatives, the Inquiry found that 'while the Board received reports of themes of complaints, these were too broad to be informative. With a serial filtering of information with no involvement from non-executive directors, the Board was distanced from the reality of complaints.' Even when presented with direct evidence of problems, the reaction of the Board, individually and collectively, 'was one of denial instead of searching self-criticism' (p. 21).

This sense of defensiveness as the first reaction to difficulty was character-istic of the organisation as a whole.

So it was that, as far as care is concerned, the Inquiry concluded that the failures had been systemic. While problems were most often rooted in inadequate numbers of staff on duty to deal with the challenge of a popu-lation of elderly and confused patients, the Inquiry, nevertheless, concluded that, 'what has been shown is more than can be explained by the personal failings of a few members of staff, with clear instances of staff being present, but lacking a sufficiently caring attitude. The lapses in care could not be explained as isolated mistakes restricted to one place or one time' (p. 13). The result was that 'a wholly unacceptable standard was tolerated on some of the Trust's wards for a significant number of patients' (p. 11) in which people in the last days of their life were 'degraded' by their treatment.

Although the Inquiry did not find evidence to substantiate the more lurid allegations printed in national newspapers – such as, for example, the claim that patients had been so left without water that they had taken to drinking water from flower vases – it still reported that 'many witnesses told me of difficulties encountered in obtaining water on different wards' (p. 94). Such treatment was only one example in a much longer list of complaints identified and confirmed by the Inquiry. In the space availa-ble here only a basic summary of some of them can be set out. They included:

- incontinent patients left in degrading conditions;
- patients left inadequately dressed in full view of passers-by;
- patients moved and handled in unsympathetic and unskilled ways, causing pain and distress;
- failures to refer to patients by name, or by their preferred name;
- rudeness or hostility;
- marked indifference;
- meals placed out of reach and taken away without being touched;
- patients not helped to unwrap the meal or cutlery;
- visitors prevented from helping feeding;
- water not available at the bedside;
- lack of involvement in decisions;
- insensitivity;
- reluctance to give information;
- provision of wrong information;
- failure to listen;
- lack of engagement with families and friends.

The force of the Inquiry's findings emerges most powerfully in the indi-vidual patient stories which it recounts. Just two will have to stand for the far greater number which the Report rehearses:

A daughter told the Inquiry that her mother required oxygen, but there was none available during her move from the ward to where the procedure was to take place. The porter said he was in a hurry and so her mother agreed to be moved without oxygen.

The patient's doctor told the daughter: 'listen ... the prognosis is very poor ... her stomach has pushed up ... she is going to die over the weekend and it is going to be a very painful death because what will happen is it can happen at any moment, any second now, it can turn, it can twist and she will die.

In fact, over the next few weeks, the patient's condition improved and she was able to walk around and use the bathroom,

Thereafter, however, the deterioration set in once again. The patient's daughter became increasingly concerned and, on raising her anxieties with a nurse she was given a medical book to look through to see if she could identify her mother's symptoms.

When asked to describe the nursing culture, she said: 'They were bullies. They bullied ... the other staff and they bullied the patients. There was no word for it ... particularly during the two weeks that Mum was dying, effectively, patients were calling out for the toilet and they would just walk by them.'

'We got there about 10 o'clock and I could not believe my eyes. The door was wide open. There were people walking past. Mum was in bed with the cot sides up and she hadn't got a stitch of clothing on. I mean, she would have been horrified. She was completely naked and if I said covered in faeces, she was. It was everywhere. It was in her hair, her eyes, her nails, her hands and on all the cot side, so she had obviously been trying to lift her herself up or move about, because the bed was covered and it was literally everywhere and it was dried. It would have been there a long time, it wasn't new.

Everyone could have seen her. That is why I was so distressed because my Mum would have been horrified if she would have known that people were walking past and could see her' (p. 54).

Governance

As the Inquiry concluded: 'The distress and suffering caused by this is almost unimaginable' (p. 54). While its focus was on treatment and care, a steady stream of witnesses pressed for an extension of its remit to explore the failure of the wider regulatory system. The collapse of care at Mid Staffs took place under the eyes of a succession of inspectorates and regulators, each of which had failed to see the evidence which the Inquiry so vividly uncovered. While the Inquiry itself was unable to take on that work, it did include, as one of its major recommendations, a call for the Secretary of State for Health to do so.

In this way, and in a governance sense, the scandal at Mid Staffs exposed many of the flaws at the heart of the New Labour model. As part of its reforming zeal, as applied to public services, New Labour Ministers had quickly come to the conclusion that the techniques of New Public Management – audit, inspection, regulation – had to be applied with renewed vigour and rigour to what it regarded as an outdated and complacent public sector. Drawing heavily on the Thatcherite analysis of such services as dominated by 'producer-capture' (see, for example, Enthoven 1985, an American academic on whom Mrs. Thatcher drew heavily for her health service reforms), policy proceeded on a 'low-trust' basis, in which the interests of users could only be protected by a series of bodies designed to hold services 'to account', and to send out a set of market signals to potential consumers. Ownership, as we have seen, mattered very little to New Labour. Regulation and inspection could guarantee the public interest, whether ownership was private (as in the case of Southern Cross), intermediate (as in the case of Foundation Trusts and the Private Finance Initiative) or public.

Yet, if such systems were to act on behalf of users, and to provide a guarantee of quality in public services, then how had they so signally failed in the case of Mid Staffs? In the aftermath, the latest configuration of the regulatory regime, the Care Quality Commission, came under fire from all sides. The Inquiry established by Labour Health Secretary, Andy Burnham, called for a specific further investigation into the failures, including its 'unhealthy organisational culture, a culture that goes to the top'.

Soon after the Inquiry conclusions were reported, the National Audit Office (NAO 2011) also produced a Report into what it said was 'a collapse in inspections and reviews' by the CQC in 2010 (despite underspending its budget) which had 'increased the risk that unsafe or poor quality care went undetected'.

It is worth just a brief pause, at this point, however, to explore something of this history of the CQC, because it turns out to be simply the latest manifestation of a series of previously failed regimes. Labour's first attempt came in 2000 with the establishment of the National Care Standards Commission. Seventeen days after its launch the government announced that it would be scrapped and replaced by a new social care regulator, the Commission for Social Care Inspection (CSCI). Within a month of that body attaining its first anniversary it learned, at a few hours' notice, that its abolition was to be announced in that day's Chancellor's budget speech. A new organisation was to be set up, incorporating CSCI, the health regulator, the Healthcare Commission and the schools inspectorate Ofsted.

Ofsted's promotion was based on its reputation as New Labour's favourite inspectorate, the most closely attuned to its marketising agenda, unafraid to pass judgement on 'failing' schools and leave parents to draw their own conclusions. CSCI, by contrast, was believed to favour a more developmental and improvement approach, lacking the hard-edged adjudicatory culture from which regulatory confidence might be created. The nature of regulatory practice, as designed for the New Labour era, is best illustrated by quoting Hudson's account of its operation in relation to child protection services. Here the process relied on a Joint Area Review (JAR), to be undertaken in each Children's Services Authority. The JAR drew on the 'parallel processes' of both Ofsted and CSCI, both of which fed into the Comprehensive Performance Assessment (CPA) of a local authority and, thereafter, into an Annual Performance Assessment (APA) of a council's children's services. Here is Hudson's (2005: 517) heroic effort to explain how these different regulatory products were intended to combine together:

> APA will play a key role in determining the aspects that will be covered in a JAR, and JAR findings will in turn be followed up in the APA – indeed, in the year in which a JAR takes place, APA will be based mainly on the relevant JAR findings. Taken together, the two will provide the CPA judgements on the service blocks for children and young people that commenced in 2005, as well as contributing to the Audit Commission's corporate assessment.

In and through these arrangements, replicated elsewhere in the public services, the New Labour project of modernisation was carried out. Its dominant message was that 'trust' could not be relied upon as the basis for the construction of welfare relationships. Instead came a determined effort to install what Newman et al. (2008: 538) term 'transactional processes', in which compliance replaces commitment and performance management replaces professional discretion. This chapter has traced some of the consequences in health and social care services.

Conclusions

The case studies presented in this chapter form the background to the reforms of health and social care services being proposed by the UK coalition government at the time of writing, and being opposed by the professional associations representing doctors and nurses. Far from breaking with the flawed principles adopted by New Labour during its term of office, and illustrated by these examples, the bill before parliament carries them further forward, applying to the NHS much the same structure as has been in place in the social care sector for 20 years.

This puts GPs in the role of commissioning and purchasing services for their patients, and introduces competition between providers as the central dynamic of the whole of the rest of the system. It relies on the managements of a multiplicity of hospitals and clinical services to force through efficiency measures which will enable them to win contracts from these purchasers, and market forces to bring about the collapse and disappearance of those unable to thrive in this environment.

As we have shown, it is not choice for service users that flourishes under these conditions, but business acumen among suppliers; and for those citizens unlucky enough to be cared for by the most ruthless or the least competent of such organisations, the consequences are grim. There are two main reasons for these outcomes.

First, there are now a whole range of international companies looking for opportunities to penetrate the United Kingdom's health services, either to manage or to provide treatments. The rationale for giving so much decision-making power to GPs – that they are in direct contact with patients and best know their needs – makes no allowance for the fact that many of them have neither the experience nor the desire to be commissioners of services on this scale. While some consortia may turn themselves into social enterprises, including a range of local community groups and complementary health providers in their surgery buildings, the majority will probably contract with commercial companies to do these tasks; they in turn will apply a business logic to their work.

Health services comprise a set of high-tech procedures and sophisticated pharmaceutical treatments which are susceptible to rapid scientific improvement, and to application to human conditions in ways involving carefully calibrated and measured processes; and a far larger number of activities which are interpersonal, involving communications and simple manipulations or assistance. It is obvious that the former allow scientific knowledge and dexterity to be well rewarded, for companies developing new products and devices as well as for skilled practitioners. It is in this minority of health care activities that profits are readily to be made, and where commercial companies will seek to make inroads into the public service elements in the NHS.

On the other hand, the routine work of care for elderly and disabled people with long-term conditions is not susceptible to these gains through new technologies or skills. Here the only way to save costs and produce profits is to intensify work for staff or to lower standards of provision. The scandals discussed in our case studies illustrated what happened when organisations in both private and public agencies applied this business logic to their work.

The danger of the proposed reorganisation is that a polarisation of standards, which is already apparent in NHS hospitals, will be consolidated by the new system. International companies will move into the potentially profitable high-tech sector and the public hospitals and clinics will cut back the quality of their services to their most vulnerable patients, in order to try to compete. The NHS has already been running on a myth that it treats all patients as equal, when in fact it has applied far higher standards to patients having elective surgery than to those admitted in emergency (as the Mid Staffs scandal showed), and to younger patients than to the great majority, who are old.

The latter point was illustrated by a series of reports towards the end of 2011. The Care Quality Commission found that 50 per cent of wards for elderly patients fell short of government standards in nutrition, hygiene and human dignity, and 20 per cent for patient safety (CQC, 2011). The Patients' Association found similar shortcomings in these wards in pain relief, assistance with toileting and help with eating and drinking (Wasson, 2011). And a report commissioned by the NHS itself found that a quarter of all patients on hospital wards in England and Wales were suffering from dementia, but were not being adequately cared for because nurses lacked the time and training to do so (National Dementia Audit, 2011).

This leads to the second point: organisations driven by the requirement to achieve efficiency and profitability are very unlikely to create an environment in which empathy and support are sustained in the care of those who require it most, and especially those with long-term needs. Indeed, it seems that the training and management of nurses in particular is now far more interested in the procedural and technical aspects of the work than the interpersonal ones. This was echoed in the criticism by the Equality and Human Rights Commission of the standards of treatment given in acute hospitals to people with learning disabilities (Equality and Human Rights Commission, 2011).

All this will be familiar to social workers, both from their own experiences within their organisations and from their contacts with service users in care homes and wards for elderly patients in hospitals. It is a distressing legacy of the reforms of these services under New Labour, but there is a danger that it could get worse under coalition government reorganisation and austerity. An alternative basis for policy and practice in these services is urgently required.

main points

- The economic and social changes traced in the first three chapters of this book have had a direct impact on health and social care services. Over the past 30 years, these changes have focused on prising open such public services for profit-making purposes.

- The results of marketisation and privatisation have been traced in the case of Southern Cross, a company where huge profits were extracted from financial strategies which ultimately left it unable to trade, and which placed its residents and those who work for it at risk. As a company 'too big to fail', the public purse has had to help deal with the consequences of private market failure.

■ The new paradigm for public services has had a direct impact on the quality of care provided to users. In the Mid Staffs case, this chapter has illustrated the systemic way in which governance arrangements, intended to guarantee and protect the public interest, failed to identify or rectify the collapse in care which occurred within that Trust.

■ Every fundamental reason for failure at Southern Cross and Mid Staffordshire has been adopted and installed at the heart of proposals, by the coalition government, for future health and social care services in England.

taking it further

■ Drakeford, M. (2008) 'Going Private?' in *Modernising the Welfare State: The Blair Legacy*, M. Powell (ed), Bristol, Policy Press.
■ Pollock, A.M., Price, D., McCoy, D., Treuherz, T., Roderick, P., McKee, M. and Reynolds, L. (2012) 'How the Health and Social Care Bill 2011 Would End Entitlement to Comprehensive Healthcare in England', *The Lancet*, 26 January.
■ Scourfield, P. (2012) 'Cartelization Revised and the Lessons of Southern Cross', *Critical Social Policy*, 32:1, 137–148.

chapter 5

Collective action, locality and community

Social work has always been concerned with people's relationships in groups and communities. In this sense it might be seen to be ahead of mainstream social and economic policy, which has traditionally been preoccupied with quantifiable issues – employment levels, rates of taxation and benefit provision, expenditures on education, health and social care and so on – and to have found the concepts of community and association somewhat nebulous. Social work has been in some ways better positioned to take up the challenge of a new concern for well-being (Kahneman *et al.*, 1999; Layard, 2005) since the start of this century, because it is aware of and deals in qualitative aspects of these relationships (Jordan, 2007).

But to take advantage of this head start, social work in the United Kingdom needs to shake off much of the baggage of the myopic focus on individuals and mechanistic methods of intervention that it acquired in the previous 30 years. In that period, it became largely detached from community work (Jordan with Jordan, 2000), and lost many of its capacities to understand individuals in their cultural contexts. To regain its links with the community perspective, it needs to shed its fantasies of exclusive expertise in the analysis of 'problem behaviours', and its claims to professional power stemming from these.

It is a truism that all the things now done in social policy and social work by states and firms were formerly done by families, groups and communities. We will analyse the factors which led to their being first collectivised and then partly privatised, to show how political, economic and social change might favour a revival of cooperative local collective action. Can what appeared to be a spontaneous evolution of societies towards larger-scale organisation – the professionalisation of services and the power of bureaucrats and managers – be turned around, to allow greater participation by and accountability to citizens?

With industrialisation and the growth of cities came working-class mutual aid and pooling of assets, in insurance, credit, housing and retailing, as well as trade unionism and savings clubs. But large sections of the poorest inhabitants of cities were excluded from these initiatives, because they had no time or resources to contribute; and at times of recession and unemployment, or during epidemics, even skilled workers were unable to afford to pay their dues. This led to the rise of political parties demanding state intervention in the economy, and eventually also state redistribution of income and provision of services, all over Europe (de Swaan, 1988).

Class struggle shaped the politics of the first half of the twentieth century; it led to the polarisation between capitalist and state socialist countries in the years after the Second World War, and to the creation of welfare states, in part as bulwarks against communism. The changes in the world economy analysed in the first three chapters have not reduced the relevance of class for life chances, but they have shifted the bases on which collective mobilisations can be organised. In the affluent countries, mass production no longer supplies the environment in which shared solidarities are part of daily experience, and common action around grievances can readily be taken. The state has been no less active in economy and society, but this has often been at the behest of capitalist interests, rather than to protect working-class citizens from the impact of their predations.

Individualism and consumerism are the cultural features of affluent societies which now block collective action, but they have been fostered as much by governments' promises of rising prosperity as by the marketing strategies of firms. People have been encouraged to regard 'independence' as the badge of good citizenship (DSS, 1998, p. 80), and material possessions as the evidence for quality of life. We ask how the prospect of a decade with slower economic growth will affect this ideology, and whether people will develop new ways of cooperating in the face of this changed reality.

Although a start can be made in such a process through small-scale collective projects and initiatives, a shift in culture demands the support of governments in enabling a new orientation towards mutuality and association. In the United Kingdom, disillusion with the coalition administration, which failed to follow through on either the Big Society idea or the community empowerment espoused by the Liberal Democrats, should not obscure the importance of this agenda. We will demonstrate its significance for social policy and social work under conditions of austerity.

So there is a need for new kinds of mobilisations, in groups and communities of all sizes, within a new collective infrastructure which enables such activities. But before we turn to the details of such developments, we need to analyse how collective action gets started and is sustained. One of the most influential theories in the political movement to restrict the scope of government action and promote the privatisation of public services concerned the logic and dynamic of group cohesion in common causes. This theory postulated a need for material rewards or punitive sanctions to sustain such action; it held that organised groups (such as trade unions) used their economic power against the interests of unorganised individuals, and it insisted that free markets represented a better approach to most of the challenges facing affluent societies (Olson, 1965, 1982).We will argue that this view has distorted policies towards collective action, especially in the Anglo-Saxon countries.

The evolution of cooperation

For social work and social policy to engage with a shift towards the revival of civil society, community and cooperation, they need to have a sound understanding of the processes by which these are either sustained or subverted by economic forces and government policies. In this section, we will set out an account of how groups and communities developed into larger societies, and how economic advance and state power transformed the ways in which members of such societies lived together.

After a prolonged period in which economic and political orthodoxy insisted that all collective phenomena must be analysed in terms of the rational, self-interested decisions of the individual participants, it is an intellectual effort to reconsider societies from the perspective of *group* evolution – how human social units were formed, and how they competed with each other. But this effort is necessary in order to grasp the full implications of the post-crash situation.

Human beings are physically puny (by the standards of the larger predators) but need big amounts of protein to feed our heavy brains. So we needed to cooperate in groups to survive; archaeological and anthropological research suggests that the size of brain needed for more sophisticated interpersonal negotiation evolved along with communication skills. As human populations grew, more social organisation was required, more brainpower demanded more nutrition and so on. As groups competed for food and territory, larger tribes gained competitive advantage over smaller units.

The formation of these larger tribes depended on their ability to limit competition and rivalry among members, and to absorb outsiders from other groups without conflicts. Research using computer simulations has confirmed the hypothesis of Boehm (1982, 1993) that these capacities of tribes strongly influenced evolutionary dynamics (Bowles *et al.*, 2003), with culture playing the role in this process that instinct plays for social insect species like ants and bees (Frank, 1995). Although hunter-gatherers generally rejected any forms of authority or leadership in favour of an informally negotiated social order, the emergence of altruistic and inclusive practices and institutions, such as the sharing of food, meant that non-kin could be treated as fellow members of a community with common interests in survival.

Groups were the bearers of these practices and institutions, through cultural transmission, just as individuals were the bearers of genes (Boyd and Richerson, 2002). The combination of social and genetic processes explains how behaviour which was costly for individuals – such as risking their lives in battles with other groups, or looking after frail and sick members – were beneficial for the group, and contributed to the evolutionary success of human societies in the first 90,000 years of anatomically modern mankind's history (Bowles *et al.*, 2003, p. 135). It is the ability to cooperate with a wide range of others which explains how human beings came to dominate the planet, despite our physical vulnerability and voracious appetites.

However, the evolution of societies took a new turn with the control of key assets such as water sources by certain groups, and the increases in population that were enabled by technological innovations for agriculture, mobility and war. Rulers emerged, along with military discipline, organised religion and finally writing, bureaucracy and specialised work roles, as what we call civilisations appeared in North Africa and the Middle East. Even then, most communities continued to be held together by processes of communication which used cultural traditions, sustained through institutions for cooperation.

So in human ecology the struggle between groups, tribes and communities as much as the struggle with natural adversities shaped development, and the sheer size of societies was often a key advantage. Ancient empires were the most advanced civilisations of their time, as well as the most prosperous economies. But alternative political structures sometimes proved superior; tiny Greek city states defeated the mighty Persian Empire in the fifth century BC, before going to war with each other, and beginning a long decline.

Europe's prosperity lagged well behind that of China and the Muslim countries until the later Middle Ages. Then banking and trade, followed by science and technology, allowed Europe to forge ahead, despite incessant national and civil conflicts. Finally by 1913, the European powers and the United States ruled the world, their empires trading with each other in the first period of global economic integration. Capitalism dominated all other forms of productive organisation; its systems of private property and profit were imposed on subject peoples, much of whose wealth and land was expropriated for use by colonialist rulers. But vast areas of communal social life and traditional economic relations coexisted with modernity, technological sophistication, mass production and the luxury lifestyles of the upper classes, even in Europe itself. For example, in 1900, only the United Kingdom, Belgium and Germany had more workers in industrial jobs than in agriculture; in France, the latter outnumbered the former by more than 2 million, in Italy by almost 4 million, in workforces of around 19 million and 16 million, respectively, and most of these were working on part-subsistence family farms (Mitchell, 1975, sec. C1).

The communal life of the countryside had been paralleled by the development of a new type of associational civil society in the towns of Europe and North America. In the eighteenth century, the arts academies, literary societies, coffee-house groups and political clubs of bourgeois London, Vienna and Paris had been followed by the growth of working-class trade unions, mutual insurance associations, savings and burial clubs, educational groups, building societies, and even new churches in the nineteenth century (Thompson, 1968). In this way, the individual civil liberties that emerged in more anonymous and more prosperous urban settings were balanced by the collective action of these membership groups.

The First World War and the economic instability of its aftermath disrupted the political and social equilibrium of the previous era, and polarised societies; the rival totalitarianisms of Stalin's USSR and Hitler's Germany produced authoritarian versions of state collectivism to challenge the liberal regimes of the United Kingdom, the United States and France. Post-war welfare states were part of the attempt to rebalance European societies, In terms of the demands of individual freedom, collective solidarity and democratic accountability (Judt, 2010). Particularly in Germany, Austria, Belgium, the Netherlands and Italy, they tried to strengthen a shattered civil society by involving associations of capitalists and workers in the administration of benefits and services, as well as funding churches and charities to supply social assistance and care.

Significantly, only in the Stalinist version of Marxism-Leninism did any theory of political economy up to this time ever subordinate social relationships to the dominant economic logic of the ruling ideology. While it was true that capitalism subverted every form of social organisation and communal risk-sharing that stood in its path, it is also true that each age saw at least one oppositional social and political movement to assert the claims of community and solidarity (local, national or class) against atomisation through such processes (Polanyi, 1944). These movements were often backward-looking; they were seldom coherent, and often lacked political effectiveness, but they supplied rallying points for the claims of loyalty and mutuality against impersonal market forces.

Even the economic theory of the first three quarters of the twentieth century allowed for the importance of non-economic, qualitative factors in the life of societies, and in their abilities to survive and flourish (Pareto, 1909, 1916; Pigou, 1920; Robbins, 1932; Keynes, 1936). It was readily conceded that the requirements of national security, political stability or quality of life could overrule efficiency and growth of incomes as criteria for policy decisions. All this was to change with the imperialistic claims of economics in the late years of the century, and the versions of individualism and consumerism which they supported.

Welfare states and communities

Social policy and social work are part of the structure of institutions which were created after the Second World War, to build a different sort of society, in which neither Stalinism nor fascism would disfigure the political landscape with their suppression of freedom and the rights of minorities, but economic life would also not be reduced to stalemate by conflicts between capital and organised labour. But – as we will argue in this section – little attention was given at that time to how the role of groups, associations and communities would be protected and preserved, or even to how active participation of citizens in public life would be encouraged.

This was because of the continuing fear that organised groups would subvert democracy and the market economy by forms of militant extremism of one kind or another, especially in countries such as Italy, Greece and France, which still had large communist parties whose actions were strongly influenced by the leadership of the USSR (Judt, 2010, chapter 3). In this sense, welfare states in Europe, and especially in Germany, Austria and Italy, were reconstructing their institutions in ways intended to include all the potentially powerful interests in society through representative organisations, incorporated into the political and economic process. Collective action, whether by trade unionists or fringe political groups, or even by those seeking local or regional autonomy, was something to be restrained or diverted. Welfare states were part of building a new set of strong national governments in Western Europe, to face down the USSR and its satellites in the east of the continent, and to construct harmonious relations with each other, thus avoiding the disaster of yet another destructive European war.

So social policy was focused on solidarity and pooling of risks at the national level, aiming as much to limit conflicts between groups and communities as to create rights and services for citizens. It was as much about regulation and control of populations, and strife-free relations between organised interests, as about enabling them to thrive and prosper. Social work was less influenced by these priorities, especially in Continental Europe, where it remained the province of voluntary, often faith-based, organisations, under the principle of 'subsidiarity'; in the United Kingdom and the Nordic countries it was run by local governments (Lorenz, 1994). But even in the former countries, it took its cue from the overall national strategy for economic and political harmonisation, rather than the encouragement of active engagement.

Beveridge report

In 1942 Sir William Beveridge published his report – *Social Insurance and Allied Services* – which was to form the basis of the post-war welfare state. Here is an extract from it:

> It has been found to accord best with the sentiments of the British people that in insurance organised by the community by use of compulsory powers each individual should stand in on the same terms; none should claim to pay less because he is healthier or in more regular employment. In accord with that view, the proposals of the Report marks another step forward to the development of the State insurance as a new type of human institution, differing both from the former methods of preventing or alleviating distress and from voluntary insurance. The terms 'social insurance' to describe this institution implies, both that it is compulsory and that men stand together with their fellows. [para 20]

This raises the question of how institutions such as public services work to enable citizens to find informal ways of meeting needs, creating value and sharing risks. As we saw in Chapter 3, a 'social order' consists in the cultural practices through which individuals engage with each other, both to give meaning to their actions and to negotiate how to live, work and celebrate together. These interactions are the ones which actually form the local order, and provide the ideas and standards through which people experience and interpret their daily lives. But they take place within the framework of institutions (such as families, groups, communities and official organisations), and are influenced by the discourses of businesses, the media, religion, politics and so on.

The aim of welfare states, largely accomplished in the 1950s and early 1960s, was that the public services would supply a framework in which people would see each other primarily as fellow citizens, enjoying the benefits of membership of a national democratic system which promoted social justice and the common good, and that a major element in this was achieving 'full employment'. Even though material inequalities persisted (Marshall, 1951), this equality of political and civic status was supposed to override these in everyday interactions at work and in the public sphere, while family values would guide relationships in the private world of households. But this left groups, associations and communities as a residual sphere, in which the informal social order was to be constructed out of some of the cultural resources of the political framework of official organisations, some through media and advertising, and some from the domestic life of family and kinship.

Mass participation and collective organisations in the post-war period

Membership of mass organisations peaked in the post-war period. Employment in manufacturing industry reached 39 per cent of the workforce in 1951, a concentration which it was never to attain again. Manual workers had always been a stronghold of trade union membership so, as manufacturing expanded so membership of collective labour organisations also rose, matched by increases in union membership amongst women and white-collar workers in the public services. At the same time, membership of the main political parties also peaked in the 1950s at around three million for the Conservative party and one million for Labour. It was a period when people saw the prospects of their individual advancement as intimately bound up with the wider collective of those whose interests they shared. By 2009 it had fallen to a quarter of a million and 166,000. respectively (McGuiness, 2012).

This residual role has recently attracted far more attention from social scientists and public policy experts, mainly because communities and associations have decayed, especially in the affluent Anglo-Saxon countries, and among poorer people. In the post-war period they were still very strong, because they allowed those who had endured the Great Depression and the two world wars to share in the sense of having survived and transcended these experiences, and turned them to good account for the sake of a new generation, whose lives would be far more prosperous and peaceful than their own had been. The achievement of welfare states was to allow these survivors of a terrible period in European history to see their children getting far better educations and employment opportunities than they had had, as well as better health and housing; social work was targeted on the minority whose needs were not so well met by the public services, and who therefore did not share in this optimistic culture.

The 'Seebohm Report' into the future of social services reported in 1968. Here is how it summed up the development of such services in the post-war period:

> The services with which we are mainly concerned have developed from different points, some reflecting and building upon the work done by voluntary organisations; some gradually being separated out from the Poor Law, while

others grew as a response to the difficulties encountered in providing other local authority services...

...the erratic course which the development of the personal social services has taken is attributable to other factors as well as these different points of origin. Many of them dealt and still deal with people or families whose problems or behaviour mark them out as deviant and enlist little if any public sympathy and understanding.

Source: Report on Local Authority and Allied Personal Social Services (Seebohm Report, Cmnd 3703, paras 54 and 56)

(It is worth noting that the state socialist countries of Central and Eastern Europe were able to offer their citizens something similar in this period of post-war reconstruction – hard work for the adult generation, but better prospects through education and skills for the new one. But social work was not a feature of these systems, or at least not an officially acknowledged one.)

Community, then, was the sphere in which these ideas from the public sphere were mediated in the everyday conversations of people; but little attention was paid to how this was done, or whether there could be more effective bridges built between the official world and this informal one. It was where things were done by means not suited to government agencies or business enterprises, requiring command of local cultural resources of language and nuance. As two eminent social scientists put it much later:

> Communities can sometimes do what governments and markets fail to do because their members, but not outsiders, have crucial information about other members' behaviours, capacities and needs. Members use this information, both to uphold norms...and to make use of efficient insurance arrangements that are not plagued by the usual problems of moral hazard and adverse selection...This insider information is most frequently used in multilateral rather than centralised ways, taking the form of a raised eyebrow, a kind word, an admonishment, gossip or ridicule, all of which may have particular salience when conveyed by a neighbour or workmate whom one is accustomed to call one of 'us' rather than them. (Bowles and Gintis, 2002, p. F423)

Yet the apparent stability of affluent societies in the 1950s and early 1960s was about to be shaken by a series of upheavals, taking the form of collective action by young people, women, black citizens, gay and lesbian groups, disabled people, benefits claimants, trade unionists and others. Economic change – the beginnings of globalisation and the start of the process of decline in old industrial heartlands – was accompanied by revolts against the restrictions of the post-war culture, and this was expressed in protests and demonstrations against the state itself, and often against the public services (Jordan, 1973, 1974, 1976).

Disabled people's movement

case study

Although there are examples from the nineteenth century onwards of efforts to highlight and withstand the discrimination faced by disabled people, it was not until the late 1960s, inspired by the examples of the civil rights movement in the United States, and women's movements more generally, that disability rights activism really began. In the 1970s, the movement developed and embraced the 'social model', in which the challenges faced by disabled people were externalised – no longer regarded as a 'medical' problem located within individuals themselves, but seen as a product of the wider context – economic, social and environmental – in which barriers to full participation were created. Collectively disabled people shifted the spotlight onto the way in which they were discriminated against, rather than their status as individual victims of illness or accident. In more recent times, disabled people's organisations have been in the forefront of the independent living movement and has been an important part of this broader movement for disability rights. It is based on the premise that people with even the most severe disabilities should have the choice of living in the community. This can be accomplished through the creation of personal assistance services allowing an individual to manage his or her personal care, to keep a home, to have a job, go to school, worship, and otherwise participate in the life of the community.

All this could be seen as a failure of the official sphere of politics and government agencies to keep adequately abreast of changes in the social order, and of the sphere of associations and communities to bridge this gap. Perhaps because the public services were designed primarily as means of restraint or control, rather than to enable active participation, the new generation, far from being grateful for the improvement in their lot, chafed at the limitations imposed on them by their elders and by the systems and organisations they had created. And because the associational and communal worlds of their parents were mainly traditional and backward-looking, they had to initiate whole new forms of collective action, focused on change, within which to frame their demands.

This illustrates how cooperation and community serve two purposes simultaneously – to transmit culture and to enable it to adapt to new circumstances. Just as our Stone Age ancestors were required to innovate in the face of catastrophic natural phenomena such as droughts and ice ages, so we too must find the means to change our shared ways of making sense of the world and living in it together to its transforming landscape. Culture is a form of restraint on individual self-interest, and it requires us to moderate our demands and limit our claims on others. But it can also suddenly take the form of spontaneous collective action to express demands and claims, as in the Arab Spring of 2011, or the Occupy movement worldwide. The late 1960s and early 1970s was a period when this was happening all over the affluent world (and also in the Soviet Bloc, as in the Prague Spring).

case study

The Prague Spring

The Prague Spring began on 5 January 1968 when Alexander Dub ek was elected as the First Secretary of the Communist Party of Czechoslovakia. Dub ek put in motion a set of reforms aimed at decentralising and democratising the regime which had previously operated firmly within the Soviet block. Restrictions were loosened on freedom of the press and freedom of speech. For a few brief months, the new liberal regime began to emerge across a wide range of activities, from politics to the arts. It was not to last for long. On the evening of the 21 August, tanks from the Soviet Union, Hungary, Bulgaria and Poland entered Czechoslovakia. During the invasion, 72 Czechs and Slovaks were killed. Alexander Dubĉek was overthrown, and his reforms reversed.

Seen from the perspective of the new century, these emancipatory movements were very successful in blowing away many of the stuffy, repressive and limiting features of post-war culture, and challenging injustice at the interpersonal and inter-group level. They also introduced feminist, anti-racist and anti-oppressive ideas (Statham, 1978; Dominelli, 1988) into social work education and training, and created a milieu in which established discriminatory practices were no longer acceptable. But they had two serious limitations in their impact on society as a whole.

First, although women, black people, Lesbian. Gay, Bisexual and Transgender (LGBT) and other groups gained enormously from the culture shift that was achieved, these advantages allowed them to enter the public sphere on more equal terms, though still facing discrimination in some communities. Economic change was simultaneously moving against the interests of less skilled workers and those with no property holdings, more than compensating, in a negative sense, for the gains from cultural transformation, in the United States and United Kingdom especially. In the areas of concentrated poverty and social exclusion which quickly appeared in the 1980s, women were still routinely abused, gays, black and minority ethnic people assaulted and disabled people bullied, for example, in the harassment by teenagers of David Askew, a 64-year-old man with a learning disability in Greater Manchester. Indeed, her Majesty's Inspector of Constabulary reported that a million complaints of anti-social behaviour and harassment in England came from disabled people (BBC Radio 4, 2010).

Second, and even more important, these successes made governments very wary of collective action of all kinds. In the 1970s and 1980s, this applied especially to trade union action against the restructuring of industry and the public sector, and to the United Kingdom and the United States under Margaret Thatcher and Ronald Reagan. They were able to portray these and other protest movements as attempts to capture the state in the interests of organised groups which were the enemies of liberty and civility – the 'enemy within'. In an ideological shift sustained by the right-wing press and think tanks, they often succeeded in associating individual freedom with free markets, and much collective action with restrictions on such liberty.

This view was supported by social scientific theory of collective action which argued that individuals would only participate if they were given 'selective (material) incentives' as members of exclusive groups, who gained economic and political advantage at the expense of other citizens with no opportunities to join such actions; and that the loyalty and solidarity of these organisations was maintained by threats of sanctions against defectors (Olson, 1965). In a later text, Olson argued that nations rose to prosperity and power while such interest groups were held in check, and stagnated or declined when they gained a hold over society's structures (Olson, 1982).

This theory was part of a systematic shift in the social sciences, in which free market economic thought replaced both Keynesian economics and sociocultural theory as the basis for all mainstream analysis. This changed approach demanded that all collective phenomena be analysed in terms of the calculative decisions of individuals, in strategic pursuit of their interests. It implied that groups would tend to be homogeneous, in terms of their incomes, ages and tastes, and that for this reason it could be expected that communities would fragment into districts with residents of similar economic profiles, confining the poorest to those neighbourhoods with the least favourable facilities. The public choice school of thought (Buchanan, 1968, 1976; Buchanan and Tullock, 1962; Starrett, 1988) argued that it was only when individuals were enabled to express their choices over collective goods by 'voting with their feet' in these ways that efficiency in public services could be achieved, and unacceptable coercion avoided.

All these developments upheld the tendency in affluent societies for aspiring individuals to see emancipation in personal terms, as rising above traditional cultural restraints and becoming 'reflexive', the authors of their own life narratives, selecting their own standards and projects from a wide range of cultural resources in a pick-and-mix way (Giddens, 1991).

This was highly ironic, given that the movements which enabled the cultural shift from which this generation benefited were political in their goals, and collective in their methods; an outcome of increased individualism, fragmentation and depoliticisation was absolutely not their aim.

In the next section, we will consider the consequences for community of these changes, and how the barriers they represent to future collective action might be overcome.

stop and think

■ What place did 'community' and 'diversity' play in the planning of the 1945 welfare state? How soon did social change begin to challenge the assumptions on which the post-war settlement was based? What sort of groups were in the forefront of that challenge? How did governments after 1979 react to these new forms of collective action?

Sacred selves and neglected communities

Both social policy and social work are centrally concerned with the bonds which link people, the way they share resources and the processes by which they manage their interdependence. Social policy deals more in the organised systems through which these relationships are conducted, while social work tries to influence their functioning at the micro level. But in the 1980s, developments in societies and in government policies, in response to global economic change, threatened the bases of both the organisational and the interpersonal aspects of welfare states and the social relations they had enabled.

At the policy level, market-minded regimes in the United Kingdom and the United States set out to make labour markets more 'flexible', by disbanding controls and regulations over pay, conditions and job security (Standing, 1989). They also cut back on universal income maintenance payments and expanded selective, means-tested ones (Lister, 1997), and they privatised several public services and introduced new, businesslike methods of financial accountability and management into the rest (Clarke and Newman, 1997). Finally, they introduced greater conditionality and compulsion into benefits systems (Mead, 1985). All these changes influenced regimes in other countries, first in Australia and New Zealand, and then in Europe. They were adopted and intensified by the Democratic Party under Bill Clinton in the United States, and by New Labour under Tony Blair in the United Kingdom (Jordan, 1998, Jordan with Jordan, 2000), so that the overall organisational framework for social policy and social work became one of economic incentives and contracts, promoting individual choice by citizens as consumers, and neglecting the loyalty, solidarity and mutual assistance on which all social bonds ultimately depend, in favour of ideas about abstract 'rights and responsibilities'.

case study

Prime Minister Blair made his first speech as Prime Minister on 2 June 1997, at the Aylesbury estate, Southwark. Here is an extract from it:

This new alliance of interests to build on 'one nation Britain' can only be done on the basis of a new bargain between us all as members of society...

The basis of this modern civic society is an ethic of mutual responsibility, or duty. It is something for something. A society where we play by the rules. You only take out if you put in. That's the bargain...where opportunities are given, for example to young people, there should be a reciprocal duty to take them up.

At the level of personal and communal relationships, this new framework reinforced a growing trend in societies for citizens to see themselves as the authors of their own life narratives and creators of their independent individual identities (Giddens, 1991). As we saw in Chapter 3, this emphasis on the self and its development had been a cultural feature of some societies since the days of hunter-gatherer tribes, but its new version added to this the fantasy that modernity had created a kind of person (a 'sacred' self with unique identity and value) who could shake off traditional social constraints and improve themselves autonomously (Douglas, 1987, p. 99).

Governments used this fantasy as a means of rule, encouraging individuals to see themselves as 'independent' and 'self-responsible', fulfilling their potential through projects funded by bank loans and credit cards, and relying on public services only when they failed (Rose, 1996; Cruikshank, 1994). In this way, social relations generally became more competitive, status sought through material success more provisional, and people more insecure and edgy about their place in society. It also put enormous strain on close personal relationships, in which people invested so much of their emotional and social 'capital' to achieve their life projects (Beck and Beck-Gernsheim, 1995).

In addition to this, the new approach to public policy aimed to equip citizens to choose with whom to share collective infrastructures and facilities. The changes in social relations just described already meant that people tended to bolster their identities and status by seeking to live in districts, and join social and sports clubs, with others of similar incomes; this segregated societies into relatively homogeneous groupings, breaking up old communities and excluding poor people from mainstream neighbourhoods and lifestyles (Jordan, 1996).

The emphasis on choice in public services did nothing to counteract these forces of fragmentation and exclusion; better-off people tended either to get the best services available or to opt for private provision. The best example of this was the way in which parents in the affluent Anglophone countries moved to districts with schools that achieved high levels of passes in public examinations (Jordan *et al.*, 1993); this was further enabled by New Labour's publication of league tables, giving such families detailed information on which to make these choices.

The damaging effect that all these social trends and policies had on local communities, and on social solidarity more generally, did not go unnoticed. Social and political theorists pointed out that human beings were communal in their historical evolution, and that all morality was rooted in the cultures and practices of groups, tribes and nations (Macintyre, 1981; Walzer, 1983; Etzioni, 1992). These 'communitarian' ideas were expressed in direct opposition to the influential public choice school of thought, which derived its principles from individualistic market economic analysis. They were espoused by both Bill Clinton (Waddan, 1997) and Tony Blair (Jordan with Jordan, 2000), but only as a basis for policies to combat social problems in the most deprived communities such as crime, drug and alcohol abuse, truancy and prostitution.

research box 5.3

The decline in social relations and the isolation of such communities was not reversed, in the United Kingdom or the United States. As part of a large-scale survey, Bynner and Parsons (2003, p. 266, table 10.19) found that among male respondents in social class V (unskilled manual workers) born in 1946, 37 per cent were members of trade unions (compared with 43 per cent of the whole male sample for that cohort) at age 26. Among those born in 1970, and surveyed at age 30, only 6 per cent of social class V men were members of unions, compared to 17 per cent overall. Conversely, among social class V men born in 1958 (the 1946 cohort figures were not available), 13 per cent had at some time been arrested; among those born in 1970, 47 per cent had been arrested. (Bynner and Parsons, 2003, p. 290, fig. 10.9)

Given that Clinton and Blair energetically pursued policies to reform the public services on the business model, to promote mobility and choice as well as self-responsibility among citizens, and hence to encourage the polarisation of residential districts and the exclusion of the poor, it was not surprising that these policies did little to counteract much stronger forces towards individualism, rivalry, insecurity and the homogeneity of social groupings. Internationally, social exclusion became a big topic for research, especially in Europe (Jordan, 1996), and the World Bank sponsored major projects to study 'social capital' (Putnam, 1993, 2002), the informal links by which people achieved their purposes outside markets and government agencies (Jordan, 2008). None of this significantly offset the corrosive effects of market forces and the contract model of government on affluent societies.

stop and think

■ How did the new emphasis on individualism and consumerism alter attitudes towards welfare services in general, and the benefit system, in particular? What was the impact of such a changed emphasis on social relationships and on relationships within communities?

It was against this background that two important figures in the UK Conservative Party, David Cameron as the new leader and Iain Duncan Smith as a former leader, set out to frame a new approach to public policy on a range of social issues. In the light of the coalition government's record on welfare and National Health Service (NHS) reform, one may doubt how far these new ideas shifted the party from Margaret Thatcher's legacy, but at least a set of alternative perspectives reached a wider audience. In the next section we will consider how these ideas relate to the community and community work traditions.

Restoring civil society

We have traced some of the origins of individualism and consumerism in the affluent states, and especially the Anglophone ones, to the rise of an economic model of government and social relationships which abhorred collective action as a process for empowering participative citizens, but applauded it as the expression of preferences for public goods by citizen-consumers – the public choice school, which became a political orthodoxy between the late 1970s and the crash of 2008. Both social policy and social work were deeply implicated in these developments, as public services, including social care and child protection, came to be organised, managed and even practised according to the precepts of this school of thought. Although the orthodoxy was first adopted in the United States and the United Kingdom, it came to influence all these countries, even the social democratic, Nordic states.

For example, if social workers stop to reflect on why so much of their practice is prescribed in detailed management-imposed procedures, focused on individuals and families rather than groups and communities, and involving extended records, with tick-boxes and checklists, they need look no further than the introduction of this model into their organisations – none of this existed in the 1970s, and the very language in which it is expressed would have been incomprehensible to practitioners of that period.

Any transformation of social relations must address this pervasive culture of contracts, targets, quality standards and business-speak which pervades every organisation, as much as it must challenge the assumptions underpinning celebrity culture, the unaccountability of the media barons, unrestrained executive pay, excessive household debt and inconsiderate behaviour in public places. But a culture shift of these proportions occurs only about once a half-century; this crisis of capitalism and democracy is a one-off opportunity.

In general, the political left has failed to seize the chance of a radical critique of affluent societies, and it has been left to hybrid thinkers like Phillip Blond, the self-proclaimed 'Red Tory', to put forward new analyses. He has argued for a redistribution of power and resources towards individuals and communities, and a revival of the kind of mutual associations, cooperatives and friendly societies which allowed working-class people to escape poverty in the late nineteenth century – forms of collective action subverted as much by big business as by state monopoly provision of benefits and social services.

research box 5.4

Friendly Societies, most popular in the nineteenth century, were local financial cooperatives which provided members with many services which the welfare state was later to provide. For example, Friendly Societies often provided financial assistance for those who needed to see a doctor and couldn't afford the costs. Many Societies also provided 'self-help' in the form of what would now be described as 'life-long learning' or citizenship. Every members' benefits were supported by every members' contributions. By the late nineteenth century, Britain had over 30,000 Friendly Societies.

Some of the most prominent Friendly Societies were the Order of Oddfellows, the Foresters, the Shepherds and the Free Gardeners.

In many ways, Blond's thinking meshed with CSJ's (2009) plan for reforming the tax-benefit system, as well as their diagnosis of 'Broken Britain' (CSJ, 2006). It was quite significant that (in an aside) he endorsed Samuel Brittan's (1995) proposal for a universal, unconditional Basic Income scheme to replace both social insurance and income support (Blond,

2010, p. 32). He also condemned the monopoly of credit by large international banks, as a major contributing factor to the financial crisis:

> 66 The great housing crash is primarily the result of the absorption of all local, regional and national systems of credit into one global form of credit…The strategy of market manipulation deployed enormous amounts of capital in speculative arbitrage (just five US banks had control over $4 trillion of assets in 2007). (Blond, 2009c, p. 3)

Accordingly, Blond recommended new local organisation, developing from the transfer of wealth from global and national concentrations of business and banking centres to the economic periphery. He argued for relocalising the banking system and strengthening local enterprise, providing new resources through breaking up big corporate monopolies in finance and production. A whole range of new banks, trusts and credit agencies would fund new cooperatives and guilds, giving rise to a new social movement, recreating the culture and institutions of the mutual and cooperative organisations of the later nineteenth century.

case study

The collapse of the Dunfermline Building Society in 2009

In March 2009, Dunfermline Building Society collapsed, as a result of management decisions to expand rapidly into commercial property prior to the financial crisis. When the property cycle turned, it faced such serious potential losses that the Bank of England had to intervene to prevent its complete collapse, effectively nationalising the business. The cost to the Treasury of protecting depositors amounted to some £1.6 billion.

There was certainly evidence for the kinds of concentration of capital which according to Blond contributed to the crash – for instance, all but one of the local building societies, founded over a hundred years earlier, which had converted themselves into banks in the previous decade, collapsed spectacularly, and in the case of Northern Rock actually precipitated the credit crunch.

stop and think

- Can you identify some of the ways in which the public choice orthodoxy of the late 1970s and 1980s had an impact on social work practice? What fresh ways have been suggested for a redistribution of economic ownership and opportunity? Are there ways in which these new possibilities echo the concerns of community-based and mutual-aid services of the pre-welfare state period?

In the event, of course, the coalition government in the United Kingdom took none of these measures, focusing instead on reducing the budget deficit, and actually cutting many of the possible sources for local economic and social revival, while using all the proceeds of selling nationalised banks as contributions to state solvency. But Blond's prescriptions for the revival of civil society through cooperative collective action, which had been echoed by David Cameron (2009, 2010) in his pre-election speeches, are still worth considering in their own right. To what extent do they address the decline in community analysed in previous sections, and do they make economic sense as ways forward in the post-crash environment?

In terms of social policy development, his proposals represent a radical shift from the design of welfare states. We have shown how their primary purpose was to create national solidarities and avoid damaging conflicts, not to encourage participation, cooperation and community, and that public services and state regulation, along with monopoly capitalist interests, have actually discouraged these activities. The goal of his new institutions is to promote organisations which have struggled into existence against the tide of economic and social change – such as social enterprises and credit unions – in order to reorientate people towards groups which aim at meeting their own needs, increasing the value available to them in their lives, and protecting themselves against risks.

One obvious doubt about this proposal is that it would actually favour more skilled and resourceful local residents, who would capture the assets distributed by central government, and use them to consolidate their advantages. This criticism has already been made of one of the only Big Society initiatives to be implemented by the coalition government, the free schools; the organisational tasks of setting up and managing such establishments are beyond the energies and expertise of most citizens, so the applicants have tended to be better-off people with specific educational agendas, or firms, or even private schools, struggling to survive during the economic downturn.

More generally, even if resources could be focused on poorer residents, there would be risks of local conflicts between those favoured by redistribution of this kind, so rivalry, or even organised conflict, could occur; these could acquire ethnic or faith-based overtones in some districts. Such fears reflect the motivations of the founders of welfare states, but also the riots of 1981, 2001 and 2011, where issues of rivalry between ethnic groups played a part.

Again, there would also be a risk that inexperienced local groups with access to such funds would not have the necessary business skills to invest them wisely, and could incur massive losses, or could end up in the hands of swindlers. The new organisations would have to have strong systems of accountability to members and stakeholders. Local or regional mafias could otherwise develop around these opportunities.

Another whole set of doubts surround evidence from other societies. Blond admires European countries which did not go as far in centralising state power or concentrating capital as the United Kingdom has done since the Second World War. But the evidence of at least one of these, Italy, is not encouraging. The Italian industrial sector is the second largest in Europe after Germany's, so its economy is not unbalanced in favour of a financial sector in the way the United Kingdom's is. Italy, like Spain, also has a very flourishing cooperative sector in every type of production, from clothes to food and wine; it has regional government and strong regional cultures and loyalties. Yet Italy is one of the economic basket cases of the EU, with a growth rate the second slowest in the world after Zimbabwe; it is not a good advertisement for Blond's ideas.

More fundamentally, Blond's focus on local communities and institutions ignores the necessity for a national framework for the kinds of solidarities and risk-pools that alone can offset the fragmenting effects of global capitalism. A Basic Income scheme would require just such a commitment of a whole national society to equality of status, inclusion and social justice; so too would the funding of an adequate National Care Service. The transformation which we advocate as an alternative to austerity, and in which social work could make a more positive contribution to social well-being, would be impossible without these society-wide solidarities.

Box 5.1 Connecting social work to post-crash economics

1. Conventional capitalism is clearly broken, especially its capacity to distribute employment and pay sufficient for decent living standards.
2. One of the main ways in which that is apparent is in the way it continues to attempt to maintain an unsustainable divide between being in work and out of work. The Centre for Social Justice (CSJ) proposals for Universal Credit appeared, when they were first published, to make some inroads into that position.
3. Breaking down the distinction between work and non-work is important for economic and social reasons. Economically, successive industrial revolutions (including the current one, in ICT, robotics, etc.) have reduced the need for labour. That means that the system can produce goods abundantly, but it leaves a society blighted by inequality and a rising tide of individuals and families cut off from a highly privileged elite.
4. A Basic Income would help fix both problems: economically it potentially distributes work more equitably, and allows for the demand side of the equation to be addressed. Socially, it would allow for a proper recognition of work which currently goes unrewarded – care work inside the family, for

> example – and opportunities for unpaid activities which contribute to
> improvements in the quality of life in communities.
> 5. In such a world, social work is able to regain some of the ground which it
>   has lost in the last 30 years – turning it again towards collective and
>   local solutions to problems which have been individualised and
>   pathologised.

Despite these criticisms, the merit of these proposals is that they challenge social policy and social work to carry out a fundamental reassess-
ment of their goals and methods. The crisis points to the need for new,
participative citizenship and collective action. Even if the specifics of
Blond's plans are rejected, he points towards the sort of radical thinking
which needs to be done.

stop and think

■ Can you identify some of the key features of the 'Red Tory' agenda for
  social and economic reform? What criticisms can be made of the policies
  associated with such an approach? To what extent has the post-May 2010
  coalition government put into practice the ideas associated with that
  agenda?

Conclusions

Under Third Way regimes, social policy and social work became enmeshed
with the New Public Management approach (Clarke and Newman, 1997),
with contract and public choice theory and with a very limited interpretation of communitarianism (Driver and Martel, 1998). The age of austerity demands a major shift, part of which will involve a greater commitment
to community and collective action, with officials and professionals more
accountable to local groups and associations, and more orientated to
enabling them to cooperate to achieve their ends.

One persistent criticism of the ideas explored in this chapter is that they
are backward-looking, and based on yearning for a past age of rural village
life, social roles defined by class, the domesticity of women's activities
and the normative dominance of the churches – a nostalgia for the world
of *The Archers* (Raban, 2010). But this underestimates the potential of
active citizens to work together to overcome new challenges; it also
misrepresents the opportunities arising from new technologies, new

means of communication and new forms of organisation. As Bowles and Gintis (2002, p. F433) say, reliance on informal, multilateral, communications-based forms of 'community governance' is growing in affluent societies.

'These interactions arise increasingly in modern economies, as information-intensive team production replaces assembly lines and other technologies more readily handled by contract or *fiat*, and as difficult-to-measure services usurp the pre-eminent role, as outputs and inputs, once played by measurable quantities like kilowatts of power and tons of steel. In an economy increasingly based on qualities rather than quantities, the superior governance capabilities of communities are likely to be manifested in increasing reliance on the kinds of multilateral monitoring and risk-sharing...'

This is true not only for centres of innovation in production and media like Silicon Roundabout on the outskirts of London, but also for new kinds of services to meet social needs (Participle, 2011). Face-to-face forms of working allow people with very different ideas and experiences to cooperate in tackling problems and finding solutions which use their skills in effective ways.

It is also highly compatible with the kind of opportunities which would be available in a society in which all citizens had a Basic Income. Not only would this give groups of young people, or older ones with new ideas, the chance to experiment with innovatory approaches, it would also allow paid workers or entrepreneurs to combine with volunteers. The security of a guaranteed subsistence income would encourage risk-taking as well as risk-pooling.

Above all, there is a growing recognition that the forms of organisation and management characteristic of the boom years of illusory economic growth, based on a bubble of bank credit, blown up out of the savings of Chinese, Japanese and Middle Eastern savers, have been proved inadequate. It is necessary not only to find new forms for cooperation, but also to prepare new kinds of active citizens for the challenges of austerity.

The Big Society is widely perceived as an excuse for public spending cuts, symbolised by libraries staffed by volunteers and youth clubs with no funding. There are real dangers that coalition policies will return UK society to something like a pre-1945 form, with all but the rich exposed to the risks of global market forces. But the fact remains that there are possibilities in community and cooperation to improve citizens' quality of life without extra public spending. The clues to how this could be achieved can be found in the research evidence on people's self-assessed well-being (Layard, 2005; Helliwell, 2003; Frey and Stutzer, 2002), which shows that relationships are considerably more important than the last third of their incomes in estimations of happiness, and that participation in communities is also an important dimension. This points towards the reorientation of priorities analysed in this chapter, and the construction of life-quality from interactions with others in groups and associations, rather than individual material consumption (Jordan, 2008, 2010).

Indeed, this is rapidly emerging as a new theme in the publications of think tanks at both ends of the political spectrum. For the Policy Exchange, Arthur Seldon (2012) argues that the transformed economic prospects for citizens of the affluent countries demand a society built around activism, trustworthiness, virtue and responsibility among citizens, and a thoughtful government promoting these qualities through education and social policies. In such a society, the significance of good relationships and cooperation would be clear to all; both capitalism and the state will need citizens of this kind in the new environment, and governments have a responsibility to enable their emergence.

'The future does not need to be like the present – it can be better for all, even in the economic climate likely to affect the country for the new decade. Indeed, the adverse economic outlook makes the case for active government policy all the more pressing' (Seldon, 2012, p. 19).

Similarly, the Royal Society for the Arts has argued that only active citizenship can fill an 'aspiration gap' between resources and expectations under austerity. Citizenship should embody *both* autonomy *and* solidarity with others; members of such a society should recognise that state services like education and health are not provision for needs so much as opportunities for relationships with people whose skills can enhance their own (Rowson *et al.*, 2012). In other words, it is the quality of interactions with public service professionals, rather than what they 'deliver', which is important for well-being (Jordan, 2008).

Social work therefore needs to rediscover its historical commitment to quality of relationships as the basis of its activities, as well as its group and community focus. In this way, it could become the cutting edge of a transformed social policy of well-being, rather than a front line in a return to authoritarian methods.

main points

■ In some ways, social work is well placed to take up the challenges of the post-2008 era. To do so, it will need to escape the shackles of individualistic and mechanistic ways of working which have grown up over the last 30 years.

■ Social work itself emerged in a tradition in which loyalty, solidarity and mutual assistance were regarded as amongst its key qualities and ways of working. Now such qualities need to be harnessed again, in support of cooperative, local and collective ways of solving common problems.

- Local action of this sort will need strong accountabilities, to ensure probity and advance equality.
- A social work practice imbued with the knowledge that the fate of any one of us is bound up in the fate of us all has a real opportunity to supplement and strengthen the large-scale solidarities of Basic Income, at a local level.

taking it further

- Harris, J. (2008) 'State Social Work: Constructing the Present from Moments in the Past', *British Journal of Social Work*, 38:4, 662–679.
- Ferguson, I. and Woodward, R. (2009) *Radical Social Work in Practice: Making a Difference*, Bristol, Policy Press.
- White, S., Wastell, D., Broadhurst, K. and Hall, C. (2010) 'The "Tragic Tale" of the Integrated Children's System', *Critical Social Policy*, 30:3, 405–429.

6 Intergenerational justice and the family

The most obvious casualties of the second phase of the crisis (2010–12) have been members of the generation just reaching adulthood, and seeking to establish their place in the economies and societies of the affluent countries. As austerity measures have been imposed, it is this generation who have paid the highest price in terms of fees, charges, reduced rights and narrowing opportunities. In particular, as jobs became scarcer and some education grants and social benefit rates were cut, their prospects of establishing themselves in incremental careers, with promotion and pension entitlements, receded, and the age at which they could expect to get a foot on the property ladder rose. Instead, they faced official pressure to take low-paid, dead-end jobs, on pain of losing their minimal incomes.

When a 26-year-old graduate working as a street trader, Mohamed Bouazizi, set himself on fire on 17 December 2010, in protest against being repeatedly moved on by officials in his town in southern Tunisia, his subsequent death sparked the uprising in that country which spread to become the revolutionary Arab Spring. These revolts were rightly regarded as claims for civil and democratic rights, against the corrupt dictatorships of that country, Egypt, the Yemen, Libya, Syria, and several smaller states; but they were also the expression of the frustration of a well-educated new generation, whose prospects were blighted by economic stagnation and the monopolisation of power by an elderly, plutocratic club of rulers and their cronies.

Yet the situation of this same generation in the mature democracies of Europe, North America, Australasia and Japan had some of the same features. Entrenched political elites took turns in office, but had clearly run out of ideas on how to fix broken economic systems. Labour market 'flexibilisation' had undermined employment security, career and salary structure. Occupational pensions in the private sector had ceased to offer security in old age, and entitlements to state pensions were also being made to require longer working lives. Above all, the youngest generation lacked any political channels to express its interests and needs; it could not negotiate with governments or with other interest groups.

So it was not surprising that young people took to the streets in all the affluent countries, protesting about the political stalemate and the economic impasse. While some of the biggest demonstrations were in the indebted southern European states – Italy, Spain and Greece – it should not be forgotten that the largest *pro rata* protests were in Israel, or that the clearest constitutional issues were in Hungary. So the protests were about structural issues affecting populations, and not just about government retrenchment.

These were issues of gender and ethnic relations, and of class ones too, with potentially new classes emerging from the collapse of previously stable economic and social formations, especially in countries like Greece and the other southern European states. But for the longer term they posed questions about the future for an insecure and excluded cohort entering working age.

In this chapter we will ask whether this situation represents a relationship of injustice between the older generations – who benefited from welfare states in their youth and adult years, and retained many of their rights as the young generation were losing theirs, who had enjoyed career opportunities even when they lacked paper qualifications, and who often also held valuable stakes in property markets and generous pension entitlements – and the youngest one.

This topic is complicated by issues of how expectations have changed over the past 50 or more years. Some of the material gains enjoyed by the generation born just before, during or just after the Second World War were culturally nurtured by commercial interests for the sake of profits. The idea of households consisting of parents and children, with the grandparents living elsewhere, was largely a product of this era, and served the interests of the construction industry. More sinisterly, the sexualisation of early childhood allowed companies to market all kinds of merchandise to this age group. The rise in material living standards was not accompanied by a proportionate increase in quality of life (Layard, 2005).

We have also shown how individualism and consumerism flourished as twin manifestations of the cultural changes associated with forms of capitalism which were more subtly exploitative, and with the retreat from welfare state collective security. However, many of the gains made by that generation – such as a greater accommodation of diversity, improved status for women and more relaxed and informal interactions in most settings – were hard-won and significant, and relied on greater material equality and better opportunity structures for their achievement.

Intergenerational justice is not a new topic in social policy, but up to now it has mainly preoccupied theorists rather than politicians or analysts of welfare systems (Fitzpatrick, 2003, chapter 7). One issue which has most concerned moral and political philosophers about the welfare of later generations is the human propensity to discount the future, saving too few resources against risks. Contract theorists have tried to frame versions of justice in which the savings rates of one generation reflect their responsibilities to their (unknown) descendants, who form part of the totality of humankind, present and future (Rawls, 1972; Barry, 1999). Communitarian thinkers place more emphasis on the relationships and reciprocities between past and future generations, whose identities and well-being are intertwined through cultural transmission, and who hence need to treat each other fairly (de-Shalit, 1995).

The crisis makes these abstract questions far more concrete and urgent, with the impact of climate change and resource depletion being recognised just as the dynamic of economic growth falters. The huge issue of environmental sustainability will be discussed in the next chapter. But of growing concern is the evidence that people now young adults will be worse off than their parents, less healthy, and even live shorter lives. Historically, in most societies generations have been able to make provision for their children and grandchildren (as families, and collectively through welfare systems), unless they have been overrun by enemies or affected by natural catastrophes. But if the mechanisms through which capitalism turns savings into the investments required for growing prosperity have failed in the affluent economies, then the savings rate alone cannot be the only relevant factor.

This can be illustrated by the contrasting cases of China and Japan, both countries with very strong savings cultures, and major sources for loans to the affluent West. China's rapid growth, founded on the processes which fuelled industrial development in the West in the past two centuries, will increasingly need to rely on rising consumption by its own citizens, which in turn will require wage rises and redistributive social policies. China can be expected to be a major contributor to global economic development in the new century, through investment in Africa and Latin America as well as through domestic expansion, but it is not certain that it can lend to the affluent countries on the pre-crisis scale.

By contrast, Japan's older generation of savers have largely financed the enormous sovereign debt of their state, but this has not allowed the government to discover policies for increasing national income. The Japanese state continues to borrow on a scale beyond that of European debtor governments, and to represent a gloomy model for the West of stagnation and the declining work security and career prospects for the young generation. In other words, the famous thrift of older Japanese citizens cannot produce improving prospects for their children and grandchildren, under present political stewardship.

In this chapter, we will consider the implications of all this for social policy and social work with families, and whether intergenerational issues can become specific targets of institutional systems and redistributive schemes. These questions arise most obviously in relation to housing markets, because the plight of the youngest cohort is symbolised by their difficulties in being able to afford to leave their parental homes, while so much of the wealth of these elders takes the form of houses. But it also arises in relation to jobs, where older workers are simultaneously encouraged to work more years to increase their savings towards the unknown future costs of social care, and aware that this blocks access to careers for younger people.

research box 6.1

The age of home buying

In 2010 and 2011 the National Housing Federation in England commissioned research into the prospects for younger people, hoping to get onto the property ladder. The subsequent report, from Oxford Economics, concluded that the average single 21-year-old (in 2010) 'who regularly saves, receives no additional financial support and has no children will be 43 before being able to buy a first home'.

At the time of the research, the average house price in England stood at 10.3 times the average income, at £216,493. Traditionally, buying a house in the United Kingdom has been based on regular employment, in jobs which have prospects of promotion and salary increases over a career. The affordability squeeze is the product of the breakdown in such employment patterns, on the one hand, and a collapse in the supply of new housing, in the post-2008 era. In 2010–11 only 105,930 new homes were built in England, despite rising population. This was the lowest peacetime total since 1923. New house building is running at less than half the rate that new households are forming. Younger people are the most severely affected by these changes.

At the same time, the lack of affordable housing for purchase has an impact on waiting lists for social housing for rent. Over 4.4 million people were on the waiting list for social housing in England in 2009.

In the United Kingdom, a report by the Institute for Fiscal Studies (IFS) in January 2012 predicted that the average family with two children would be £1,200 a year worse off by 2015, and that 400,000 more children would be living in poverty (IFS, 2012). Any changes in generational relationships would therefore have to be made against a background of reducing household resources.

- How might the relationship between the generations best be understood? Is it simply a set of economic exchanges? Are there important cultural and social reciprocities which also need to be navigated and negotiated? Can you identify some key underlying factors which shape intergenerational relationships in contemporary Britain?

Generations and households

Although cultures are the most important influences on family patterns and lifestyles, economic forces also affect the ways people share their lives with partners, children and wider kin. As a general rule, two of the clearest consequences of a reduction in the pace of growth of economies are a lower birth rate and a slower rate of formation of households. After the collapse of the Soviet Bloc in 1989–90, the restructuring of Central and Eastern European economies (which experienced sharp recessions) was accompanied by fewer births and fewer new households being formed. Similarly, as rates of economic growth slowed in Italy and Spain after 1990, traditionally high birth rates turned to some of the lowest in Western Europe, and adult offspring left the family home at a later age.

Up to the time of the crash in 2008–09, the United Kingdom and the Scandinavian countries had the highest birth rates in Europe. But in the United Kingdom there were strong long-term trends towards smaller-sized households, women having children later, and more people living alone, especially beyond middle age, as married women's earnings played a larger role in household incomes, and rates of divorce rose (until the turn of the century) (*Social Trends*, 2011). Compared with their continental European counterparts, young British people more readily left their parental homes in their twenties, and more of them were able to get their feet on the ladder of homeownership, often starting to buy a property jointly with a partner before getting married.

This did not imply that transitions to adult life were smooth and simple for young people. The casualisation of employment and the need to navigate risk and insecurity in establishing a reliable trajectory for earning were factors in making such processes hazardous (Furlong and Cartmel, 2006). But all these problems were greatly intensified by the crisis.

Along with declining incomes and job prospects, and rising inflation, the main factor in more adult children living with parents, and access to homeownership being far longer delayed, was the whole structure of the housing market. Availability of 'affordable' social housing had been declining since the sell-off of the local authorities' stock of council houses (once 30 per cent of the total market in accommodation) began in the 1980s. But to this was added a sharp fall in new construction of private homes after the financial crisis, which resulted in a rise in the costs of renting in that sector also.

To complete a vicious circle for the young generation, banks became much more cautious about lending, especially to first-time buyers; the number of mortgages approved fell from 130,000 in 2006 to 50,000 in 2010 (Bank of England, 2010). At the start of 2011, the Council of Mortgage lenders calculated that the proportion of first-time buyers purchasing a property without help from family or friends fell from 63 per cent in 2005 to 17 per cent in 2010. It would take 14 years for the average earner to save a deposit enough for the average property, and many lower earners would never be able to save enough (Resolution Foundation, 2011). The Housing Minister, Grant Shapps, described the situation for younger people as 'horrendous', but could offer no prospect of government housing policy achieving more than 'stability' of prices (*The Guardian*, 1 January 2011), while another leading Conservative, cabinet minister David Willetts (2010), denounced the selfishness of the 'baby boomer' generation in a book which highlighted the housing issue.

These statistics also illustrate how the wealth of the generation of UK citizens now aged 44 or over, who own something like £1.5 trillion of the nation's £2.5 trillion housing assets, calculated as prices less mortgages, but excluding property owned for commercial letting (Inman, 2011a), skews the opportunities open to the youngest generation. Of the 83 per cent of first-time buyers who do receive family help for a deposit, most presumably get this from that group of relatives; but the lack of such a willing and asset-rich source of assistance leaves the majority unable to access a mortgage.

---

research box 6.2

1948: the best year to be born?

Given the gap in economic prospects between the generations, traced in this chapter, it's worth asking the question: 'When was the best year to be born?' Much research concludes that 1948 comes out on top. 1948 babies were the first to be delivered in National Health Service (NHS) hospitals; benefited from Family Allowance; received free education under the 1944 Education Act; the 11-plus extended the opportunity of attending university (with means-tested student grants from 1962) to many that would never have entertained the possibility before. National Service was abolished in 1960, and there were no wars to fight in.

Research by Prudential Insurance identifies 2008 as the last year the majority (52 per cent) could retire at 60 on a final salary pension. By the start of the current decade, the figure was nearer 30 per cent and falling – and by 2050 the retirement age will be 68, with pension recipients having paid more, and worked longer, to get less in old age. The chief economist of the Institute of Public Policy Research, Tony Dolphin suggest that the 1948 generation will have had the best of the housing market too. The 1970s housing boom coincided with 1948 generation's first steps on the property ladder. House price inflation was to benefit this generation, with an average house costing £1,751 in 1948 now costing £160,159.

The choice for the vast majority of today's young people, who do not share in the good fortune of the 1948 generation, is therefore between staying in the family household or paying rent for a flat, and these rents have been rising faster than overall price inflation because of the shortfall in overall housing supply since the crash. Lack of reliable employment and earning prospects play a large part in such decisions, but it is this feature of the crisis situation which most clearly links the plight of the young with the relative good fortune of the older generation, and raises issues of intergenerational justice in the most direct way.

The fact that such a high percentage of the small numbers of successful mortgage applicants do receive help from family, and the growing numbers who continue to be accommodated in their parents' homes, indicate that the family as a system of housing support works for a proportion of individual young people. But in aggregate, the decisions about how to deploy their housing wealth taken by the asset-rich generation work against the interests of the young. Between 1997 and the first quarter of 2008, homeowners used their resource to increase their borrowing, in order to buy expensive items such as cars, or to improve and enlarge their properties; in one quarter of 2006 alone, this borrowing rose by £13.7 billion. But since the crash started in the second quarter of 2008, they have been paying down their mortgages, by a total of £50 billion by the beginning of 2011 (Inman, 2011a).

The problem posed for the economy as a whole, and the housing market in particular, by these decisions in aggregate has been that they exacerbated the failings of the ways markets were operating. The borrowing of 1997–2008 helped inflate the bubble and the excessive lending by the banks; the debt reduction withheld potential spending from the economy, and specifically from new house construction. At the national scale, the use of their wealth by the older generation was actually damaging the interests of the generations of their children and grandchildren.

This situation indicates a need for change in government policy and among groups and communities of citizens. Government policy should look for ways of encouraging asset-rich people to come together to invest in trusts and funds for building affordable housing schemes and running social housing provision. The older generation could in this way be induced to recognise that they can contribute collectively to the amelioration of the obstacles faced by their children and grandchildren.

At present, they have strong incentives as individuals instead to buy housing for commercial letting, and indeed this form of ownership has increased, even during the prolonged crisis. Because returns on savings are so low, as interest rates continue to be held down, most resource-rich older people have a strong incentive to buy property to rent out. Indeed, as we saw in Chapter 2, there is a kind of social movement, promoted by a group of entrepreneurs, to enlarge the class of rentiers in this way, as the only opportunity for people on middling incomes to improve their relative position in the economic order of the United Kingdom.

This example shows how injustice between generations is not often the consequence of intentional actions by one cohort; it is more likely to reflect the unintended consequences of millions of individual decisions. This is the classic argument for institutional changes which will make collectively fairer outcomes more possible, the rationale on which the structures of welfare states were founded.

A debt-burdened generation

Another factor reinforcing the labour market disadvantages of the young generation in the England has been the trebling of university fees and the cuts in Education Maintenance Allowances. Although coalition government ministers have emphasised that fees will be covered by student loans, and grants paid to the poorest college students, these changes have greatly increased the long-term costs of further and higher education at the very time when prospects of repaying this indebtedness over a working life are the least promising.

Education maintenance allowances

case study

Despite a pre-election promise not to scrap Educational Maintenance Allowance (EMA), the coalition administration at Westminster announced an intention to do just that, in the October 2010 spending review. On 25 October 2010 *The Guardian* newspaper included a set of case studies of young people, reflecting on the impact of that change in their own lives. Here are two of those examples:

I moved away from Cornwall to do my A-levels because I wanted to raise my aspirations. No one on my mum's side of the family has ever gone on to further education, and no one has a job at the moment. I didn't want to end up on benefits. I now live with my nan, but she is in her late sixties and her pension doesn't stretch too far, so the EMA is vital for me. I didn't have access to a computer at home, so last year I saved it all up and bought a laptop for my college work. Ultimately, I want to join the police, but I wanted to get a degree first so I could progress more quickly. But with rising tuition fees, I'm wondering if it is really worth it.

Lee Christian, 17, is studying for A-levels at Harlow College

The cuts announced in the spending review seem to be hitting people who are already having a tough time the hardest. My mum died when I was seven, so my dad is the only wage earner in our household. He lost his job two years ago, so money is really tight and I rely on the EMA to cover my travel costs from Basingstoke to college in Winchester every day. It's only an 18-minute journey, but it costs me over £350 a term in train fares. And now I hear we're also going to have to weather a 3% rise in rail fares. I do wonder if the government is putting up tuition fees because it wants to discourage young people from going to university and set their sights a bit lower. I still want to go to university, because I want to be a barrister, and I need a degree for that, but the prospect of running up over £40k of debt is depressing.

Katy Horgan, 16, is studying for A-levels at Peter Symonds, a sixth-form college in Winchester, Hampshire, UK

It could be argued that the system of grants enjoyed by most students before the Thatcher era was unsustainable, partly because of the vast increase in the numbers entering higher education and partly because it involved subsidisation of advantaged young people by those who had had no such educational opportunities. However, the steep rise in costs of further and higher education imposes an unfairness of a different kind. This burden of debt for a whole generation is particularly counterproductive for society as a whole, because it deters young people from investing in education and professional expertise at exactly the time in the economic cycle when they should be encouraged to improve their long-term prospects, because their short-term ones are so limited. As economies like Finland's and Singapore's show, an excellent educational system and high proportions of graduates in the workforce can greatly improve the performance of a developed economy, in which symbolic analysis forms a major part of productive activity.

The increase in student debt was a direct consequence of the political decision to make universities self-funding, and to force them to compete with each other for fee-paying students as well as for research funds. This policy followed the American model of higher education, but it was the application to this sector of the economic orthodoxy discussed in Chapters 2 and 5. Universities had been induced to compete for funding since the early 1990s, and New Labour had introduced the system of tuition fees, but with a cap restricting these to around £3,000. The new measures taken by the coalition government reduced state support for higher education so as to strengthen competitive market forces in the system.

This followed the logic of public choice theory by treating universities as exclusive 'clubs' for their members, and encouraging them to seek to attract students according to the perceived benefits of the quality of their degrees, their other facilities and the total experience they offered. This constructed choice of university places by students as a calculative individual one, as in the choice of a sports club (Buchanan, 1965), or a house in a gated community (Foldvary, 1994); it allowed young people to group together for study on the basis of their abilities, their aspirations and their tastes in collective living.

But this was a very inappropriate model, especially in view of the transformations in the labour market described in Chapters 2 and 5. If the future of economy and society are dependent on new forms of cooperation in groups and communities, and hence as much on skills in communication and negotiation as on knowledge and expertise, the experience of higher education should seek to widen students' contact with others of their age cohort as extensively as possible, not to segregate them into homogeneous, class-based establishments. Parental choices of residential districts and schools already produce this effect at the stage of secondary education (Jordan *et al.*, 1994), higher education should seek to offset these effects, not to reinforce them.

---

research box 6.3

Sutton Trust

In 2011 the Sutton Trust published a research report into intergenerational social mobility in England. It concluded that there are enduring social mobility gaps between those of differing family backgrounds, and that this trend can be picked in the educational outcomes of children as young as five.

The study made comparisons between nations, demonstrating how cultural, economic and educational aspects, amongst others, influence mobility levels. England's relatively high attainment gaps and low mobility, for example, shows that genetic endowments from parents to children cannot be the sole drivers of social mobility as this could not explain the significant and consistent international differences in mobility.

The report concludes that higher inequality appears to reduce equality of opportunity and intergenerational mobility. Countries with large gaps between rich and poor, such as the United Kingdom and the United States, appear to be destined to remain the least mobile into the future. Income inequality and educational inequality are described as feeding off each other, creating a cycle of ever decreasing mobility. Those at the top of the polarised scale are able to invest ever-greater resources into the education of their children, ensuring they maintain their advantageous position in society, leaving those at the bottom without the opportunities to achieve upward mobility.

Already, social mobility in England is lower than at any time since the Second World War (Suttton Trust, 2011); social class is a powerful determinant of life chances even before the full impact of the economic crisis has been felt. The intergenerational injustice consolidated by the new university fees system is that many of the parents and grandparents of the current young generation benefited from both the expansion of university education and the new opportunities for employment (especially in the public sector) of the latter half of the twentieth century. The young generation will be restricted by debt, but also by the limited labour market openings for those holding degrees from the particular university they attended; those from the least favoured establishments would be unlikely to have the same range of opportunities as were enjoyed by the previous post-war cohorts of graduates.

Indeed, those with the degrees perceived by prospective employers as least attractive face a new kind of poverty trap. Although they are not required to start to repay their loans until they earn more than £21,000 a year, they may struggle to reach much above this level for many years, leaving a receding prospect of paying of their whole debt. It will be a bit like the situation of those with low earning power who have a mortgage, and qualify for interest payments when on benefits; they may be trapped outside the labour market by the need to earn substantially more than their benefit rate in order to meet the mortgage instalments demanded (Jordan *et al.*, 1991).

Against this background, the anger expressed by student organisations protesting against the fees increases in March 2011 is understandable. They felt themselves to be a generation with considerably fewer routes into the mainstream than their seniors, and this sense of exclusion exploded into collective fury. But the perception of being relegated to the margins of society was even stronger among those with few or no educational qualifications, living in deprived districts, as we will discuss in the next section.

It might be argued that the changes taking place in the funding of higher education have made the situation of English students more like that of their counterparts in Germany, France or Italy, who do not graduate until their late twenties, and usually support themselves from part-time work during their average ten years of study. But that long-standing model does not leave most graduates with large debts; the extensive and leisurely paced programmes of continental universities are designed to allow students to pay their way through university, and they gain a considerable premium from their degrees on graduation.

So the political elite in England has constructed a further and higher education system which will trap many young people in debt, restrict social mobility and contribute to the 'squeezed middle' phenomenon for the foreseeable future. But it has also reduced the chances for this generation of breaking out of their limits and contributing to a transformation of economy and society, by socialising them into narrow, class-based solidarities, and hence restricted the scope for the kinds of cooperative innovation on which future quality of life will depend.

In this section, we have focused on debt among students in further and higher education, in many ways among the more advantaged of their generation. None of this should distract from the problems of those with fewer educational qualifications, many of whom face even larger problems in gaining the income they need during the transition to adult life, and who can run up even larger debts with fewer prospects of paying them off.

An unrepresented generation

The student protests and the riots in the English cities in 2011 shocked many observers, and were not the kinds of collective action which David Cameron hoped to encourage. But they showed that the young cohort of the population were not willing to be passive in the face of intergenerational injustice, and that there were no institutionalised means for them to represent their views or pursue their interests as a group within the UK political system. During and after these actions there were no attempts to negotiate with leaders over their demands, no institutions in which these might have been conducted and no attempts to remedy these gaps in the democratic process.

The main reason why there were no meetings (of minds, or in the sense of negotiations) between the political authorities and the protesters can be understood in relation to the Arab Spring revolutions, the demonstrations in European cities and the Occupy movement worldwide. These were political phenomena of a new form, organised in a new way, through the technologies of mobile phones and the Internet, Facebook and Twitter, and coordinated through millions of interpersonal communications among participants across national borders.

Whereas political power is organised hierarchically, even in the most democratic systems, these actions were organised through *networks* (Powell, 1990, 2006), which had no formal structures, and which coalesced around mass gatherings and small discussions, without ever consolidating into chains of command and control. Mason (2012a and b) argues that this form of movement represents a revolutionary wave on a par with those of 1789 in France, 1848 all over Europe (including Ireland) and 1989 in the Soviet Bloc countries, but one defined by the technological means which enable its participants to communicate with each other, and to 'organise' without the trappings of offices and hierarchies.

> ❝ The ability to deploy, without expert knowledge, a whole suite of information tools has allowed protesters across the world to outwit the police, to beam their message into the newsrooms of the global media, and above all to assert a cool, cutting edge identity... It has given today's protest movements a massive psychological advantage. (Mason, 2012a, p. 10)

Echoing Powell, Mason points out that networks are better at adapting to a situation where the quality of information is crucial to success, and where information itself is fluid. Hierarchies are superior only for transmitting orders and responses, and the situational context is predictable. Once the young generation had a common set of grievances around which to mobilise, and could identify with others in revolt against authorities in other countries, their notorious lack of interest in formal politics (a growing number in the United Kingdom do not register to vote) was no disadvantage; the potential for networking through new technology trumped the rigid structures of control.

research box 6.4

The 'Precariat'

Guy Standing has pioneered the concept of a 'precariat', a new 'class' consisting of 'a multitude of insecure people, living bits-and-pieces lives, in and out of short-term jobs, without a narrative of occupational development', who, unlike the proletariat, have relations of production which are 'defined by partial involvement in labour combined with extensive 'work –for-labour', a growing array of unremunerated activities that are essential if they are to retain access to jobs and to decent earnings'.

This emerging class is divided internally, sharing only common fears and insecurities; but when united the precariat is a powerful force. The protests in Europe, the uprisings of the Middle East, and further mass protests around the world are the manifestations of this 'class in the making'. In the United Kingdom the precariat's position can be demonstrated by young unemployed individuals being forced to participate in unpaid work in order to gain access to jobseeker's allowance, as part of the Work Programme.

Membership of the precariat has grown since the global financial crisis, resulting in more temporary and agency work, outsourcing and firms abandoning non-work benefits.

'Because of flexible labour markets, the precariat cannot draw on a social memory, a feeling of belonging to a community of pride, status, ethics and solidarity. Everything is fleeting...The precariatised mind is one without anchors, flitting from subject to subject, in the extreme suffering from attention deficit disorder.'

Putting faith in labour market flexibility, mass commodification and the restructuring of social protection are all factors of a neo-liberal reality which has swelled the ranks of the precariat.

Mason argues that the common grievances were readily identified among a generation whose prospects had suddenly been transformed by the crash. Not only were a large proportion of them 'graduates without a future', for whom the promise that years of study and sacrifice would be rewarded with well-paid and secure jobs had been traduced; instead, they found themselves among a cohort of unemployed claimants without prospects, or part of a 'precariat' doing insecure, low-paid or temporary work (Standing, 2011). Instead of a generation split into a majority of well-educated mainstream young people with a stake in capitalism and the political order and a minority excluded from the benefits of that system, they had been transformed into a potentially single mass network, united by technology and youth culture, with a common interest in confronting the authorities and the means to do so.

This gave rise to the danger for the hierarchical order that it could be engulfed by an uprising which united the unruly forces of the youth from the deprived districts and the sophisticated networks of disaffected graduates. In the United Kingdom, the agonising about the riots in the summer of 2011 reflected these fears, as the government became aware that it had no effective means, short of repression through the criminal justice system and the sanctions of the benefits regime, for combating such a force. Mason may overemphasise the plight of 'graduates without a future', and exaggerate their potential role; Standing's work places more weight on the wider significance of 'precariousness', and the emergence of a whole new class of casualised workers worldwide, who could become the vanguard of a political movement for change.

It would be neither justifiable nor feasible to try to reduce the networking potential of young people. As we saw in Chapter 5, both economic and social change in the new context demand networks of active people, finding innovative ways to cooperate for production, well-being and the meeting of needs. The political class needs to find ways to open up a dialogue with the young generation, allowing their views and interests to be represented in the democratic process.

But public- and voluntary-sector services, including social work ones, should also look for ways in which representatives of the young generation can be involved in policy decisions and in priority setting and management. Only in this way can they avoid becoming part of the hierarchies of power from which the whole generation now feels alienated and excluded. Such representatives should see themselves as communicators from a constituency of their own age cohort, not as young people to be absorbed into the power structures of their organisations, or as token advisors.

They should also deploy young people, using new media of communication among networks of their generation, as outreach workers, to try to involve large communities and specific groups (or gangs) in discussions about social issues. This may create new opportunities to do effective work in deprived areas, or with intractable problems.

Unless this is done, social work and social policy risk becoming the instruments by which older generations oppress the young one. Because they are hierarchically organised and managed, they will have great difficulty in communicating with young people and being relevant to their lives. Worse still, they will be used to try to contain the forces for change represented by the young, and to discipline and punish them for their attempts to rectify the injustices they suffer.

stop and think

■ Does social work have a contribution to make to repairing intergenerational links in contemporary Britain? Does the history of social work help or hinder such a prospect? Are there ways in which social work itself would need to change, if any contribution were to be possible?

Families

In human history, the family has proved to be a remarkably adaptable institution; its demise was frequently forecast in the twentieth century, but it survived in more diverse forms. Multigenerational households, and those containing other kin, diminished as a proportion of all households; couples produced fewer children, more of them divorced, and hence more one-parent families were created. In the United Kingdom by 2010, the most common family household contained two parents and one child, but this constituted only 46.3 per cent of all families (*Social Trends*, 2011, ST41).

Yet by the time of the second phase of the crisis, some of these long-standing trends seemed to be in the process of being reversed in the United Kingdom. Since the turn of the century, divorce rates had been falling; not only were offspring remaining longer in the parental home as costs of independent accommodation grew, but there were even signs that households containing more than two generations were on the increase, as care costs for older people soared.

If economic necessity was demanding that family members find a *modus vivendi* in shared households for longer, this seemed to challenge the culture of individualism which had prevailed for the previous 20 or more years. The idea that each person had a duty to themselves to realise their full potential through a 'project of self' (Rose, 1996) was always one which put a strain on close relationships (Giddens, 1991, 1998; Beck and Beck-Gernsheim, 1995, 2002). The rejection of traditional norms governing the roles of men and women, in favour of negotiated equality, leading to authentic 'intimacy' (Jamieson, 1995) made each partner accountable for the other's emotional development in a way which tested many relationships to breaking point. The needs of children were not adequately accommodated within this model; until they were old enough to be autonomous and self-developmental, they made demands which impinged on the self-realisatory projects of their parents.

Historically, social work was rooted in the ideas that children needed loving families, and that adults needed loving relationships; its methods were developed around practice with families, aimed at defusing violence and conflict, and enabling positive interactions. Its claim to professional expertise lay mainly in its ability to encourage the expression of feelings among family members, to improve communication and understanding, and to promote the development of shared emotional and practical resources among members (Jordan, 1972, 1983, 2007).

However, in the United Kingdom in the 1990s, and especially under New Labour, the emphasis of social work interventions shifted towards protecting vulnerable individuals (children, frail elderly people or those with disabilities) from abuse by other family members. In particular, public services for children and families came to be focused on the task of assessing risks of harm to children, at the expense of support for parents or mediation between family members. Research showed that, among the large numbers of families referred to these services (650,000 in England and Wales by 2007), a great proportion received no specific help or counsel, and social work attention focused on the small percentage deemed to be at risk (Parton *et al.*, 1997, 2006). This had the effect of stigmatising all users of these services, and spreading a fear of child care social workers as harbingers of children's removal from the family home (Waterhouse and McGhee, 1998, p. 280).

Against this background, the New Labour government chose to launch its flagship Sure Start programme of multi-agency centres for families with pre-school children, in which all the relevant professionals worked together, and parents were encouraged to play an active part; these evolved into Sure Start Children's Centres by the last years of the New Labour administration. These undoubtedly produced many benefits for children and families, and provided unstigmatised opportunities for support and advice. But they did not reduce the number of referrals to social services departments, or shift the style of practice away from investigation and surveillance.

Following the notorious death of Baby Peter Connelly, a child well known to child protection workers, health visitors, paediatricians and the police in Haringey, the coalition government in 2010 commissioned a report on child and family work by Professor Eileen Munro of the London School of Economics. While endorsing the overall strategy of the new government in relation to collaboration between agencies in relation to the most difficult, multi-problem families (Munro, 2011, chapter 1), she was critical of the management and methods of social services departments, and of the procedural guidance within which they carried out their work.

Her plea was for a different approach to practice, which made less use of 'rational–technical' analyses of family situations, and more of professionally grounded intuitions, based on the reflective consideration of emotional responses to interpersonal situations. Using evidence from recent advances from neuro-psychology, she argued that social workers should pay more attention to these qualitative aspects of their interactions with children and parents, and that this would allow them both to assess risks of harm more accurately and to offer more reliable help with family relationships than the current style of anxious monitoring enabled. She drew attention to the ways in which management structures in these departments were far from suited to sustaining the approaches she recommended (Munro, 2011, chapter 2).

This report was important, both in its signal of a shift away from the proceduralism and technical focus of the Third Way era and in its endorsement of a greater reliance on professional expertise, which demanded organisational changes as well as a different emphasis in training. In these respects, social work was in the vanguard of a cultural change in the public services, promised in the Conservative Party's election manifesto, but not followed through in other services in its first year in office, or with any sign of it happening thereafter.

Here the consequences of the crisis are ambiguous. On the one hand, the coalition government seems as keen as ever to insist on individual citizens aspiring to self-responsibility. When they show signs of lacking this ethic of autonomy and enterprise, government policies, such as the Work Programme, are designed to instil and reinforce it, if necessary under punitive sanctions. But the reality is that people's everyday lives require them to negotiate and cooperate about an increasing range of needs.

This should give a signal that public services will be increasingly required to offer opportunities to mediate in families over the emotional stresses of a changed economic outlook, over increased interdependence, and the lowering of expectations of individual self-development. Instead, the goal might more be one of supporting families in the quest to recognise and develop the common interests and mutual needs which allowed them to live together in relative harmony.

Here a contribution was made by the report of the Good Childhood Enquiry (Layard and Dunn, 2009), which specifically addressed the issue of a culture shift away from the competitive social environment of the previous 30 years. Like the report of the Joseph Rowntree Foundation on its survey into *Contemporary Social Evils* (Unwin, 2009, p.4), the authors blamed 'excessive individualism' for many of the negative influences on well-being of children in the United Kingdom, which had been assessed as one of the lowest in the EU and the OECD (Bradshaw *et al.*, 2007, Innocenti, 2007).

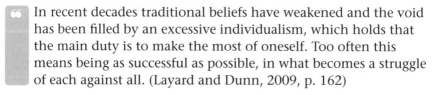

> In recent decades traditional beliefs have weakened and the void has been filled by an excessive individualism, which holds that the main duty is to make the most of oneself. Too often this means being as successful as possible, in what becomes a struggle of each against all. (Layard and Dunn, 2009, p. 162)

If the family is to supply many of the remedies for correcting intergenerational injustice, it is important that social work and the public services provide a framework in which issues can be negotiated openly and with goodwill. This does indeed require a shift from both the rational–technical risk assessment approach and the perception of all social institutions as promoting individual autonomy and self-development. Social work has an important contribution to make to such a transformation.

Conclusions

The Arab Spring was a warning to the affluent countries, not only because of the geopolitical upheaval it caused, but also as an indication of the potential for intergenerational conflict in the affluent countries. If young people's prospects of attaining the status of full and equal citizenship of their society are blocked, and if their prospects of economic advancements are thwarted, they have little to lose from rebellion. By creating a situation for our young people which is structurally similar to that in the Arab dictatorships, we stand to experience similar uprisings.

This threat contains some ironies for the generation which grew up after the Second World War in the United Kingdom. The 1950s were experienced by this cohort as a period of conformity and repression, with little room for cultural innovation or individual idiosyncracy, especially for women, for whom domestic duty defined their social roles, for gay people, while male homosexual activity was still illegal, and for ethnic minorities, who were expected to assimilate to the white majority's norms, it was a uniformly limiting environment.

The 1960s saw the emergence of youth culture as an expressive outpouring of energy and enterprise, as well as the start of emancipatory movements for women and minorities. But the outcome of this accelerated social change was evidenced more in the greater freedom of individuals to develop their lifestyles and their personal identities than in long-term gains by those at the lower end of the status hierarchy. Now we see that those who turned their liberty into wealth and power form a ruling class in UK society whose repressive influence over the young generation is almost as strong as their parents' was over them, though it is exercised by different means. Today's young people are free to express themselves through ideas, music, art, clothes and adornments which would have been considered outrageous in the 1950s; but they do not have the same access to jobs, earnings, income security or the prospects of a career.

All the issues discussed in this chapter are complex, and involve conflicts of interests other than intergenerational ones. For example, the gains made by minority ethnic groups in the United Kingdom in the decades before the crisis were not evenly shared. Some groups, notably those of Indian and Chinese heritage, were more successful in gaining access to good educations, jobs and property than others. For all of them, those who remained in relative poverty and disadvantage were much more likely to continue to suffer from racism and discrimination than those who escaped into middle-class environments and employments.

So – for example, in the English city riots in deprived districts – elements of class- and ethnicity-based resentments against the authorities were as significant as generational ones. But this does not undermine the analysis presented here, because issues of intergenerational relations pervade society as a whole.

We have argued that there is a relationship of injustice between the generations which demands new institutional solutions. The distribution of housing wealth is fundamental to this injustice; funds for financing new homes and loans to young people should be established, to attract investments from the assets of the older generation. The indebtedness of students has been greatly increased by the rise in university fees in England; government should be pressured to reverse this. And above all, the public services and local and national government should seek ways to involve and consult with young people in order to ensure that their interests are represented, and that they do not become detached and alienated from the state and the political process.

It is equally important that young people should be included in the shift towards collective action and cooperation at the level of communities – indeed, that they should take a leading role in it. At present, youth culture, under the influence of advertising and the media, is predominantly constructed around material consumption and hedonism. But the signs that this is changing are already visible in the protest movements directed against finance capitalism. The next step would be for the young generation to organise more around meeting their collective needs, and pursuing their economic interests.

In all this, the introduction of a Basic Income scheme, guaranteeing a subsistence level of provision unconditionally, would be an enormous help in enabling young people to overcome their generational disadvantages. Because it would enable them to combine study, paid work and volunteering in flexible ways, it would promote the new forms of cooperation on which future economic organisation will rely. It would also make young people more attractive as recruits to traditional firms and public sector organisations, whether in part-time or trainee roles, as the first steps on career ladders.

The Child Trust Fund

case study

The Child Trust Fund (CTF) was, perhaps, the most radical social policy experiment of the New Labour era. Drawing on the work of Asset-Based Welfare theorists (see, for example, Sheridan 1991, Prabhakar 2009 and Morel *et al.* 2011), it was rooted in the belief that, in modern Britain, access to assets (in the form of savings, houses, pensions and so on) is sharply unequal, both within and between the generations. The CTF meant that every child born after September 2002 would, on attaining the age of 18, have a sum of money set aside which they would then be able to use to help shape their futures. The government provided £250 for each child, on birth, and £500 for children in less well-off families, in an example of what was known as 'progressive universalism'. The Trust Fund was to be topped up, by the Government, when a child became 7 and 14. Family and friends were also able to add to the funds available for any child. Early research (see Gregory and Drakeford 2006) suggested that young people from the most disadvantaged backgrounds were most likely to use their Trust Funds to extend their education, help find work or secure accommodation. In the terms discussed in this chapter, the Fund represented a sense of distributional justice, across the generations, promoting opportunity and social mobility. As an unconditional payment, made on the basis of citizenship, it shared a number of key characteristics with Basic Income thinking. Abolition of the CTF was one of the first actions of the incoming coalition government in June 2010.

Since the 1970s, the political elites of the affluent countries have all feared collective action by militant groups or trade unions in strategically vital sectors of their economies. This has made them disinclined to promote involvement in the political process or in the economy, preferring to manage societies through hierarchical organisations and market incentives. As we have shown in this chapter, technological change has allowed networks of active, communicating citizens to emerge as an alternative form of coordination, which represents an opportunity for the future of societies, but a challenge to these authorities. As experts in the deployment of these technologies, young people are natural networkers, as the disorders have already proved.

The advantages of networks over hierarchies are particularly relevant for the kinds of economic activities – symbolic analysis, creative ideas and innovatory methods – in which these countries still enjoy competitive advantages. But these will not thrive in a cultural environment in which the talents of young people are held back by rigid, authoritarian structures, This should be the lesson of the Arab Spring for the West; the energies of the young will be directed against the injustice, oppression and exclusion practised by their elders if they are not freed from these shackles to build a better future.

Welfare states, and specifically social insurance systems, were essentially pay-as-you-go schemes in which each new generation funded the pensions and health care of the oldest one in the population. As people lived longer after retirement, these came under strain, but it was the failure of the dynamic of employment and income growth in the affluent countries which finally meant that radical change was required. This is why the potential and the needs of young citizens will remain unmet until there are new institutions for solidarity and redistribution through the state (Basic Income) and in the economy and society (networks for cooperation and community).

- The post-2008 crisis has thrown issues of intergenerational justice into sharp relief. A fairer settlement, between and across the generations remains a key challenge for future social policymaking. In doing so, excessive individualism will need to be replaced with a new concern for collective and collaborative ways of solving problems and supporting personal progress.

- Closely interconnected with intergenerational justice are issues of social mobility. Growing economic inequality, since the 1970s, has been strongly associated with decreasing mobility between social classes.

- As a craft practised primarily with families, social work could have an important part to play in reconnecting generations and helping find new ways of making young people powerful actors in shaping their own futures.

taking it further

- Layard, R. and Dunn, J. (2009) *A Good Childhood: Searching for Values in a Competitive Age,* London, Penguin.
- Munro, E. (2011) *The Munro Review of Child Protection: A Child Centred System*, London, Department for Education, available at: http://www.education.gov.uk/munroreview/downloads/8875_DfE_Munro_Report_TAGGED.pdf.
- Standing, G. (2011) *The Precariat: The New Dangerous Class*, London Bloomsbury.

7 Sustainability in social work and social policy

One aspect of intergenerational justice that was postponed from our discussion in the previous chapter was the responsibility of present generations to hand on to future ones a physical environment which can sustain at least the quality of life which we have enjoyed. But the social policies of the twentieth century were all based on the idea that current rates of economic growth could continue indefinitely. It was only when environmentalists started to draw attention to the fact that the global economy's demand for natural resources was rapidly coming to exceed their supply (Brundtland Commission, 1987, p. 26), and the phenomenon of global warming was identified, that this assumption came under scrutiny.

Social policy had been grounded in a set of economic arrangements which were 'productivist' (Offe, 1992, 1996; Gough *et al.*, 2004), in the sense that the principles for just distribution of roles and resources and the concepts of equality of citizenship in which they were embedded relied on the expansion of gross national product (GNP) for their realisation. This model prioritised paid employment, male earnings and work activities, increases in output per worker/hour (productivity), state-organised welfare systems (hierarchically managed) and technological sophistication. Towards the end of the twentieth century it also became associated with the notion that the integration of the world economy through free movement of the factors of production (globalisation) could benefit all the earth's inhabitants.

So it was only fairly recently that social policy analysts began to turn their attention to approaches which were 'non-productivist' (Offe, 1992, 1996; Fitzpatrick, 2003), exploring possibilities of new foundations for equality, social justice and improved well-being in sustainable economic development, balancing the demand for and supply of natural resources, and avoiding damaging harms to the ecology of the planet through pollution and carbon emissions. This challenge has gained relevance and urgency with the crisis of 2008–12, because productivist versions of capitalism can no longer be assumed to supply rising incomes, let alone rising welfare provision, for the majority of the populations of the affluent countries, even if they can continue to do so for those of the industrialising countries of the wider world.

The main elements in this new approach are an emphasis on quality of social relationships as well as on quantity of consumption; on unpaid work for 'social reproduction' as well as paid employment for the production of commodities; on recognition of the value of a diversity of identities and lifestyles as well as on justice over the distribution of assets; on small-scale, low-tech and labour-intensive work as well as high-tech, large-scale production; on local and communal solidarities as well as national ones organised through the state; and on preservation of the resources in cultures and environments as well as improvements in efficiency and productivity (Fitzpatrick, 2003, chapter 6).

Except for environmental conservation, all these elements in a non-productivist version of sustainable social policy have been discussed in our analysis so far. In this chapter we will consider how they can be combined with ecological principles in a transformation of societies which is a genuine, viable alternative to the authoritarian austerity into which productivism has degenerated during this crisis of capitalism and government.

One of the ironies of the neo-liberal and Third Way periods in the development of social policy and social work was that they moved them in the opposite direction from the one envisaged in this alternative design. The economic approach to public service funding and management created organisations which were businesslike, used contracts to achieve compliance with their objectives for cost control and quality assurance, supplied detailed information to citizens as consumers to maximise their choices between providers and so on. In all these respects, they made the public sector more productivist in its design, ethos and methods, especially when they also used the creation of new agencies and activities to expand paid employment and economic growth in less favoured regions.

So public sector social work, especially in the United Kingdom, finds itself organised in systems which are in many ways antagonistic to the features of its cultural heritage which could offer most to the non-productivist approach. By tradition, social work emphasises quality of relationships, interdependence between people, an ethic of care, respect for diversity and the advantages of small-scale cooperation and community. But it finds itself managed according to ideas and methods focused on competition, efficiency, procedure and the measurement of outputs and outcomes. In all these ways it is currently blocked from its potential contribution to a transformative approach.

research box 7.1

In order to assess the validity of claims that electronic recording systems such as the Integrated Children's System have caused social workers to spend less time working directly with families, the Centre for Child and Family Research at Loughborough University was commissioned to compare data on the activity of child and family social workers collected in a study in 2001–02, with similar data collected in 2007–08. At both time points, front line social workers reported that they spent 80 to 90 per cent of their time on indirect activities, and felt that they had insufficient time for direct work with children. The data from 2007–08 did show an increase in the number of hours spent on administrative tasks and indirect work for most social work processes, but time spent on direct work with children and families had also increased. The main message from the research suggested that while the balance of direct and indirect work remained heavily skewed towards the latter, the tasks required of children and family social workers within the *Every Child Matters* framework have become even more time-consuming.

Source: Holmes L., McDermid S., Jones A. and Ward H. (2009) How social workers spend their time. Research Report DCSF-RR087. Nottingham: DCSF.

This even applies to the voluntary and community sectors, which under New Labour became increasingly reliant on funding from central and local government contracts, to carry out work that was specified by these authorities according to their understandings of the tasks of public policy. Although they had previously represented alternative values and methods from the ones promoted by government, this dependence on official funding drove them to become more business-orientated and to adopt more managerialist organisational hierarchies.

After tracing the non-productivist approach to feminist and anti-racist thought as well as Green ideas, we will show how these might combine in social policies to which social work would make a central contribution. Instead of being on the margins of the drive towards a just and inclusive society, as it was during the era of the post-war welfare state, it could become an essential expression of the model for improving quality of life in the absence of rapid economic growth.

Valuing others

Any alternative to the model of social policy that relies on perpetual economic growth, placing unsustainable demands on the planet's natural resources, must first show that it can offset the tendencies of this phase of capitalism to intensify paid labour, reduce workers' rewards and rely on government schemes to enforce productive obligations, to improve well-being in other ways. This is because important political decisions are being made all the time about policies concerning economic growth and the environment, in which the long-term strategies of the affluent countries have to be negotiated with those still benefiting from gains in human development through industrialisation and rapid growth of GNP.

For example, it now seems that the supplies of fossil fuels available for extraction, and the amounts of carbon discharged into the atmosphere by burning them, are not in themselves the absolute barriers to further growth they once seemed to be. Processes – unpleasant, expensive and damaging to the local environmental amenities, but not in themselves physically unsustainable, such as 'fracking' for natural gas, and underground burning of coal for gas (BBC Radio 4, *Today*, 24 January, 2012) – have, on their own terms, been successfully piloted. If combined with equally expensive and complex systems of carbon capture, they could allow, some argue, the continuation of global economic growth for a far longer period than was for a time considered a feasible or realistic possibility.

But the costs of such a trajectory of development would be so high, and the consequences, in terms of concentration of global economic power in the hands of a few high-tech corporations, so significant, that the least socially and politically attractive features of the crisis would be strongly reinforced by this choice. It would widen the growing gap between those with a stake in global capitalist expansion and those excluded from the benefits of these forms of development. If instead the decision was made to go for some combination of increasing low-tech energy production (such as solar, wind and wave power) while running down those forms using fossil fuels, this would be more compatible with the kind of societies which exist in the affluent countries at present. Yet arguments for this strategy must also show that it does not entail an unacceptable decline in the quality of life of whole populations in these societies, as Green policies have been accused of risking.

The first element in the case for the sustainable alternative to the growth-at-any-cost strategy is derived from the value of human relationships for quality of life. Faced with a choice between a greatly intensified process of heavy industrial extraction of resources, production of energy and storage of emissions, leading to greater inequality of earnings and more polarised social relations, or a lower rate of growth, we should consult the work of Wilkinson and Pickett (2009) on the contribution of equality to well-being, health, longevity and social harmony. But we should also make sure that we understand the microprocesses by which quality of life is sustained in societies which are not at the top of the league in terms of income and growth rates before making a rational collective decision.

In Chapter 3, we analysed the way in which everyday interactions give people a measure of their worth as members of a set of relationships by communications about their place in the social order – either positively, in terms of affection, respect and the sense of belonging, or negatively, in terms of hostility, stigma and exclusion (Jordan, 2008). These not only supply the moral regulation of their shared lives, which are made meaningful by the same processes, they also give them the resources on which their well-being (or lack of it) depend.

From a philosophical perspective, this insight was developed through the concept of *recognition*, partly by the German moral theorist Axel Honneth (1995, 2000) and partly by feminist writers such as Iris Marion Young (1990) and Nancy Fraser (2000). Recognition is a word which seeks to capture the sense of esteem gained in affectionate, respectful and inclusive relationships, and its absence connotes the lack of these. It is appropriate for the kinds of struggles for full citizenship engaged in by the women's, black, LGBT and disabled people's movements in the 1970s and 1980s, and for their achievements in getting themselves accepted as equal holders of the rights of citizenship.

However, as Fraser acknowledges, recognition is not a substitute for a stake in the material prosperity of society, its civil and political freedoms. It means that employment and welfare rights should be equally available for those with caring responsibilities, those of different skin colours, cultures and sexual orientations, and those who have physical and mental incapacities. It emphasises the importance of translating these principles into the fabric of social interactions, so that certain categories of citizens are not assigned roles and status on the basis of characteristics other than their abilities, needs and choices, and that all get full value for their diverse contributions to the common good, defined as embracing qualitative as well as quantitative flourishing.

Recognition for contributions other than those to material production, and enjoyed in ways other than material consumption, broadens the understanding of what it is to improve quality of life. If this can be achieved without economic growth, for instance, by reorganising some activities so as to involve a broader spectrum of people, and increased engagement in satisfying communications between them, it may be preferable to producing and consuming more. Or if some rearrangement of the way society is regulated redistributes power to a larger number of citizens without damaging overall prosperity, this too may be preferred.

All this represents a potential step forward from an approach to social policy in which the public services and the normal lives of citizens in associations and clubs was put on a business footing, with every role given the title of an organisational position, and every relationship described in the vocabulary of contracts and compliance. The New Labour version of civil society and democracy was a largely vacuous one; the primary duty of citizens was 'to earn, shop, save and pretty much shut up' (Fitzpatrick, 2003, p. 108).

case study

Brixton pound

The Brixton Pound (B£) is an 'alternative currency', designed for use in places where conventional money is in short supply, but where there is no shortage of need, nor of goods or services for exchange. The Brixton currency shares the general ambition of such initiatives of supporting local trade and production while improving the circumstances of those whom the mainstream economy has left behind. The B£ is the United Kingdom's first local currency in an urban area, and the fourth 'transition town' to have its own currency. It draws on an even wider, and older, history of communities under stress inventing 'new' money, to get round a shortage of old. The residents of Brixton are encouraged to exchange pounds sterling at special issuing points, spend the B£ with participating local businesses, ask for B£ as change, accept B£s if they are a trader in Brixton, and to give B£s as gifts or as pay for informal activities such as babysitting. You can even 'Pay by Text', and by signing up to this service you receive £11 of 'B£e' for every £10 sterling that you pay in.

The B£ project was initiated be a group of volunteers from Transition Town Brixton, a community-led organisation specialising in energy issues and climate change. The Brixton £ is an example of how local residents have taken action to try to preserve their local businesses, promoting the consumption of local produce. It relies on high levels of trust and a willingness to act collectively, beyond the state. Other similar currencies have been set up in Totnes in Devon, Lewes in Sussex and Stroud in Gloucestershire.

So these views broaden the idea of justice to include how people treat each other in informal transactions, and this opens up the possibility for activities organised through unpaid exchanges or non-monetary systems of reward to be included in the calculation of what is to be counted as relevant for its assessment. In particular, therefore, it brings the world of families, households, kinship, neighbourliness and community into the questions to be addressed by public policy. This puts care, and social work's place in its quality and organisation, at the heart of social policy.

stop and think

■ In what ways have environmental concerns cast a new light on thinking about economic growth in late capitalism? What sort of activities become newly valued when such concerns are given fresh priority? Are there new possibilities for social work in such a new social and economic order?

Interdependence and care

In the long period between the rise of Margaret Thatcher and Ronald Reagan and the onset of the economic crash, the dominant ideas in politics were ones derived from market economics, and these came to be reflected in popular culture and in the organisations of the public sector. Economists colonised the worlds of family and community life, and insisted that their analyses were superior to those of the other social sciences in predicting behaviour in every sphere. For example, the Nobel laureate Gary Becker claimed that people's 'utility function' (their 'preferences' in every sphere of activity) could explain their choices of friends and partners, whom they loved and sympathised with, their habits and addictions.

'This extension of the utility-maximising approach...is remarkably successful in unifying a wide class of behaviour, including habitual, social and political behaviour. I do not believe that any alternative approach – be it founded on "cultural", "biological", or "psychological" forces – comes close to providing comparable insights and explanatory power' (Becker, 1996, p. 4).

On this account, human beings could be best understood as calculating the highest pay-offs available for each of their decisions; if they chose to look after each other, this was a matter of preference or 'taste'. It is hard to imagine a cultural environment less hospitable to the practice of social work than one in which these views were orthodox, or an organisation milieu for managing it less suited to a sensitive and creative version of its deployment as an approach to social policy than this one.

Yet despite the continued hegemony of these ideas under both neoliberal and Third Way governments, other analyses were emerging, mainly from feminist thinkers (Elshtain, 1981, 1998; Gilligan, 1982), which reasserted the centrality of interdependence and care for human societies. In reaction against the imperialistic bombast of the (male) economists who had risen to the top of the social science tree, it was understandable that they presented this alternative analysis as one which was derived from an approach to relationships which was characteristic of women, and contrasted with the drive for material possessions and power of the masculine competitive ethic.

But later theorists of this school of thought quite rightly insisted that no theory of citizenship and justice was complete or adequate which neglected the bonds and reciprocal caring actions which made up the networks of societies, and that any political or moral theory which started from individuals with preferences and interests would be likely to neglect these aspects. Tronto (1993), Sevenhuijsen, 1998, 2000), Noddings (2002) and Williams (2001) all assert that the ethic of care must be regarded as part of the starting point for the analysis of justice in social relationships;

people have intimate, neighbourly and communal relationships from their earliest years, in which they are raised, and which form part of their conceptions of the 'social goods' relevant for justice and citizenship.

Edgar Cahn and the Time Dollar Youth Court

Dr. Edgar Cahn, a former special counsel and speechwriter for Bobby Kennedy, created the concept of Time Banking in the 1980s. Quite simply, 'time dollars' are earned by people helping out in their community. These are then spent when the owner needs help themselves. The system started off as a simple like-for-like exchange – for example, someone offering a lift to the shops in return for an hour of babysitting – but has evolved into more sophisticated models, with community groups and social agencies swapping training, expertise and skills. One element, however, remains constant in all the different variations: contributions are measured in time. An hour of gardening is worth the same as an hour of brain surgery. The movement is now fully international, with time banks having been established across the world.

In 1996, Cahn founded the Time Dollar Youth Court in Washington DC. The court enlists young people with the aim of improving juvenile justice in the city. Almost every young person brought before the Courts in Washington DC is black. It is now one of the largest youth courts in the United States, the majority of recruits being former offenders. Young people who appear before the Time Dollar Youth Court are judged by their peers. The punishment involves contributing a set number of hours to activities determined by the Court. Almost without exception, one element in those hours will be a stint sitting as a juror in future cases. There are no rules of evidence at the Court, so jurors are able to ask any questions, or seek any information which they believe to be critical to understanding an individual's situation. The belief that each individual is an asset, with something positive to offer – to give, as well as to receive – lies at the heart of Cahn's time bank proposition, and can be seen vividly in practice at the Time Dollar Youth Court.

Fitzpatrick (2003, pp. 117–8) points out that this represents a strengthening factor in the social force of ideas of justice (because our interdependence is part of our everyday experience, and because care is a universal value), but also a challenge, because we care more about those individuals, groups, faiths and nations which have won our loyalty and demonstrated care for us. However, the issue for social policy is how to build on preexisting patterns of interdependence and care, and create institutions that broaden these to include those on the margins of society, along with respecting diversity and difference.

The link with sustainability here is that, while markets promote acquisitiveness and consumption, and productivism relies on growth derived from these, interdependence and care focus on the reproduction of cultures and collective forms of life, from families to communities. It has long been recognised that capitalism has an inbuilt logic that drives it towards turning the world into One Big Market, and that this involves the destruction of all forms of solidarity and mutuality which protect people from its forces of creative destruction (Polanyi, 1944). While this is symbolised by television pictures of the giant machinery of logging companies felling the Amazonian rain forest, destroying the environments previously conserved by their hunter-gatherer peoples, it is also reflected in the ways that consumerism has undermined the shared rituals of family life, and competition among producers has led to the decline of trade unionism in the United Kingdom during the past 40 years.

So sustainability provides a link between concern for the protection of the physical environment from the ravages of industrial production and the priority of human relationships and mutual support in the life of societies. It points to the need to attend to how we care for and care about others, and to defend those institutions for interdependence from subversion by economic forces (including ideological erosion by advertising and the media).

Social work in the United Kingdom should be at the forefront of a movement to uphold the values and practices of interdependence and care, but it has somehow let this role slip out of its grasp. On the defensive since the child protection scandals of the 1970s which have punctuated news bulletins ever since, it has become locked into a defensive form of technical practice, trying to keep its head down and hoping to avoid bad publicity. This is in contrast to the optimism about its future that prevailed in the 1960s, when it seemed to be part of the emancipatory spirit of that time.

In many ways this is an issue of self-confidence for the profession. In social work education the leading texts still assert the importance of social relationships, and teaching still focuses on empathy and expertise in communication with people with emotional problems and interpersonal conflicts. Authors such as Bob Holman, Jan Fook and Lena Dominelli are internationally renowned for their contributions to community development, professional skill and anti-oppressive practice, respectively. Neither the breadth of theoretical analysis nor the depth of the knowledge base is adequately reflected in the rather impersonal, formulaic guise that practice is supposed (by policymakers and managers) to take (though in fact the best practitioners still defy these expectations to work in much the same ways as their predecessors did).

Another paradox of the past decades is that the enormous proportional growth of service work (relative to manufacturing, extraction and construction) has not increased well-being and quality of life, as measured in people's self-assessments of their personal happiness (Jordan, 2008). It might have been assumed that this growth in the quantity of time and energy devoted to meeting each other's requirements would have improved our relationships and our enjoyment of our lives, but in fact these figures have flat-lined since the 1970s in the affluent countries.

Two studies of low-paid women service workers in cleaning, catering and residential care in the United States and the United Kingdom give clues about why this has been. Barbara Ehrenreich (2002) and Fran Abrams (2002) both found that these workers faced heavy management pressures to increase the pace of their performances, to do more in less time. Driven into these forms of employment to sustain household incomes, and often carrying out tasks that released other women to work in better-paid services who probably faced similar pressures, they were part of a cycle in which more and more work was turned into service employment to fund consumption, but with unsatisfying outcomes.

In the next section, we will consider whether there are ways out of this cycle which would also be steps towards sustainability, and how progress might be made towards this goal.

stop and think

■ Can you identify some key characteristics of a newly sustainable approach to economic growth? Conventional analysis concentrates on the material *reward* which can be derived from economic activity. In what ways might a focus on *recognition* amend or supplement such an analysis?

New ways of thriving

These connections between overwork, stalled well-being, inequality, injustice and overconsumption have been increasingly recognised, and the Green movement has in turn linked them with sustainability through the dangers to the environment from depletion and pollution. An alternative economics of sustainability is rapidly being developed, and was provisionally set out in his *Prosperity without Growth* (2009) by Tim Jackson.

His report for the Sustainable Development Commission emphasised the role of novelty in the commercial dynamic of growth. Firms constantly innovate in their methods of production and in their output, and market their products as integral to desirable lifestyles. Consumers are conditioned to associate status with the ownership and display of goods; people from the Stone Age onwards have always communicated through their possessions and through displays of clothing and adornments (Douglas, 1970), and advertising has simply developed such behaviour into more refined, competitive and addictive forms.

Tim Jackson Report: 12 steps to a sustainable economy

Building a sustainable macroeconomy

Debt-driven materialistic consumption is deeply unsatisfactory as the basis of our macroeconomy. The time is now ripe to develop a new macroeconomics for sustainability that does not rely for its stability on relentless growth and expanding material throughput. Four specific policy areas are identified to achieve this:

1. Developing macroeconomic capability
2. Investing in public assets and infrastructures
3. Increasing financial and fiscal prudence
4. Reforming macroeconomic accounting

Protecting capabilities for flourishing

The social logic that locks people into materialistic consumerism is extremely powerful, but detrimental ecologically and psychologically. A lasting prosperity can only be achieved by freeing people from this damaging dynamic and providing creative opportunities for people to flourish – within the ecological limits of the planet. Five policy areas address this challenge.

5. Sharing the available work and improving the work–life balance
6. Tackling systemic inequality
7. Measuring capabilities and flourishing
8. Strengthening human and social capital
9. Reversing the culture of consumerism

Respecting ecological limits

The material profligacy of consumer society is depleting natural resources and placing unsustainable burdens on the planet's ecosystems. There is an urgent need to establish clear resource and environmental limits on economic activity and develop policies to achieve them. Three policy suggestions contribute to that task.

10. Imposing clearly defined resource/emissions caps
11. Implementing fiscal reform for sustainability
12. Promoting technology transfer and international ecosystem protection

'Above all, there is an urgent need to develop a resilient and sustainable macro-economy that is no longer predicated on relentless consumption growth. The clearest message from the financial crisis of 2008 is that our current model of economic success is fundamentally flawed. For the advanced economies of the Western world, prosperity without growth is no longer a utopian dream. It is a financial and ecological necessity.'

The tragic consequences of these cultural processes for some individuals are evidenced in assaults and even murders of teenagers for designer items of clothing, footwear or technology. But growth can also become addictive for governments, when their macroeconomic management strategies come to rely on rising consumption, and the employment and earnings that citizens need to fund it.

So the necessary conditions for a shift to an alternative economics include both a cultural and a governmental transformation, and these are connected. Jackson argues that over time it will be possible to wean people off competitive consumerism by reducing perverse incentives, by making people less insecure about their status in the mainstream and by redistributing income more equitably. On the side of government, he favours a programme for investment in sustainable technology (especially for energy production), and in the public infrastructure, to make it more conducive for the enjoyment of shared cultural, sporting and political experiences, and less focused on consumerist ones.

Another of Jackson's recommendations was for work to be shared more evenly among the population, through a shorter working week, and this formed the basis for a set of radical proposals by the New Economics Foundation (2012). Their report argued that this was the best means to combine improvements in social justice and well-being with conservation of the world's natural resources, and they chose 21 hours as the rough average of the amount of paid work done in a week by all UK residents of working age. The strategy they advocate relies on vastly increased mutual aid to substitute for this cut in the number of hours of paid work done by those with higher salaries.

They argue that, as well as contributing to greater equality through redistributing employment, the reduction in consumption this will entail will allow increases in activities that are more productive of the social value which is so important for well-being, like care for children and other family members, friendship, volunteering, taking outings, and further education. All these things would make us more satisfied with our lives and 'society a better and more convivial place to be', as well as doing less environmental damage (NEF, 2012, p. 6).

To achieve this, they recommend that we become more aware of the distribution of paid and unpaid work, which at present is skewed in terms of far longer hours for the higher earning groups of the former, and far more for women of the latter. The aim would be to make care work more visible and valued, and to lower the norm of what is regarded as a full week of paid employment, redistributing both more evenly among the population of working age.

Current patterns are, they argue, a legacy of industrial capitalism, but new technologies have made them outmoded; yet instead of liberating people from the tyranny of the clock, they have been accompanied by an intensification of effort and longer hours of work. A rebalancing of the economy should include a revaluation of the care work done mainly by women, and changing the relationship between time, money and consumption, also shifting power relationships between social groups. But in addition it would require a different kind of social policy, getting people, the planet and markets working together for sustainable social justice (Coote *et al.*, 2009).

This relies on the reduction in working time being translated into more eco-friendly and more communal, cooperative patterns of leisure and collective life, reducing consumption without lowering real living standards. It would involve reversing decades-long trends in lifestyles, with more people growing and cooking their own food, repairing household items and machinery rather than replacing them, walking and cycling more, and making more use of public transport. The aim of this transformation would not only be to reduce carbon emissions and conserve natural resources, but also give people more control over their time to live well.

The aim of work redistribution would be to improve the well-being of both the unemployed and the overworked. The authors argue that, given this opportunity, women would be able to negotiate with men to achieve a fairer distribution of unpaid tasks in the home, and that shorter working hours would allow fathers to become more involved with their children. It would also enable a more gradual transition to retirement, with more people being able to stay in employment for longer. Other benefits would be an easier way to combine earning with caring, more time to participate in associational and cultural life and for nurturing social virtues and capacities, more collective action to meet social and environmental needs, and for reflective contemplation. They suggest that it would also benefit business by making workers more alert, aware and hence productive, and the economy by making it more adaptable to the big issues of globalisation and environmental crisis.

All this paints a very optimistic picture of the prospects for radical change, though the authors recognise the need for a transitional process, the details of which are acknowledged to be a work-in-progress for the

Foundation. Employers are clearly a potential source of resistance, much of it rational, to their proposals. Business assumes that it is able to select and recruit the best staff for the roles it requires, and it is no coincidence that the highest paid tend to work the longest hours. Employers get rid of or avoid recruiting those they regard as less potentially productive workers; they deploy all employees in ways calculated to extract the most output from them. The idea of sharing out employment more evenly among a far larger pool of people, of widely varying aptitudes, would certainly not appeal to them.

On the supply side, there would be likely to be as much resistance from those whose hours would be curtailed as among those for whom 21 hours of employment would be seen as burdensome. People are not necessarily equally industrious and employment orientated; there is much to be said for a system which allows those who prefer leisure or non-commercial pursuits to choose these in preference to paid work, not least for the sake of productive efficiency. Why should organisations be required to recruit all those who would rather spend the day fishing, cooking or growing plants, and why should skilled anglers, cooks and gardeners be made to be inept workers in offices, factories or shops? By the same token, why should those who find their work absorbing and fulfilling not be permitted to do it for more than a small fraction of the available time?

For these reasons among others, it is surprising to see that the authors, while acknowledging that an unconditional Basic Income for all would be the logical income maintenance counterpart to the approach they suggest, actually reject this out of hand as too costly. Instead, they rely on other, potentially equally or more expensive, measures to compensate for loss of income and to prepare people for the very new world which this approach would usher in, including training schemes and extended, upgraded public services.

If it is accepted that it would be better to achieve the same goals in ways that went more with the grain of people's abilities and inclinations, it would seem that a gradual transition to Basic Income, starting with the kind of scheme prefigured in the thinking behind the Centre for Social Justice's report in 2009, would be a preferable approach. That scheme would not have achieved many of the aims of employment redistribution or revaluing of unpaid work, because it would apply only to those currently at the lower end of earnings or outside the labour market. But over time and step by step it could have been extended, eventually integrating the whole of the tax-benefit system, and enabling citizens to combine different kinds of work in much the same ways as those envisaged in the Foundation's report. (In the event, the coalition government's welfare reforms have failed even to take a convincing first small step in this direction.)

■ If, in the future, work will be in short supply, and insufficient to sustain the incomes of many people, then what strategies might be adopted to [re]distribute purchasing power in the future? Is work sharing a practical proposition? Would a Basic Income approach be more effective and equitable?

Implications for social work

Given these reports' explicit connections between care and social justice as well as with environmental sustainability, why is social work never mentioned in them? And given that social work has always laid claim to concern with well-being and quality of relationships, and that social justice is central to its values (BASW, 2003), why are social workers not among the leading figures in these movements?

Part of the answer seems to lie in social work's quest for recognition as a profession. It has been more anxious to establish its credentials as an exclusive expertise in solving specific problems or ameliorating specific conflicts, rather than allowing itself to become associated with movements for social change, or with developments in society at large.

This strategic orientation over several decades has backfired, because it has played into the tendency under liberal capitalism to see social work as a way of dealing with a poor and excluded minority in society, and with individuals who do not match up to the competitive requirements of the economy. In this way, it has acquired some of the stigma attached to its clients, without getting much credit for the help it has given them.

It has also been corralled into a narrow role in child protection and assessments of needs and resources among those seeking social care. Under New Labour, new agencies were established to tackle issues like youth unemployment, asylum seeking and social exclusion, and the government preferred to train people for social work-like roles in these new initiatives, and to use the profession for limited tasks with strong associations with social control and the rationing of government resources (Jordan with Jordan, 2000).

'Voices from the front line: state social workers and New Labour' by Chris Jones

Chris Jones conducted interviews with just over 40 state social workers in local authority social services departments in the north of England from 1999 to 2001, listening to their accounts of 'seemingly endemic organisational change' in the first few years of a New Labour government.

Here are some examples of how the day-to-day working experience had changed for those he interviewed:

> We are now much more office based. This really hit home the other day when the whole team was in the office working at their desks. We have loads more forms which take time to complete. But we social workers also do less and less direct work with clients. Increasingly the agency buys in other people to do the direct work and we manage it.

Contact with clients had become 'more fleeting, more regulated and governed by the demands of the forms which now shape much of the intervention'.

> Our contact with clients is more limited. It is in, do the assessment, get the package together, review after a spell and then close the case and get on with the next one as there were over 200 cases waiting for an assessment.

The neo-liberal emphasis on regulation and managerialism is outlined by this community care social worker:

> Social work is more and more about numbers with managers wanting to hit so many targets which involves turning cases over quickly. They want a case in, sorted and pushed out. We have many unallocated cases so there is great pressure on everyone to take the maximum number of cases. I think this emphasis on turnover is cosmetic, to make it seem that we are giving a service to the public. But we don't give anything. We have nothing to give.

The kinds of cultural shifts envisaged by the reports examined in the previous section would potentially create opportunities for social workers to be more involved in local communal activities to address need, in which citizens took the lead and formed the main body of participants. This approach would be closer to the experience of countries like Canada,

Australia and New Zealand, where many social workers are employed by small community organisations, to advise on the best strategies and methods to adopt, and to address specific problems among residents.

This might be unattractive to many of today's social workers, because it would take them out of the security of a tight management structure and well-defined tasks under detailed guidance, as well as removing them from the opportunities of promotion and incremental pay rises in such organisations. But the limitations imposed by these structures inhibit the development of real expertise in complex situations (Fook *et al.*, 2000), and isolate them from the most important social currents in societies.

Another direction in which the profession has developed over the decades is away from involvement in economic life. Its founding figures placed no such barriers on practitioners, who encouraged small-scale craft production by poor people, and especially by women (Cormack, 1945). In the developing world, this tradition is even stronger; social workers regularly help women organise to grow food or initiate schemes to supply clean water. This is an example of where social workers in the affluent countries can learn from their counterparts in Africa and Latin America. We have argued elsewhere that social workers could and should take a lead in helping devise ways of improving the circumstances of their users, through promotion of local, cooperative means of generating economic activity and supplying ethical financial services (see, for example, Drakeford and Gregory 2008).

In general terms, the implication of these new perspectives on sustainable directions for social policy and society point towards a style of practice that makes itself more accountable to ordinary citizens, and allows them more say in decisions about the roles and tasks of the profession. This is in line with a much broader understanding of the term 'care' which is deployed in the sustainability literature. Care is not defined as a way of helping people who are unable to look after themselves, but as attentiveness to the needs of all others, flexibility in divisions of paid and unpaid work roles and awareness of the need to negotiate over fairness in the ways that responsibilities, for example, in parenting, are allocated. It also involves care for the environment, both physical and social.

There may also be lessons from the former Soviet Bloc countries of Central and Eastern Europe. While it is something of a myth that there was nothing like social work in these societies (Šiklova, 2001), there was little official acknowledgement of the need for a profession dedicated to addressing social problems. This meant that it was a subversive act when, in the late 1980s, some citizens in Hungary and Czechoslovakia started to call themselves social workers, and to help the poorest groups in their societies to organise to improve their situation (Jordan, 2001). But after 1989, social workers were quickly organised in hierarchical management structures, very much like their counterparts in the United Kingdom.

This illustrates that – at moments of rapid change and economic crisis – social work is capable of assisting in emancipatory and transformative action. But there is a strong tendency for the forces of authority to ensure that it is used as an agency for control of potential subversion, if not for the actual oppression of minority or deviant groups. We hope that social work will rise to the challenges of the second phase of the long crisis of capitalism and democracy.

Conclusions

The sustainability agenda for social policy is the only one which addresses all the challenges posed by the economic and political crisis; it is also the only one which incorporates a potential for a positive, transformative role for social work. It sees the faltering of the capitalist version of growth (relying on the commercialisation of previously informally organised activities) as a potential opportunity for social justice and equality, and emphasises better relationships as part of what is required for a sound approach to the environment. But the path it maps out for achieving its goals requires major cultural shifts, which might be criticised as paternalistic if imposed by experts, or as utopian if left to processes of spontaneous adaptation by citizens.

This does not imply that the economy must not grow, but that it must do so in a more balanced way, with less consumption for its own sake and less reliance on processes which cause environmental damage. It means that those activities which increase and flourish should not always be ones undertaken by high-tech processes or owned and managed by global corporations. It also points to the need for development in cities like Hull, Newport and Doncaster, and not just in Aberdeen, Cambridge and Milton Keynes; polarisation between the prosperity of cities in the United Kingdom has occurred at the same time as between regions, and growth should aim to rebalance this, not exaggerate it further.

Much of the change needed to accomplish this shift has started to happen spontaneously. For example, the ideas of Colin Tudge (2010) about increasing local food production on a huge scale through small-scale cooperative farming, which seemed absurdly utopian when they were first published, have begun to be turned into reality on the fringes of cities in the United Kingdom by groups of ordinary people, in response to the crisis. The whole town of Todmorden, on the Yorkshire–Lancashire border, has committed itself to sustainable food production (BBC Radio 4, *The Food Programme*, 22 January 2012).

We have argued for many of the features of the sustainability agenda – more equitable sharing of work, more recognition for the value of caring, more emphasis on quality of relationships, more active participation, fairer distribution of income – quite independently of their implications for the environment. The pressing need to reduce carbon emissions and conserve fossil fuel supplies simply strengthens the case for these directions in policy. But the central weakness of the agenda – symbolised by the Greens' failure to achieve an electoral breakthrough – is how it can be reconciled with democratic development, especially in first-past-the-post systems. Representative democracy in market societies has hitherto not supplied the openings for sustainability to capture the public imagination. Advertisers and the consumerist agenda still hold sway in popular culture and their tacit supporters in the political one.

But such scepticism about the future chances for the adoption of the sustainability agenda ignores popular disillusion with representative democracy itself, and with the manifestations of the latest phase of capitalist development in the crisis. If Green ideas are not yet readily accepted, there is increasing evidence that traditional parties' nostrums are seen as largely stale and outdated, and their purveyors out of touch with the experiences of ordinary citizens.

This means that there is a key role for the young generation in challenging conventional wisdoms and political leaderships, and developing new ideas and strategies. Here it seems likely that those based on sustainability must be very prominent in the minds of those, like members of the Occupy movement, who are actively searching for new solutions to the crisis situation. If something akin to the sustainability agenda emerges from their deliberations, the fact that they came to it by debate and discursive reasoning will be a strength, not a weakness.

In the same way, although the Basic Income proposal has hitherto, like the sustainability agenda, been advocated mainly by academics and think tanks – except in the 1970s, when it was adopted by a social movement of poor people (Jordan, 1973), and in the 1930s when a version of it was advanced by a militant group of diverse activists (Drakeford, 1997) – it could perhaps best be propelled into democratic politics if it was espoused by a youth protest group or anti-capitalist movement, rather than taken up as part of a conventional programme , as it was by the UK Liberal Democrats before the 1992 general election (Ashdown, 1988). Its persuasive power might be greatest if it was presented as a response to the failure of conventional policies in the face of the crisis.

The other strength of the case for Basic Income lies in the manifest failure of the cobbled-together income maintenance systems in the affluent states, and especially in the United Kingdom and the United States. The fact that the coalition government in the United Kingdom has embarked on a partial integration of the tax-benefit system indicates that the existing mess cannot endure much longer, but it needs the impetus of a supportive movement among young people to drive reforms on towards a full Basic Income scheme.

We have argued that this would be an essential condition for the transformation of social policy and society we envision, and – despite the reservations of the New Economics Foundation report – for the sustainability agenda also. It would enable all the other features of a better society to be implemented over time, by democratic processes.

In this chapter we have argued that social work could play a central, positive role in this transformation, if it can cast off the shackles of its own insecurity and limited aspirations. Now that well-being is far more widely recognised as residing more in the quality of relationships of all kinds (civic and associational as well as neighbourly, familial and intimate) there is a golden opportunity for it to take on a more expansive, generous and democratic concept of its mission and role. In an age of austerity, the alternative is to be an instrument in the hands of the oppressors.

main points

■ Low growth economics over the years ahead has shifted the attention of social policy analysts to sustainable futures, based on sharing and conserving finite resources. Quality, rather than quantity of consumption, is set to be the test of prosperity, both economic and social.

■ In this future, social work has a new relevance in helping shape quality of life, based around interdependence and an equal recognition of the rights of citizenship.

■ One way of rebalancing both social and economic life would be to share out the available work more equally amongst all those able to undertake employment. A better alternative would be to provide an unconditional Basic Income for all citizens, as advocated in this book.

taking it further

■ Fitzpatrick, T. (ed.) (2011) *Understanding the Environment and Social Policy*, Bristol, Policy Press

■ Jackson, T. (2009) *Prosperity Without Growth: Economics for a Finite Planet*, London, Earthscan.

■ Mantle, G. and Backwith, D. (2010) 'Poverty and Social Work', *British Journal of Social Work*, 40:8, 2380–2397.

8 Conclusion: Responses to the social crisis

We have argued that the crisis of capitalism and democracy in 2008–12 was accompanied by a social crisis at least as profound. The obvious manifestations of this were growing inequalities (as the real incomes of the richest grew as fast as ever, while those of middle and lower earners fell); rising unemployment, especially among the young generation; and falling standards of care for older and disabled citizens. This in turn has led to a crisis in social policy and social work, many of whose assumptions have been based on projections of continual economic growth and the prospects of increasing material prosperity for each successive generation.

In the case of social work, in the United Kingdom it had come to occupy a slightly embattled, defensive and self-effacing role, following the prescriptions of governments and managers, under the watchful eyes of inspectors, and concerned mainly with protection of society's most vulnerable individuals from abuse or neglect by others in their lives. This was a far cry from the optimistic and expansionary view of the profession's future envisioned in the 1960s and early 1970s, when it was seen as potentially contributing to a new era of emancipation and social progress.

The history of social work suggests that it can easily become the tool of oppressive political authorities, as in Germany and elsewhere in Europe in the 1930s (Lorenz, 1994). Its problem in relation to such forces is that it can deceive itself that it is ameliorating suffering or offering opportunities for escaping the worst hardships of a ruthless regime's activities, when actually it is oiling the wheels of these policies. These dilemmas are likely to arise again in the age of austerity, for example, as the UK government looks for ways of intervening in the lives of the 120,000 'problem families' blamed for rising social expenditures and disorder. Even if less authoritarian ways are found for addressing their difficulties, social workers (or someone doing work that is essentially the same as they do) will be focusing on a minority who are being blamed for the wider problems of a whole society in crisis.

On the other hand, social work is at its most positive as an influence on social relations when it forms part of a broader trajectory of social policy, or carries forward the ideas of a social movement, which associate it with such values as social justice and equal citizenship. In other words, what really matters, we would argue, is not so much the technical competences which practitioners deploy, or even the benevolence of their intentions, but the ways in which their practice is linked with other tides in the collective life of a society.

This is why the analysis in this book has taken the form, not of an account of what social workers need to know about social policy, nor indeed of the political economy underpinning social policy, but of how the long crisis of capitalism and democracy impacts on the public services and their tasks, and how the role of social work is directly affected by this. But we have also tried to show that there are alternative trajectories in which it could play a much more positive part.

Above all, we consider that affluent societies face a choice between approaches to the challenges posed by the crisis that consolidate the polarisation of income and opportunity of those with a stake in global financial, technological and productive advances (the elites of wealth and power, and the managers and skilled workers employed by international companies), and those whose fate is linked to their local economies and communities; or approaches that attempt to forge solidarities (such as Basic Income schemes and National Care Services) and collective action (both formal and informal) that offset the conflicts of interest involved in the first.

It seems clear to us that the young generation have most to lose from the first approach, because so few of them are gaining access to the advantages enjoyed by membership of the club of growing global material prosperity. But in the longer run we all stand to lose if the path chosen provokes increasing social conflict, and is also unsustainable in its environmental consequences. We have suggested that social work is inescapably embroiled with this choice of approaches. In this concluding chapter, we will rehearse some of the day-to-day examples of policy decisions which raise the fundamental questions about our direction of travel signposted in this book.

The important point is that these instances are seldom illustrated by clashes between political leaderships in the affluent countries. Over the past 50 years, the parties which developed welfare states to their fullest expression in the 1960s (mostly Labour or Social Democrats) have gradually come to adopt variants of the free market orthodoxies of their Liberal and Conservative opponents. This tendency reached its height with the Third Way; Bill Clinton's and Tony Blair's programmes and campaigning styles were imitated by leaders of these parties throughout these states, and the ideas behind their reforms of the public sector were adopted in most of them.

So the opposition they now offer to the increasingly dominant regimes of austerity hawkish governments of the Right, or technocrats installed to do their bidding (as in Italy and Greece), is muted to the point of inaudibility. To recognise alternatives it is necessary to pay attention to small acts of resistance and protest – court cases, the findings of investigative journalists and street demonstrations.

Just as the Arab Spring was not launched by an opposition political group, but by the desperate action of a single young man in an obscure town in southern Tunisia, so the alternatives to the grim face of austerity programmes are more likely to emerge from the suffering margins of society. Social workers are more likely than most to encounter such voices, if they allow themselves to hear them.

Court case: 'forced labour'

The case of Cait Reilly, a 22-year-old geology graduate who was required to work as an unpaid shelf-stacker and cleaner at Poundland as a condition for continuing to receive Jobseekers' Allowance, hit the headlines when her lawyers announced that they would be applying for judicial review of the issue of whether this constituted forced labour, and was therefore a violation of her human rights by the UK Department of Work and Pensions. The original report of this case in the *Daily Mail* (12 January 2012) was taken up by the Sydney *Herald Sun* in Australia within hours, and also by the *Huffington Post* in the United States, indicating that it touched a nerve in the affluent Anglophone countries.

She had been working as a volunteer in a museum when she was asked to attend a day session with the supermarket's management, and was later informed by benefits officials that this constituted a commitment to a period of 'training', including this fortnight of unpaid work. If she had refused, her benefits entitlement would have been forfeited.

The case was interesting because it revolved around the fact that the firm offered nothing constituting a training experience that would enhance claimants' skills, and was therefore not beneficial to their prospects of a job, especially if they were already doing voluntary work of the kind that Ms. Reilly was undertaking, and to which she subsequently returned. Because they were doing unpaid work under threat of losing benefits, the coercive features of their labour were more obvious than they would have been if, for example, they had reluctantly accepted part-time, low-paid employment. Her lawyers were at pains to distinguish this case from the more usual one of sanctions being deployed to enforce acceptance of labour for firms paying minimum wages for unpleasant tasks or unsocial hours.

Yet we would argue that the concept of 'forced labour' in fact applies across the board to many of the employments now being filled by officials and firms under contract to the Work Programme. The fact that this particular scheme was clearly adopted without question by 'advisors' who regarded it as a routine exercise of their powers points to an unreflective abuse of the sanctions in the welfare-to-work regime.

It also symbolises the powerless situation of an educated young generation who find themselves without career prospects. The notion of 'activation' implies that schemes such as the Work Programme enable claimants to be included in a process through which they are given access to the opportunities for entering the world of work. It represents them as becoming agents of their own advancement into jobs and careers through this process (Behrens and Evans, 2002), in which they participate as partners.

Yet research on programmes for unemployed young people in a number of countries – Sweden, Germany and Spain (Wolf and Knopf, 2010) and the United States (Caroleo and Pastore, 2003) – all indicate that, in so far as this is true at all, it is only the case when the labour market is relatively buoyant, and young claimants therefore have a number of options for survival. When there are many applicants for every desirable job, the experience of 'activation' is experienced as exactly the opposite – a further reduction in the limited autonomy that they have in the key decisions affecting their lives.

We have argued that social policy and social work should instead aim to help young people to mobilise in collective action to address the structural elements in their situation, and to organise to meet their needs, improve their quality of life and protect themselves from oppression and exploitation. This was the aim of organisations of unemployed people and other social assistance claimants in the 1970s (Jordan, 1973), and they had considerable success, not only in helping members win appeals against refusals of or reductions in benefits, but also in devising strategies for evading pressures to take unsuitable employments. Some of them also enabled their members to organise in providing cooperative shops, vegetable plots and social entertainments.

At that time, public opinion was broadly supportive of claimants in such causes, but today no such positive reactions could be relied upon. The great majority of the messages published by the *Mail on Line* in response to the paper's report on Cait Reilly's case were very unsympathetic, and some correspondents even seemed to imply that the more onerous the labour duties imposed on young claimants such as her, the more approving of the official government programme they would be. One message 'explained' that Jobseekers' Allowances were not for the costs of subsistence, but to pay for travel to interviews and other work-search expenditures.

Our standpoint is that the whole orientation of social policy and social work should shift away from this attempt to impose work obligations, and towards the encouragement of autonomy, enterprise, solidarity and participation among the young generation. This of course would be enabled by a Basic Income scheme, which would make all attempts to coerce citizens to undertake unwilling labour on behalf of society illegal. The role of social work in this field would then become one of helping claimants and others to organise in their own interests. But in the present policy environment and climate of public opinion (at least among readers of the *Daily Mail*), this would be a direction for practice that would encounter considerable hostility.

Investigative journalism: the role of the police in the social order

Since the suicide attacks on New York on 11 September 2001, and London on 7 July 2005, security has been a far higher priority of governments in these and other affluent countries. The challenge for the 'Free World' (as it used to call itself during the Cold War, in contrast with the pathologically paranoid security states of the Stalinist Soviet Bloc) is how to be vigilant and effective in dealing with these threats without slipping into policies and methods that undermine the very liberties that are threatened by theocratic terrorists.

Since the significance of the security services and the police was heightened by these attacks, there has been a creeping tendency for anti-terrorism legislation to be used as a cloak for clamping down on all kinds of protest, or even on much milder manifestations of citizen's curiosity about power and authority (such as taking photographs of buildings). As the crisis deepened, and demonstrations against greed and incompetence in the financial sector, and the austerity policies of governments, appeared on the streets of cities, these tendencies were more evident.

However, in the United Kingdom, the first signals of unaccountable arrogance and petty corruption having pervaded the culture of the police force, especially in London, came from investigative journalism by *The Guardian's* reporter Nick Davies into phone hacking on behalf of the *News of the World* in the early summer of 2011. Both celebrities and the families of victims of tragedies, such as the murdered schoolgirl Millie Dowler, complained that their mobile phone messages had been intercepted illegally, and that many of the incidents to which these calls related, and in some cases their numbers, could only have been known to reporters through information supplied by the police. In the wake of public outrage over a string of revelations of this kind, and especially of the hacking of Millie Dowler's phone after her death, the *News of the World* was closed down by its owner, Rupert Murdoch.

Immediately following this, the Metropolitan Police Commissioner, Sir Paul Stephenson, and several of his most senior officers resigned over inappropriate relationships with the press and the failure to carry out adequate investigations of previous phone-hacking allegations. Subsequently, several lower-ranking officers were arrested on charges of receiving payments for information given to journalists. The hearings of the Leveson Enquiry into the regulation of the press did nothing to dispel the view that, over the first decade of the century, the power and unaccountability of the tabloid newspapers, to which prime ministers of the United Kingdom had being paying craven court, had been consolidated by a relationship with a police force which saw its own power and unaccountability bolstered by the favours it did to the press.

All this was of concern in its own right, but it gained significance because of the greater prominence of the police in maintaining an acceptable level of public order during a time in which a security threat from terrorists coincided with a movement for protest against capitalism, and an outbreak of rioting, itself sparked by an incident in which the police shot a young black man. Were police actions, strategies and cultures consistent with a democratic political order which could allow legitimate resentment against economic failure to find expression, and to lead to the social changes needed for healthy political development?

There were many indications that they were not. As we have seen, the report on the causes of the riots in the English cities in early August 2011, *Reading the Riots* (Newburn *et al.*, 2011), found that one reason given by participants for their involvement was oppressive and aggressive policing, especially the use of stop-and-search powers, which were 26 times more likely to be used against young black than white men. The incident which sparked the riot, the shooting of Mark Duggan, raised many unanswered questions about the police's actions, and the poor handling of the protests outside the police station, combined with police defensiveness about that incident, contributed to the riots getting out of hand.

But of equal concern should be the way the police have tended to elide threats to public order like these with legal and democratic protests, and to attempt to screen off demonstrators from the wider public, symbolically marginalising them from the everyday life of citizens.

> Last month City of London police sent a letter to the banks titled 'Terrorism/extremism update for City of London business community'. It warned of the following 'substantial' terrorist threats: Farc in Colombia, al-Qaida in Pakistan, and Occupy London. It advised banks to 'remain vigilant' as 'suspected activists' from the Occupy movement were engaging in 'hostile reconnaissance' – language that might have been used to report spies in the second world war. When asked to explain the letter, the police told *The Guardian* that it had been circulated to 'our trusted partners'. The banks are the trusted partners of our impartial law enforcers; those who

> seek to hold them to account are terrorists. ... [T]he pensions march in central London was sealed off with three-metre steel walls, meaning that no-one except for those marching could see what was happening or read the banners. The protesters were, in other words, prevented from explaining their purpose to the public. (Monbiot, 2012, p. 26)

These examples indicate how fears about security erode democratic processes, and frustrate the attempts by citizens to find collective expressions for their grievances. There are real dangers that these forms of creeping authoritarianism gradually expand and affect the fabric of societies. It is ironic that this should be happening at the very time when movements to overthrow police states were bringing revolution to developing Arab countries.

But the effects of these slow and insidious subversions of liberty and a proportionate response to dissent and non-conformity are not confined to the political sphere. In some states in the United States, the police are now routinely involved in keeping order in schools, even arresting pupils for minor infractions in school rules which are not offences in the outside world, such as throwing paper aeroplanes or failing to pick up crumbs from the canteen floor. Police, some with dogs, patrol the corridors and playgrounds of state schools, issuing tickets to those seen as disruptive or disobedient, including over 1,000 primary school pupils in the previous six years.

'Each day, hundreds of schoolchildren appear before courts in Texas charged with offences such as swearing, misbehaving on the school bus or getting in to a punch-up in the playground. Children have been arrested for possessing cigarettes, wearing "inappropriate" clothes and being late for school' (McGreal, 2012, p. 8).

There are at least two dangers for social work in this authoritarian drift. First, it creates a culture of oppressive regulation in the public sector itself, which is bound to infect practice, for instance, in juvenile justice. Practitioners are implicated in policies which deploy authority in these heavy-handed ways. This is ironic because the heyday of optimism and expansion of social work in the United Kingdom was in the 1960s and early 1970s, when it was associated with the overthrow of a similar paranoid authoritarianism that had prevailed at the height of the Cold War, and with the reform of juvenile justice systems in England and Scotland (Packman, 1968, 1976). Social work was especially instrumental in the reform of oppressive and abusive regimes, such as those in some Approved Schools in the 1950s and beyond (Milham *et al.*, 1970).

Second, the intergenerational injustices analysed in Chapter 5 cannot be corrected unless young people are free to mobilise, both to protest against them and to organise in their own interests. We have argued that social workers should support such mobilisations, and this means offering constructive criticism with police strategies, not simply going along with them.

If the crisis represents an opportunity for a new kind of social order, even against a background of austerity, it is important that the police do not use fears about security as a rationalisation for heavy-handed control or discriminatory tactics against minority youth. Even if government policy does little to reduce these tendencies in policing, social work can play a part in criticising and changing them, as they are likely to be counterproductive in the long run.

New social movements? The precariat and the 'squeezed middle'

In democracies, no political movement or party can hope to succeed unless it is able to command support from a broad section of people with incomes just above and below the average for that society. During the Third Way era, this is exactly what Bill Clinton and Tony Blair, along with their equivalents in Australia and New Zealand, and their imitators in social democratic parties in Europe, were able to do. But Third Way policies were, as we have shown, founded on economic orthodoxies which are now discredited; they fostered the growth of bubbles in house prices and in other assets, excessive consumer credit and overblown financial sectors using smoke and mirror methods and Ponzi schemes to create the illusion of growing prosperity.

Parties of the centre-left have been slow to adapt to the new situation, and have suffered electoral setbacks in most of the affluent countries. Indeed, the groupings which have seemed to gain most from the crisis have been extreme market-minded ones, such as the Tea Party in the United States, or nationalist, xenophobic and anti-EU ones like the True Finns, who almost drove the Social Democrats into third place in the general election in Finland in the spring of 2010, or UKIP in the United Kingdom.

Because centre-left parties adopted a businesslike, managerialist approach to policy and public administration in the Third Way period, it has been difficult for them to shift towards an attempt to mobilise the potential forces for social change. Indeed, politicians like Tony Blair and Gordon Brown were suspicious of political activism, far preferring to cast citizens as consumers, and the governments as technicians to organise systems of incentives and sanctions which would steer them into socially desirable pathways.

In the post-crash world, people resent the absence of a political leadership that expresses their feelings of betrayal and their resentment against the few who have gained from the crisis – often those most to blame for its onset. In the United Kingdom, politics itself has been discredited, with all politicians compromised by revelations of their venality and their excessive obeisance to media overlords.

Many of the economic and social developments foreseen in this book are likely to arise spontaneously, through grass-roots informal groups and organised associations at a local level, in response to the crisis situation. But the two major changes in social policy – the Basic Income scheme and National Care Service – which we recommend require national political leadership of a kind which has been absent since the crash. In the United Kingdom, Labour's leading figures continue to repeat the same tired mantras about being tough on welfare cheats and promoting jobs and growth (Byrne, 2012).

This is in contrast with the politics of the age in which welfare states were founded in Europe (Judt, 2010, chapter 3). In the United Kingdom, austerity was considerably more constraining than in our times, yet the Labour leadership was able to mobilise support for the sacrifices which had to be made to invest in new systems to redistribute income and supply the services for health, secondary education, decent housing and social care to all citizens. This was possible because people on the middle range of earnings were open to persuasion that they, and above all their children, would benefit from these investments – as in fact they did.

We have argued that the arguments for the Basic Income are likely to emerge from protest movements of young people, and from other members of the 'precariat' who lack regular, secure, full-time work and career prospects (Standing, 2011). But to be successful, campaigns for national implementation need to win support from older cohorts in more favourable situations, in terms of employment and earnings. At present only the Green Party in the United Kingdom is attempting to make the case for this new approach as a long-term basis for economic and social transformation.

It is a reproach to politicians in the affluent countries that pilot projects and media discussion of Basic Income are more a feature of developing economies than affluent ones. For example, Guy Standing was interviewed for the *Times of India* about current reforms of that country's income maintenance system, and the political obstacles to the Basic Income approach. He pointed out the unsuitability of both targeted and social insurance schemes for replacing existing price subsidies, and recommended a series of carefully conducted pilot projects.

He was asked about the consequences of the pilot in one district of Namibia, and explained how school attendance there had risen dramatically, use of medical clinics went up, as did numbers of HIV patients taking medication, women's status improved, crime rates fell and income equality increased. Standing argued that poor people in India would be enabled to pay off their debts and buy means for petty production under a pilot project there, such as one which was currently being carried out in Delhi (Citizens Income Newsletter, 2012, p. 5).

It could hardly be argued that India and Namibia are better placed to implement a Basic Income scheme than their affluent counterparts; nor could it be maintained that the latter's tax-benefits systems currently function effectively. Yet their willingness to debate this proposal in the press, and to hold trials of its effects, puts more prosperous states, their politicians and media, to shame. If developing countries adopt this approach, it could add to their advantages in competing with the old colonial powers of the West.

We have argued that the reforms of the tax-benefit system initiated by the coalition government in the United Kingdom point in the right direction. But they have been marred by mean-spirited cuts – most notably upper limits in rates of housing benefits, time limits on contributions-related Employment and Support Allowance, the abolition of Disability Living Allowance and its replacement by a less generous scheme, and the imposition of an absolute cap on benefits – which were not in the original blueprint (CSJ, 2009).

As yet, there is no sign of a concerted social movement to press the authorities in the interests of the 'squeezed middle'. It is only in Greece, under the impact of extreme austerity measures, that this potential political force has taken to the streets. But there are some signs in the United Kingdom that a movement might emerge, for instance, in the indignation expressed over the coalition's bungled attempt to remove child benefit for all households with a member on the higher rate of income tax (while leaving eligibility for those with two or more earners just short of this level). Such issues might serve to create a groundswell of protest among hitherto acquiescent or resigned voters.

There is also the possibility that the Labour Party leadership will finally recognise the opportunities presented by the crisis (Kelly, 2011). Already in early 2012 Ed Miliband had begun to criticise 'predatory capitalism', and to develop a case for a 'responsible capitalism' which adopts the High Pay Commission's proposals on executive salaries and attempts to build a culture of probity and moderation in board rooms. In this he must have been influenced and sustained by the campaigns of activist groups of young protesters, such as UK Uncut's against tax avoidance, Occupy's against the banks and the City, and London Citizens' for fair pay.

The other major policy issue over which national solidarity is required is one around which it is more difficult to mobilise mass support. Funding for care in old age is one of those issues that people prefer not to think about, discounting the future likely costs of needing assistance or expensive residential provision. Attempts to reach cross-party consensus broke down before the 2010 election, leaving the United Kingdom's system notably more chaotic and restrictive in its scope than those of Germany, the Netherlands and the Nordic countries.

Again, giving unequivocal support to the recommendations of the Dilnot Commission would allow the Labour Party to take a lead in raising awareness about a pressing social crisis. Here it is scandals about neglect and suffering rather than angry protests that are likely to persuade the leadership to take such a stance.

Professional development

Another theme of the book, which is common to all the social services, is the organisational structures for the practice of work with people. We have argued that in the Third Way era these were remodelled according to a business blueprint which was inappropriate for their tasks. In the United Kingdom, this took the form of detailed and prescriptive guidance, externally set targets and outcomes, management surveillance, extensive electronic recording and form filling, and an approach to interactions with service users that was procedural and mechanistic (Jordan, 2010). This environment was limiting for teachers, nurses and other health and social care professionals as well as social workers.

This was where government policy impacted on the very nature of the human service professions, and consciously tried to mould them in the directions of its model for the regulation of society, derived from the economic orthodoxy of the time. It created organisations which directly entered their work to shape the forms of intervention and styles of response adopted by those meeting the public face to face. As Eileen Munro in her interim report on child protection put it in relation to this branch of practice:

> It is important to see the quality of any one social worker's performance as not just being due to their expertise but arising from the interaction between what they bring to the job and the aspects of the work environment that make it easier or harder for them to exercise that expertise ... The lessons learned in other safety critical areas of work such as health and aviation show that studying the interplay between workers and the work environment is the most productive way of improving standards and reducing errors. (Munro, 2011, sec. 3.2, p. 35)

She went on to suggest that the basis for practice in these agencies had shifted from understanding and working with emotions to a 'managerialist', 'rational–technical' one, collecting information and making plans, often to refer on to other organisations rather than engage in direct work.

The approach had become formulaic, counting incidents as means of assessing situations, rather than attending to the quality of relationships, and communicating both challenge and support. She quoted Klein (2000) in recommending a version of human service expertise which used the professional's intuitive understanding and emotional responses, derived from parts of the brain little engaged in calculation or abstract reasoning, in the analysis of relationships and in communicating with family members (Munro, 2011, secs 3.3–3.19, pp. 33–9).

These recommendations apply to a far broader range of human services, where staff have been strongly influenced by the shift in organisational cultures which has taken place over the past 20 years. Hospitals and schools have also become 'rational–technical' in their methods, and sometimes formulaic in the ways they performed their tasks. The evidence of neglect amounting to inhumanity from some of the hospital enquiries and inspections noted in Chapter 4 indicates that a change of approach is urgently required.

But we have argued that all this was exacerbated by the other feature of this model of government and the reform of public services, the emphasis on individual choice and 'personalisation'. Far from increasing autonomy in a way consistent with freedom and democracy, it was essentially a means of rule (Rose, 1996) in which citizens were encouraged to see themselves as self-responsible and self-developmental individuals, and to neglect their roles as active members of civil society and democratic systems of governance. It also promoted a myopic focus on individual skills, capabilities, health and welfare, at the expense of the flourishing that can only be derived from engagement with others in associations and communities.

The result has been a neglect of cultural features of social life and in the functioning of organisations, as well as of group and community work among social workers. As research has increasingly traced social problems and conflicts in the United Kingdom to excessive individualism (Layard and Dunn, 2009; Unwin, 2009), this has meant that professional practice in the public services has if anything reinforced this weakness rather than offset it.

The crisis is changing all this. Starting with the young generation, collective action is growing, both to counter the effects of austerity on people's lives and to resist some of the more damaging aspects of government policy. So the direction of professional development should also be towards a new attention to the advantages of collective engagement in the meeting of needs, the improvement of well-being and protection against risks. This also implies that professionals should make themselves more accountable to groups and communities, rather than to managers and inspectors.

We have argued that this would also point human services in the direction of sustainability, because it would start to break the link between the public sector and the economic model of growth and job creation. Instead, it would orientate them towards improvements in quality of life which could be achieved by cooperation and the better use of the energies and abilities of ordinary people.

The public services are always being exhorted to increase their efficiency, but the biggest wastefulness in their organisation stems from the attempt to make them like businesses. This implies that they produce and 'deliver' services in 'packages' to individual 'consumers', in forms that can be used in a single act of ingestion, like fast food. But this model, which has underpinned the vast expansion of service industries that has emanated from the United States in the past 50 years, may be appropriate for the profitability of these enterprises, but it is certainly not suitable for the public sector at a time when prosperity without growth is the requirement of policy.

A far more efficient and effective way of working is to engage with those who are active in a field of need or value creation to help them build upon their own shared capabilities, and iron out problems. But to work in this way demands a flexibility and openness, as well as a humility, which has not been fashionable in these services over recent years. It needs professional staff to give up some of the ways they protect themselves from the demands of everyday interaction with ordinary people, in exchange for being relieved of the constant pressure to fill in forms and complete checklists.

It also requires staff to defy expectations that they will take the side of authority against the protests of the younger generation in particular – to act as if they were in Tunisia in 2011, or the Czech Republic in 1989, rather than trying to clamp down on legitimate frustration. If this is really a moment for potential transformation, it is important to be open to opportunities to help these processes unfold.

Redistributing power

The ruling elites of the affluent countries have for at least three centuries come to expect to dominate the world, and to negotiate as equals only with each other. The crisis has forced them to recognise that the rising new industrial powers, China, India, Brazil and South Africa, along with Russia, must now be regarded as at least of comparable significance in the global economy, and actually in better shape to withstand the challenges of the situation. The sight of the eurozone governments seeking the assistance of these states in constructing a bailout package in October 2011 was a sufficiently humbling one to drive this message home.

But there is a danger that the governments of the affluent countries will try to compensate for their loss of dominance in the world economy, and their lack of instruments to capture the resources of global corporations for their national economies, by bearing down more heavily on their own populations. By the middle of January 2012, credit rating agencies were signalling that austerity measures were not enough to satisfy bond markets and that sovereign debt in the eurozone was a good long-term bet. Imbalances within and between these economies, and the lack of competitiveness of some, were of equal relevance. The affluent countries, and the financial sectors they fostered as the engines of their economic systems, were the infected parts of an ailing interdependent world; they had to find their own remedies for their symptoms of distress.

We have argued that the attempt to ratchet up pressure on citizens to work harder, for longer but more 'flexibly' and for lower pay, under the direction of an apparatus of officialdom, is not the answer. Citizens need more power and control over their lives, not less, and they need to look to each other, not to the surveillance of officials, to find opportunities to thrive. Social work should be part of this empowerment, and social policy should enable it through schemes such as Basic Income.

There is no single solution to the problems of insolvent banks and governments, because these take different forms – housing bubbles in the United States, Spain and Ireland, imprudent loans to other countries' banks in Germany, Austria and Japan, financial trickery and self-delusion in the City of London and excessive personal borrowing in the United Kingdom – and corrections will take time. The important thing is for governments not to ruin the chances of their societies recovering their poise, and discovering new approaches to sustainable well-being, by trying to control them in obsessive ways.

The Conservative Party's election manifesto of 2010 pledged to redistribute power and resources from the state to individuals and communities. In its first two years in office, the coalition government did not show many signs of doing this. People are going to have to organise to take power over their lives, by looking to their own pooled resources and shared energies.

The notion that they have the initiative and ideas to do this productively is not just wishful thinking, as the experience of Ireland during the crisis illustrates. Since its sovereign debt became too great to finance on bond markets, the government has been tied into damaging austerity measures by the European Central Bank and the IMF. Its 2011 budget details were scrutinised by the Bundestag (the German parliament) before they were seen by the Dáil (the Irish parliament).

But in spite of this, some parts of the Irish economy have been flourishing. The country has become a hub for the social media and social networking industries, with large companies such as Microsoft and Facebook establishing major sites there, and new Irish enterprises springing into existence. In all, the sector employs hundreds of thousands of employees, and is anticipated to supply 40 per cent of the new jobs to be created in the next two years (BBC World Service, *News Briefing*, 14 January 2012).

This success owes much to the good educational standards achieved by young people in Ireland, and their use of social media for networking amongst themselves. But it also shows that the way forward, even under the most oppressive regime of austerity, lies in liberating the potential of this generation.

Perhaps the most radical consequence of the crisis has been that it opened a debate about the moral implications of capitalism which seemed to have been closed when the Soviet empire collapsed. It had come to be assumed that market processes and outcomes were ethically justifiable, and that, even if the philosophical arguments of Hayek and his school of thought (Shand, 1990) were flawed, there was no coherent alternative. As the crisis developed, and especially as the greed of investment bankers and company board members became notorious among the huge majority whose living standards were declining, capitalism itself came under scrutiny.

This was in no small part a result of the Occupy protests in major cities of the affluent world, which explicitly questioned capitalism's moral credentials in ways that were mocked at first by the media, but gradually gained purchase. By the middle of January 2012, the UK prime minister and leader of the opposition were almost simultaneously making speeches about the ethical flaws in capitalist systems, how to ensure that markets were made compatible with morality, and the need to restore confidence in the fairness of the economy (*The Guardian*, 20 January 2012).

We have argued that no such cleansing of capitalism can be achieved without a radical transformation of the institutions of social policy, and a cultural transformation of society. The Basic Income proposal which we recommend would supply a new ethical basis for income, and ultimately for property, and it would empower citizens as members of the political community. For this reason, it would be resisted by many vested interests, including some in the social policy community itself. What would emerge from this struggle would be something very different from the version envisaged by the marginal tinkering proposed by David Cameron and Ed Miliband in their speeches.

Social work, we have suggested, has a potentially important part to play in such a transformation, and much to gain from it. We hope it can regain its confidence in the mission to build a better society.

References

Abrams, F. (2002), *Below the Breadline: Life on the Minimum Wage*, London: Profile Books.

Ackerman, B. and Alstott, A. (1990), *The Shareholder Society*, New Haven, CT: Yale University Press.

Al Khalili, J. (2010), *The Secret World of Chaos*, BBC2 TV, 11 February.

Ashdown, P. (1988), *Citizens' Britain*, London: Fourth Estate.

Atkinson, A.B. (1995), *Public Economics in Action: The Basic Income/Flat Tax Proposal*, Oxford: Oxford University Press.

BBC Radio 4 (2009), *File on Four*, 3 November.

BBC Radio 4 (2010), *News*, 11 March.

BBC Radio 4 (2011a), *Today*, 21 November.

BBC Radio 4 (2011b), *News*, 29 November.

BBC1 TV (2011), *Panorama*, 11 November.

BBC2 TV (2011), *Analysis*, 29 November.

BBC Radio 4 (2012), *Analysis: Why Have Wages Not Been Keeping Up with Profits?*, 20 February.

BBC2 TV (2011), *Watched over by Machines of Loving Grace*, 23 August.

Bank of England (2010), *Quarterly Bulletin*, 2nd quarter.

Barry, B. (1989), *Theories of Justice*, Berkeley, CA: University of California Press.

Barry, B. (1999), 'Sustainability and Intergenerational Justice', in A. Dobson (ed.), *Fairness and Futurity*, Oxford: Oxford University Press.

BASW (2003), *Code of Ethics for Social Workers*, Birmingham: BASW.

Baumol. W. (1967), 'The Macroeconomics of Unbalanced Growth', *American Economic Review*, 57, pp. 415–26.

Baumol, W., Batey-Blackman, S. and Wolf, E. (1985), 'Unbalanced Growth Revisited; Asymptotic Stagnancy and New Evidence', *American Economic Review*, 75, pp. 806–17.

Beck, U. and Beck-Gernsheim, E. (1995), *The Normal Chaos of Love*, Cambridge: Polity.

Beck, U. and Beck-Gernsheim, E. (2002), *Individualization*, London: Sage.

Becker, G.S. (1996), *Accounting for Tastes*, Cambridge, MA: Harvard University Press.

Behrens, M. and Evans, K. (2002) 'Taking Control of their Lives? A Comparison of the Experiences of Unemployed Young Adults (18–24) in England and the New Germany', *Comparative Education*, 38(1).

Belloc, H. (1912), *The Servile State*, London: T.N. Foulis.

Belloc, H. (1924), *Economics for Helen*, London: J.W. Arrowsmith.

Beveridge, W. (1942), *Social Insurance and Allied Services*, Cm 6804, London: HMSO.

BIEN Newsflash (2010) 11 November.

BIEN Newsflash (2010) 10 December.

Blond, P. (2009a), 'The New Conservatism Can Create a Capitalism that Works for the Poor', *The Guardian*, 3 July, p. 33.

Blond, P. (2009b), 'Without a Concept of Virtue our Politics and our Banks are Doomed', *The Independent*, 1 June.

Blond, P. (2009c), 'Rise of the Red Tories', *Prospect Magazine*, 28 February, issue 155.

Blond, P. (2010), *Red Tory: How Left and Right Have Broken Britain and How We Can Fix It*, London: Faber and Faber.

Boehm, C. (1982), 'The Evolutionary Development of Morality as an Effect of Dominance Behaviour and Conflict Interference', *Journal of Social and Biological Structure*, 5, pp. 413–21.

Boehm, C. (1993), 'Egalitarian and Reverse Dominance Hierarchy', *Current Anthropology*, 34(3), pp. 227–54.

Bolton, P. and Dewatripont, M. (2005), *Contract Theory*, Cambridge, MA: MIT Press.

Botkin, D.B. (1990), *Discordant Harmonies: The New Ecology for the 21st Century*, Oxford: Oxford University Press.

Bourdillon, A.F.C. (ed.) (1945), *Voluntary Social Services: Their Place in the Modern State*, London: Methuen.

Bowles, S. and Gintis, H. (2002), 'Social Capital and Community Governance', *Economic Journal*, 112(483), pp. F419–36.

Bowles, S., Choi, J.-K. and Hopfensitz, A. (2003), 'The Co-evolution of Individual Behaviours and Social Institutions', *Journal of Theoretical Biology*, 223, pp. 135–47.

Boyd, R. and Richerson, P.J. (1985), *Culture and the Evolutionary Process*, Chicago, IL: Chicago University Press.

Bradshaw, J., Hoelscher, P. and Richardson, D. (2007), 'An Index of Child Well-being in the European Union 25', *Journal of Social Indicators Research*, 80, pp. 133–77.

Brittan, S. (1976), 'The Economic Contradictions in Democracy', in A. King (ed.), *Why Is Britain Becoming Harder to Govern?*, London: British Broadcasting Corporation.

Brittan, S. (1995), *Capitalism with a Human Face*, Cheltenham: Edward Elgar.

Brown, G. (2010), *After the Crash: Recovering from the First Crisis of Globalisation*, London: Simon and Schuster.

Brundtland Commission (1987), *Our Common Future*, Oxford: Oxford University Press.

Buchanan, J.M. (1965), 'An Economic Theory of Clubs', *Economica*, 32, pp. 1–14.

Buchanan, J.M. (1978), *The Economics of Politics*, London: Institute of Economic Affairs.

Buchanan, J.M. and Tullock, G. (1962), *The Calculus of Consent: Logical Foundations of Constitutional Democracy*, Ann Arbor, MI: University of Michigan Press.

Bynner, J. and Parsons, S. (2003), 'Social Participation, Values and Crime', in E. Ferri, J. Bynner and M. Wadsworth (eds) *Changing Britain, Changing Lives: Three Generations at the Turn of the Century*, London: Institute of Education, pp. 261–94.

Byrne, L. (2012) 'A William Beveridge for the New Century: Labour Won't Win on Welfare Reform by Default. On Jobs and Benefits We Need another Tough-Minded Social Revolution', *The Guardian*, 2 January.

Cameron, D. (2009), 'The Big Society', Hugo Young Memorial Lecture, London, 10 November.

Cameron, D. (2010), 'Labour are Now the Reactionaries, We are the Radicals – as this Promise Shows', *The Guardian*, 9 April.

Canovan, M. (1977), *G.K. Chesterton: Radical Populist*, New York: Harcourt Brace Jovanovich.

Care Quality Commission (2011), *The State of Health Care and Adult Social Care in England: An Overview of Key Themes in Care in 2010/11*, London: Care Quality Commission.

Caroleo, F.E. and Pastore, F. (2003), 'Youth Participation in the Labour Market in Germany, Spain and Sweden', in T. Hammer (ed.), *Youth Unemployment and Social Exclusion in Europe: A Comparative Study*, Bristol: Policy Press.

Centre for Social Policy (CSJ) (2006), *Breakdown Britain* (6 vols), London: CSJ.

Centre for Social Justice (CSJ) (2009), *Dynamic Benefits: Towards Welfare that Works*, London: Centre for Social Justice.

Channel 4 TV (2011), *News*, 21 November.

Checkland, S.G. and Checkland, E.O.A. (eds) (1974), *The Poor Law Report of 1834*, Harmondsworth: Penguin.

Chesterton, G.K. (1904), *Heretics*, London: John Lane.

Chesterton, G. K. (1919), *Irish Impressions*, London: Leonard Parsons.

Chesterton, G.K. (1926), *The Outline of Sanity*, Leipzig: Bernard Tauchnitz.

Citizens Income Newsletter (2012), Interview with Guy Standing in *The Times of India*, January.

Clarke, J. and Newman, J. (1997), *The Managerial State: Power, Politics and Ideology in the Remaking of Social Welfare*, London: Sage.

Clarke, J. and Newman, J. (2004), 'Governing the Modern World', in D.L. Steinberg and R. Johnson (eds), *Blairism and the War of Persuasion: Labour's Passive Revolution*, London: Lawrence and Wishart.

Cole, G.D.H. (1920), *Guild Socialism Restated*, London: Methuen.

Cole, G.D.H (1921), *Social Theory*, London: Cassell.

Cole, G.D.H. (1945), 'A Retrospective of the History of Voluntary Social Service' in A.F.C. Bourdillon, (ed.), *Voluntary Social Services: Their Role in the Modern State*, London: Methuen, pp. 11–30.

Conservative Party (2010), *An Invitation to Join the Government of Britain*, (Election Manifesto), London: Conservative Party.

Coote, A. and Franklin, J. (2009), *Green Well Fair: Three Economies for Social Justice*, London: New Economic Foundation.

Cormack, U. (1945), 'Developments in Casework', in A.F.C. Bourdillon (ed.), *Voluntary Social Services: Their Role in the Modern State, London: Methuen*

Cox, R.H. (1998), 'From Safety Nets to Trampolines', *Governance*, 18(1), pp. 28–47.

Craig, G. (2010), '"Flexibility", Xenophobia and Modern Slavery in the UK', in I. Greener, C. Holden and M. Kilkey (eds), *Social Policy Review*, Bristol: Policy Press, pp. 173–98.

Cruikshank, B. (1994), 'The Will to Empower: Technologies of Citizenship and the War on Poverty', *Socialist Review*, 23(4), pp. 29–55.

Daily Mail (2012), 'It Is My Human Right Not to Work for Poundland: Graduate who Faced Losing Benefit Sues Minister', 12 January.

Daily Telegraph (2011), 'Hospitals being Charged "Extortionate" Sums by PFI Firms to Carry out Basic DIY Jobs', 23 December.

De-Shalit, A. (1995), *Why Posterity Matters*, London: Routledge.

Dilnot Commission (2011), *Fairer Funding for All: Report of the Commission on Funding of Care and Support*, London: Department of Health.

Department of Health (DoH) (1998), *Modernising Social Services: Promoting Independence, Improving Protection, Raising Standards*, Cm 4169, London: HMSO.

Dominelli, L. (1988), *Anti-Racist Social Work*, London: Macmillan.

Douglas, C.H. (1919), *Economic Democracy*, London: Cecil Palmer.

Douglas, C.H. (1920), *Credit-Power and Democracy*, London: Cecil Palmer.

Douglas, C.H. (1931), *The Monopoly of Credit*, London: Chapman and Hall.

Douglas, M. (1970), *Natural Symbols*, London: Barrie and Rockliffe.

Douglas, M. (1987), *How Institutions Think*, London: Routledge and Kegan Paul.

Department of Social Security (DSS) (1998), *A New Contract for Welfare*, Cm 3805, London: Stationery Office.

Drakeford, M. (1997), *Social Movements and Their Supporters: The Greenshirts in England*, London:

Drakeford, M. (2000), *Privatisation and Social Policy*, London: Longman.

Drakeford, M. (2006), 'Ownership, Regulation and the Public Interest: The Case of Residential Care for Older People', *Critical Social Policy*, 26(4), pp. 932–44.

Drakeford, M. and Gregory, L. (2008), 'Anti-Poverty Practice and the Changing World of Credit Unions: New Tools for Social Workers', *Practice: Social Work in Action*, 20(2), pp. 141–50.

Driver, S. and Martell, L. (1998), 'New Labour's Communitarianisms', *Critical Social Policy*, 17(52), pp. 27–56.

Duncan Smith, I. (2009), Preface to CSJ, *Dynamic Benefits: Towards Welfare that Works*, London: CSJ.

Durkheim, E. (1898), 'Individualism and the Intellectuals', *Revue Bleu*, 4(10), pp. 7–11.

Ehrenreich, B. (2002), *Nickel and Dimed: Undercover in Low-Wage America*, London: Granta Books.

Elshtain, J.B. (1981), *Public Man, Private Woman: Women in Social and Political Thought*, Oxford: Martin Robertson.

Elshtain, J.B. (1998), 'Antigone's Daughters', in A. Phillips (ed.) *Feminism and Politics*, Oxford: Oxford University Press, pp. 369–81.

Enthoven, A. (1985), *Reflections on the Management of the National Health Service*, London: Nuffield Provincial Hospitals Trust.

Equality and Human Rights Commission (2011).

Ertürk, I., Froud, J., Suchdev, J., Leaver, A., Moran, M. and Williams, K. (2011), *City State against National Settlement: UK Economic Policy and Politics after the Financial Crisis*, London: Centre for Research in Socio-Cultural Change, Working Paper 101.

Esping-Andersen, G. (1990), *The Three Worlds of Welfare Capitalism*, Cambridge: Polity Press.

Etzioni, A. (1992), *The Spirit of Community: The Re-invention of American Society*, NY: Touchstone.

Financial Services Authority (2011), *FSA Fines HSBC £10.5 million for Mis-selling Products to Elderly Customers*, FSA/PN/105/2011, 5 December.

Frank, R.H. (1995), 'Does Money Buy Happiness?', in F.A. Huppert, N. Bayliss and B. Keverne (eds), *The Science of Well-being*, Oxford: Oxford University Press pp. 461–74.

Frank, R.H. (2011), *The Darwin Economy: Liberty, Competition and the Common Good*, Princeton, NJ: Princeton University Press.

Frey, B. and Stutzer, A. (2002), *Happiness and Economics: How the Economy and Institutions Affect Well-being*, Princeton, NJ: Princeton University Press.

Fitzpatrick, T. (1999), *Freedom and Security: An Introduction to the Basic Income Debate*, London: Macmillan.

Fitzpatrick, T. (2003), *After the New Social Democracy: Social Welfare for the Twenty-First Century*, Manchester: Manchester University Press.

Fleckenstein W.A. and Sheehan, F. (2008), *Greenspan's Bubbles; The Age of Ignorance at the Federal Reserve*, NY: McGraw Hill.

Foldvary, F. (1994), *Public Goods and Private Communities: The Market Provision of Social Services*, Aldershot: Edward Elgar.

Fook, J., Ryan, M. and Hawkins, L. (2000), *Professional Expertise: Practice, Theory and Education for Working in Uncertainty*, London: Whiting and Birch.

Fraser, N. (2000), 'Rethinking Recognition', *New Left Review*, 2nd Series, 3, pp. 107–20.

Giddens, A. (1991), *Modernity and Self-Identity: Self and Society in the Late Modern Age*, Cambridge: Polity.

Giddens, A. (1998), *The Third Way: The Renewal of Social Democracy*, Cambridge: Polity.

Gilligan, C. (1982), *In a Different Voice*, Cambridge, MA: Harvard University Press.

GMB (2011a), *GMB Response to Reports that 200 Southern Cross Care Homes May Close as It Seeks £100 Million to Prevent Collapse*, 16 March.

GMB (2011b), *Four Seasons Healthcare Accounts for 2010: How Earnings (EBITARM) of £8,408 per Resident per annum to Pay Interest on £790 million Loans and Rents*, 4 October.

Goffman, E. (1967), *Interaction Ritual: Essays in Face-to-Face Behaviour*, NY: Doubleday Anchor.

Glasman, M., Rutherford, J., Stears, M. and White, S. (2011), *The Labour Tradition and the Politics of Paradox*, London: Lawrence and Wishart.

Gough, I. (1979), *The Political Economy of the Welfare State*, London: Macmillan.

Gough, I. et al. (eds) (2004), *Insecurity and Welfare Regimes in Asia, Africa and Latin America : Social Policy in Development Contexts*, Oxford: Oxford University Press.

Gregory, L. and Drakeford, M. (2006), *Social Work*, Asset-Based Welfare and the Child Trust Fund,' *British Journal of Social Work*, 36(1), 149–57.

Haldane, A.G. and May, R.M. (2011), 'Systemic Risk in Banking Ecosystems', *Nature*, 469, 20 January, pp. 367–85.

Harding, R. (2011), 'Pay Gap Threatens US Recovery', *Financial Times*, 15 December.

Hayek, F.A. (1960), *The Constitution of Liberty*, London: Routledge and Kegan Paul.

Healthcare Commission (2009), *Investigation into Mid-Staffordshire NHS Trust*. London: Healthcare Commission.

Helliwell, J.F. (2003), 'How's Life? Combining Individual and National Variables to Explain Subjective Well-being', *Economic Modelling*, 20, pp. 331–60.

Hirschman, A.O. (1981), *Essays in Trespassing: Economics to Politics and Beyond*, Cambridge: Cambridge University Press.

Hobhouse, L.T. (1922), *The Elements of Social Justice*, London: Cassell.

Holman, B. (1998), *Faith in the Poor*, Oxford: Lion Publishing.

Holman, B. (2002), *Faith in the Poor*, Lyme Regis: Russell House.

Honneth, A. (1995), *The Struggle for Recognition*, Cambridge: Polity.

Honneth, A. (2001), 'Recognition or Redistribution? Changing Perspectives on the Moral Order of Society', *Theory, Culture and Society*, 18(2–3), pp. 43–55.

Hudson, B. (2005), 'Not a Cigarette Paper Between Us: Integrated Inspection of Children's Services in England', *Social Policy and Administration*, 39(5), pp. 513–27.

Hutchinson, F. and Burkitt, B. (1997), *The Political Economy of Social Credit*, London: Routledge.

Inman, P. (2011a), 'Baby Boomers Must Do Their Bit for Britain's Economy', *The Guardian*, 3 January.

Inman, P. (2011b), 'No Country for Young Workers', *The Guardian*, 5 September, p. 24.

Innocenti Report Card 7 (2007), *Child Poverty in Perspective: An Overview of Child Well-being in Rich Countries*, Florence: UNICEF.

Institute for Fiscal Studies (IFS) (2012), *The Impact of Austerity Measures on Households*, London: IFS/Family and Parenting Institute.

Investigation into Mid Staffordshire NHS Foundation Trust www.parliament.uk/deposits/depositedpapers/ ... /DEP2009–0861.pdf

Jackson, T. (2009), *Prosperity Without Growth: Economics for a Finite Planet*, London: Earthscan.

Jamieson, L. (1998), *Intimacy: Personal Relationships in Modern Societies*, Cambridge: Polity.

Jenkins, S. (2011a), 'Without a Growth Plan, the EU Faces Financial Waterloo', *The Guardian*, 28 September, p. 27.

Jenkins, S. (2011b), *The Guardian*, 'Without a Growth Plan, the EU Faces Waterloo', 28 September.

Johnson, J., Rolph, S. and Smith, R. (2010), 'Uncovering History: Private Care Homes for Older people in England', *Journal of Social Policy*, 39(2), pp. 235–53.

Jordan, B. (1972), *The Social Worker in Family Situations*, London: Routledge and Kegan Paul.

Jordan, B. (1973), *Paupers: The Making of the New Claiming Class*, London: Routledge and Kegan Paul.

Jordan, B. (1974), *Poor Parents: Social Policy and the Cycle of Deprivation*, London: Routledge and Kegan Paul.

Jordan, B. (1976), *Freedom and the Welfare State*, London: Routledge and Kegan Paul.

Jordan, B. (1985), *The State: Authority and Autonomy*, Oxford: Blackwell.

Jordan, B. (1996), *A Theory of Poverty and Social Exclusion*, Cambridge: Polity.

Jordan, B. (1998), *The New Politics of Welfare: Social Policy in a Global Context*, London: Sage.

Jordan, B. (2001), 'Soziale Arbeit in Osteuropa', in H.-U. Otto and H. Thierisch (eds), *Handbuch Sozialarbeit und Sozialpadogogic*, Kriftel: Luchterhand, pp. 1637–43.

Jordan, B. (2006), *Social Policy for the Twenty-First Century: New Perspectives, Big Issues*. Cambridge: Polity.

Jordan, B. (2007), *Social Work and Well-being*, Lyme Regis: Russell House.

Jordan, B. (2008), *Welfare and Well-being: Social Value in Public Policy*, Bristol: Policy Press.

Jordan, B. (2010), *Why the Third Way Failed: Economics, Morality and the Origins of the 'Big Society'*, Bristol: Policy Press.

Jordan, B., James, S., Kay, H. and Redley, M. (1991), *Trapped in Poverty? Labour-Market Decisions in Low-Income Households*, London: Routledge.

Jordan, B., Redley, M. and James, S. (1994), *Putting the Family First: Identities, Decisions, Citizenship*, London: UCL Press.

Jordan, B. with Jordan, C. (2000), *Social Work and the Third Way: Tough Love as Social Policy*, London: Sage.

Judt, T. (2010), *Postwar: A History of Europe since 1945*, London: Vintage.

Kahneman, D., Diener, E. and Schwartz, N. (eds) (1999), *Well-Being: The Foundations of Hedonic Psychology*, NY: Russell Sage Foundation.

Keen, S. (2011a), *Debunking Economics: The Naked Emperor of the Social Sciences*, Sydney: Zed Books.

Keen, S. (2011b), Interview, *The Guardian*, 21 November.

Keynes, J.M. (1936), *A General Theory of Employment, Interest and Money*, London: Macmillan.

Kindleberger, C. (1967), *Europe's Post-War Growth: The Role of Labour Supply*, Cambridge, MA: Harvard University Press.

Kelly, G. (2011), 'Why the Squeezed Middle is Here to Stay', *The Observer*, 22 May.

King, A. (ed.) (1976), *Why Is Britain Becoming Harder to Govern?* London: British Broadcasting Corporation.

Laffont, J.J. and Martimort, D. (2002), *The Theory of Incentives: The Principal–Agent Model*, Princeton, NJ: Princeton University Press.

Lane, R.E. (2000), *The Loss of Happiness in Market Democracies*, New Haven, CT: Yale University Press.

Layard, R. (2005), *Happiness: Lessons from a New Science*, London: Allen Lane.

Layard, R. and Dunn, J. (2009), *A Good Childhood: Searching for Values in a Competitive Age*, London: Good Childhood Enquiry/Penguin.

Lewis, W.A. (1954), 'Development with Unlimited Supplies of Labour', *Manchester School*, 22, pp. 159–91.

Liebe, M. and Pollock, A. (2009), 'The Experience of the Private Finance Initiative in the UK's National Health Service', Edinburgh: Centre for International Public Health Policy.

Lister, R. (1997), *Citizenship: Feminist Perspectives*, Basingstoke: Palgrave Macmillan.

Lorenz, W. (1994), *Social Work in a Changing Europe*, London: Routledge.

Luttwak, E. (1999), *Turbo-Capitalism: Winners and Losers in the Global Economy*, NY: Weidenfeld and Nicolson.

Macfarlane, A. (1978), *The Origins of English Individualism; The Family, Property and Social Transition*. Oxford: Blackwell.

Macho-Stadler, I. and Pérez-Castrillo, J.D. (2001), *An Introduction to the Economics of Information, Incentives and Contracts*, Oxford: Oxford University Press.

MacIntyre, A. (1981), *After Virtue: A Study in Moral Theory*, London: Duckworth.

Malpass, P. (1984), 'Octavia Hill, 1835–1912' in Barker, P. (ed.), *Founders of the Welfare State*, London: Heineman.

Mandelbrot, B. (1982), *The Fractal Geometry of Nature*, NY: W.H. Freeman.

Marshall, T.H. (1951), *Citizenship and Social Class*, London: Dent.

Marx, K. (1867), *Capital*, (3 vols), Harmondsworth: Penguin (1978).

Marx, K. and Engels, F. (1848), 'The Manifesto of the Communist Party', in *Marx and Engels, Collected Works*, London: Lawrence and Wishart (1976), Vol. 6.

Mason, P. (2012a), 'The Revolution Goes Viral', *The Guardian*, G2, 4 January, pp. 6–10.

Mason, P. (2012b), *Why It's Kicking Off Everywhere: The New Global Revolution*, London: Verso.

Mays, N. (2011), 'The English NHS as a Market: Challenges for the Coalition Government', in C. Holden, M. Kilkey, and G. Ramia (eds), *Social Policy Review*, 23, Bristol: Policy Press.

McGuiness, F. (2012) *Membership of UK Political Parties*, London: Commons Library Standard Note.

McGreal, C. (2012), 'Whatever Happened to Writing Lines?', *The Guardian*, G2, 10 January, pp. 8–12.

Mead, L.M. (1985), *Beyond Entitlement: The Social Obligations of Citizenship*, NY: Free Press.

Meade, J.E. (1989), *Agathotopia: The Economics of Partnership*, Aberdeen: Aberdeen University Press.

Mitchell, B.R. (1975), *European Historical Statistics, 1750–1970*, Basingstoke: Macmillan.

Monbiot, G. (2012), 'Today's Terror Threats: Farc, al-Qaida and Occupy London', *The Guardian*, 10 January, p. 26.

Morel, N., Palier, B. and Palme, J. (2011), *Towards a Social Investment Welfare State*, Bristol: Policy Press.

Munro, E. (2011), *The Munro Report on Child Protection: Interim Report: The Child's Journey*, London: Department of Education.

Milham, S., Bullock, R. and Cherrett, P. (1970), *After Grace, Teeth: A Comparative Study of the Experiences of Boys in Approved Schools*, London: Human Context.

National Audit of Dementia (2011), *Report of the National Audit of Dementia Care in Hospitals*, London: Royal College of Psychiatrists

National Audit Office (2011), *The Care Quality Commission: Regulating the Quality of Health and Adult Social Care*, London: NAO.

National Audit Office (2012), *The Introduction of the Work Programme*, London: NAO.

New Economics Foundation (2012), *21 Hours: Why a Shorter Working Week Could Help Us All to Flourish in the 21st Century*, London: New Economics Foundation.

Newburn, T., *et al.* (2011) *Reading the Riots: Investigating England's Summer of Disorder*, London: London School of Economics.

Newman, A.L. (2002),'When Opportunity Knocks: Economic Liberalisation and Stealth Welfare in the United States', *Journal of Social Policy*, 32(2), pp. 179–98.

Newman, J., Glendinning, C. and Hughes, M. (2008), 'Beyond Modernisation? Social Care and the Transformation of Welfare Governance', *Journal of Social Policy*, 37(4), pp. 531–57.

Nissan, D. and Le Grand, J. (2000), *A Capital Idea*, London: Fabian Society.

Noddings, N. (2002), *Starting at Home*, Berkeley: University of California Press.

Norman, J. (2010), *The Big Society: The Anatomy of the New Politics*: Buckingham: University of Buckingham Press.

O'Connor, J. (1977), *The Fiscal Crisis of the State*, NY: St. James' Press.

Offe, C. (1984), *Contradictions of the Welfare State*, London: Hutchinson.

Offe, C. (1992), 'A Non-Productivist Design for Social Policies', in P. Van Parijs (ed.), *Arguing for Basic Income: Ethical Foundations for a Radical Reform*, London: Verso.

Offe, C. (1996), *Modernity and the State*, Cambridge: Polity.

Olson, M. (1965), *The Logic of Collective Action: Public Goods and the Economics of Groups*, Cambridge, MA: Harvard University Press.

Olson, M. (1982), *The Rise and Decline of Nations: Economic Growth, Stagflation and Social Rigidities*, New Haven, CT: Yale University Press.

Packman, J. (1968), *Child Care: Needs and Numbers*, London: Allen and Unwin.

Packman, J. (1975), *The Child's Generation*, Oxford: Blackwell.

Pareto, V. (1909), *Manuel d'économie politique*, Paris: Giard.

Pareto, V. (1916), 'Treatise on General Sociology', in S.E. Finer (ed.), *Vilfredo Pareto: Sociological Writings*, London: Pall Mall Press (1966), pp. 97–122.

Parker, H. (1989), *Instead of the Dole: An Enquiry into the Integration of the Tax and Benefit System*, London: Routledge and Kegan Paul.

Participle Ltd (2012), *The Circle Movement*, London: Participle.

Parton, N., Thorpe, D. and Wattam, C. (eds) (1997), *Child Protection, Risk and the Modern Order*, Basingstoke: Palgrave Macmillan.

Parton., N. (2006), *Safeguarding Childhood: Early Intervention and Surveillance in Late Modern Society*, Basingstoke: Palgrave Macmillan.

Pateman, C. (2004), 'Democratizing Citizenship: Some Advantages of a Basic Income', *Politics and Society*, 32(1), pp. 89–106.

Patients' Association (2011), *We've Been Listening, Have You Been Learning?*, London: Patients' Association.

Pierson, P. (1994), *Dismantling the Welfare State*, Cambridge: Cambridge University Press.

Pigou, A.C. (1920), *The Economics of Welfare*, London: Macmillan.

Polanyi, K. (1944), *The Great Transformation: The Political and Economic Origins of Our Times*, Boston: Beacon Press.

Ponticelli, J. and Voth, H.-J. (2011), 'Cuts and Riots: They're Linked', *The Guardian*, 17 August.

Powell, W. (1990), 'Neither Market nor Hierarchy: Network Forms of Organization', *Research in Organizational Behaviour*, 12, pp. 295–336.

Powell, W. (2006), *The Nonprofit Sector*, New Haven, Connecticut: Yale University Press.

Prabhakar, R. (2009), 'What Is the Future of Asset-Based Welfare?', *Public Policy Research*, 16(1), pp. 51–6.

Prospect Magazine (2010), 'The Prospect Debate: Red Tory v. Blue Labour' (Phillip Blond and Maurice Glasman), Issue 170.

Public Accounts Committee (2011), *Oversight of User Choice and Provider Competition in Care Markets*, Report 57, London: House of Lords.

Pusey, M. (2003), *The Experience of Middle Australia: The Dark Side of Economic Reform*, Cambridge: Cambridge University Press.

Putnam, R.D. (1993), *Making Democracy Work: Civic Traditions in Modern Italy*, Princeton, NJ: Princeton University Press.

Putnam, R.D. (2002), *Bowling Alone: The Decline and Revival of American Community*, NY: Simon and Schuster.

Raban, J. (2010), Parson Blond's Foggy Sermon', *The Guardian*, Review, 14 April.

Ramesh, R. (2011), 'Forget Welfare, the Poorest People Must Now Rely on "Charity"', *The Guardian*, 31 August, p. 32.

Rand, A. (1957), *Atlas Shrugged*, NY: Random House.

Rand, A., Greenspan, A. and Branden, N. (1966), *Capitalism: The Unknown Ideal*, NY: New American Library.

Rawls, J. (1972), *A Theory of Justice*, Oxford: Clarendon Press.

Resolution Foundation (2011), *Making a Rented House a Home: Housing Solutions for 'Generation Rent'*, London: Resolution Foundation.

Rimlinger, G.V. (1971), *Welfare Policy and Industrialization in Europe, America and Russia*, London: Wiley.

Robbins, L. (1932), *The Nature and Significance of Economic Science*, London: Allen and Unwin.

Rose, N. (1996), *Inventing Ourselves: Psychology, Power and Personhood*, Cambridge: Cambridge University Press.

Rothstein, B. and Stolle, D. (2002), 'Social Capital and Street-Level Bureaucracy: Towards an Institutional Theory of Generalised Trust', paper given at a Conference on Social Capital, Exeter University, 15–20 September.

Rowson, J., Mezey, M.K. and Dellot, B. (2012), *Beyond the Big Society: Psychological Foundations of Active Citizenship*, London: RSA.

Ruane, S. (2010), 'Corporate and Political Strategy in Relation to the Private Finance Initiative in the UK', *Critical Social Policy*, 30(4), pp. 519–40.

Sahlins, M. (1974), *Stone Age Economics*, London: Tavistock Publications.

Scarman, Lord (1981), *The Scarman Report*, London: Home Office.

Scourfield, P. (2007), 'Are There Reasons to be Worried about the "Cartelisation" of Residential Care?', *Critical Social Policy*, 25(2), pp. 155–80.

Seldon, A. (2012), *The Politics of Optimism*, London: Policy Exchange.

Sevenhuijsen, S. (1998), *Citizenship and the Ethics of Care*, London: Routledge.

Sevenhuijsen, S. (2000), 'Caring in the Third Way: The Relation between Obligation, Responsibility and Care in Third Way Discourse', *Critical Social Policy*, 20(1), pp. 5–38.

Sissons, P. (2011), *The Hourglass and the Escalator: Labour Market Change and Mobility*, London: The Work Foundation.

Šiklova, J. (2001), 'Social Work in our Country from the Second World War to the Present Day', in Matoušek, O. *et al.* (eds) *The Basics of Social Work*, Prague: Portál, pp. 139–53.

Shand, A. (1990), *Free Market Morality: The Political Economy of the Austrian School*, London: Routledge.

Sheridan, M. (1991), *Assets and the Poor: A New American Welfare Policy*, Armock, NY: M.E.Sharpe.

Smith, A. (1776), *An Inquiry Concerning the Nature and Causes of the Wealth of Nations*, Oxford: Clarendon Press (1976).

Social Trends 41 (2011), London: Office for National Statistics.

Spruyt, H. (1994), *Sovereign States and their Competitors*, Princeton, NJ: Princeton University Press.

Standing, G. (1989), 'Global Feminization through Flexible Labor', *World Development*, 17(7), pp. 1077–95.

Standing, G. (1999), *Global Labour Flexibility: Seeking Distributive Justice*, Basingstoke: Palgrave Macmillan.

Standing, G. (2009), *Work After Globalization: Rebuilding Occupational Citizenship*, Cheltenham: Edward Elgar.

Standing, G. (2011), *The Precariat: The New Dangerous Class*, London: Bloomsbury.

Starrett, D.A. (1988), *Foundations of Public Economics*, Cambridge: Cambridge University Press.

Statham, D. (1978), *Radicals in Social Work*, London: Routledge and Kegan Paul.

Steiner, R. (1923), *Towards Social Renewal: Rethinking the Basis of Society*, Forest Row: Rudolf Steiner Foundation.

Stiglitz, J.E. (2002), *Globalization and Its Discontents*, London: Allen Lane.

Stiglitz, J.E. and Greenwald, B. (2003), *Towards a New Paradigm of Monetary Economics*, Cambridge: Cambridge University Press.

Swaan, A. De (1988), *In Care of the State: Health Care, Education and Welfare in Europe and the USA in the Modern Era*, Cambridge: Polity.

Tett, G. (2009), *Fool's Gold: How Unrestrained Greed Corrupted a Dream, Shattered Global Markets and Unleashed a Catastrophe*, London: Little, Brown.

Tett, G. (2011), Interview, BBC Radio 4, *Today*, 17 February.

The Gaurdian (2011) 'Response to Flak or Policy Fightback: What Exactly is the PM Proposing?', 16 August, pp. 4–5.

The Guardian (2011), 'Broken Prison System to Blame for Riots – Clarke', 6 September, p. 1.

The Guardian (2011), 'Punishment Europe' (editorial), 9 November, p. 34.

The Guardian (2011) 'Women on Top', G2, pp. 5–7.

The Guardian (2011) 'Aspiration Talk? All the Young Hear is a Sick Joke', 17 November, p. 49.

The Guardian (2011) 'Obesity is about Poverty, Not Lack of Moral Fibre', 15 December, p. 32.

The Guardian (2011), 'Courts to Dock Benefits under Coalition Plan', 8 September, p. 1.

The Guardian (2012), 'Cameron Calls for a "Fairer Economy"', 20 January, p. 2.

The Guardian (2012), 'Welfare-to-Work Boss Quits her Company, Blaming Media Furore over Pay and Allegations of Fraud', 25 February, p. 2.

The Guardian (2012), 'Government U-Turn on Work Scheme: Rules on Work Experience Changed after Threats from Major Employers', 1 March, p. 1.

The Mid Staffordshire NHS Foundation Trust Inquiry. January 2005–March 2009. http://www.midstaffsinquiry.com/news.php?id=30.

Thompson, E.P. (1968), *The Making of the English Working Class*, Harmondsworth: Penguin.

Trade Union Congress (2011), *Unfair to Middling: How Middle Britain's Low Pay Fuelled the Crash and Threatens Recovery*, London: TUC, at http://tuc.org.uk/extras/unfairtomiddling.pdf. Last accessed 28 January 2012.

Trade Union Congress (2011) *Unfair to Middling: How Middle Britain's Low Pay Fuelled the Crash and Threatens Recovery*, London, TUC. Available at: http://www.tuc.org.uk/extras/unfairtomiddling.pdf.

Tronto, J. (1993), *Moral Boundaries*, London: Routledge.

Tudge, C. (2010), 'Agriculture is in a Mess, but Politicians Don't Give a Damn', *New Statesman*, 2 May, pp. 35–40.

Tudor Hart, J. (2006), *The Political Economy of Health Care*, Bristol: Policy Press.

Unwin, J. (2009), 'Introduction' in *Contemporary Social Evils*, London: Joseph Rowntree Foundation.

Van Parijs, P. (1995), *Real Freedom for All: What (If Anything) Can Justify Capitalism?* Oxford: Clarendon Press.

Von Mises, L. (1966), *Human Action*, Chicago: Contemporary Books.

Walzer, M. (1983), *Spheres of Justice*, Oxford: Blackwell.

Wasson, P. (2011), *We Have Been Listening, Have You Been Hearing?*, London: Patients' Association.

Waddan, C. (1997), *The Politics of Social Welfare: The Collapse of the Centre and the Rise of the Right*, Cheltenham: Edward Elgar.

Waterhouse, L. and McGhee, J. (1998), 'Social Work with Children and Families', in R. Adams, L. Dominelli and M. Payne (eds), *Social Work: Themes, Issues and Critical Debates*, Basingstoke: Palgrave Macmillan.

Wilkinson, R. and Pickett, K. (2009), *The Spirit Level: Why More Equal Societies Almost Always Do Better*, London: Allen Lane.

Willetts, D. (2010), *The Pinch: How the Baby Boomers Took their Children's Future – and Why They Can Give It Back*, London: Atlantic Books.

Williams, F. (2001), 'In and Beyond New Labour: Towards a New Political Ethics of Care', *Critical Social Policy*, 21(4), pp. 467–96.

Wolf, M. and Knopf, P. (2010), *Left Behind: Youth Unemployment in Germany and Spain*, London: Faber and Faber.

Young, I.M. (1990), *Justice and the Politics of Difference*, Princeton, NJ: Princeton University Press.

Index

exploitation
  capitalist, 5, 132
  in nature, 24
  and social insurance, 45
  of workers, 2, 10, 92

Fabianism, 44–5
'face', 68
family, 14, 39, 65, 74–5, 107, 113,
    126–7, 131–52
  assets, 136–7
  'chaotic', 66, 173
  complaints by, 99
  deviant, 65, 173
  discord, 71–2
  formation, 48–9
  practice with, 146–7
  rituals, 161
farming, 44
  family, 111
  forced labour in, 52–3
  in human evolution, 110
  small-scale, 170
fascism, 32, 112
fashion, 68
feedback loop, 23
financial sector
  and the crisis, 186
  employment in, 30–1
  ethical, 169
  insurance, 95
Financial Services Authority (FSA), 95
Finland
  graduates in, 139
  True Finns in, 180
flexibility
  labour market, 10, 143–5, 186
  over unpaid work, 169
  in working life, 42
Fook, J., 161
Foundation Status (NHS), 97–100,
    102
France, 6, 45, 143
  innovation in, 8
  organised groups in, 112

university funding in, 142
welfare state in, 111
Friedman, M., 23
Friendly Societies, 123

gangs, 64
  cultures of, 83
  outreach workers and, 145
gay people
  collective action by, 115–16
  oppression of, 149
Germany, 1, 3–4, 6, 18, 27, 42, 67
  banks in, 186
  and the euro, 36, 42–3, 126, 186
  imperialism in, 53
  industrialisation, 48, 53, 110
  productivity, 8
  social care in, 12, 94, 173, 183
  university funding in, 142
  welfare state in, 111
Giddens, A., 71
Glasman, M., 45–6
globalisation, 19, 22–7, 115–16
graduates
  debts of, 142
  opportunities for, 141
  unemployment, 10, 14
  'without a future', 144
Greece, 4, 6, 27, 32, 36
  ancient, 110
  bones from, 110
  organised groups in, 112
  protest in, 13, 63, 132, 182
  technocratic government in, 175
  welfare-to-work in, 56
Greenspan, A., 24
groups
  action by, 107–8
  cohesion of, 108
  cultures of, 83
  faith, 68, 160
  individuals and, 67–9, 160
  informal, 181
  occupational, 68
  organised, 109, 112